D0143856

TOWARD A
MORE PERFECT UNION

Toward a
More Perfect Union

Virtue and the Formation of

American Republics

★　　★　　★

Ann Fairfax Withington

OXFORD UNIVERSITY PRESS
New York　　Oxford

Oxford University Press

Oxford   New York
Athens   Auckland   Bangkok   Bogota   Bombay
Buenos Aires   Calcutta   Cape Town   Dar es Salaam
Dehli   Florence   Hong Kong   Istanbul   Karachi
Kuala Lumpur   Madras   Madrid   Melbourne
Mexico City   Nairobi   Paris   Singapore
Taipei   Tokyo   Toronto

and associated companies in
Berlin   Ibadan

First published in 1991 by Oxford University Press, Inc.
198 Madison Avenue, New York, New York 10016
First issued as an Oxford University Press paperback, 1996

Oxford is a registered trademark of Oxford University Press

Library of Congress Cataloging-in-Publication Data
Withington, Ann Fairfax.
Toward a more perfect union: virtue and the formation
of American republics / Ann Fairfax Withington.
p.   cm.
Includes bibliographical references and index.
ISBN 0-19-506835-1; ISBN 0-19-510130-8 (pbk.)
1. United States—History—Revolution, 1775–1783—Moral and
ethical aspects.   2. United States—History—Revolution.
1775–1783—Social aspects.   3. Political culture—
United States—History—18th century.   I. Title.
E209.W58   1991
973.3—dc20   91-8317

1 3 5 7 9 0 8 6 4 2
Printed in the United States of America
on acid-free paper

For
L.A.W.

and to the memory of
P.R.W.
P.R.W., Jr.

ACKNOWLEDGEMENTS

I am always amazed, when I pour over the acknowledgements in books (often the best part), at the number of institutions and foundations that disgorge of their gold and the exuberance of the authors for research. I remember my first research trip. I was shoved into a room brimming with folios but noticeably lacking in those amenities that make reading pleasurable, like a chair and perhaps a table. Light of only a very modest nature filtered in from a distant window and warmed a sleeping tarantula. The folios that interested me were, of course, on the top shelf so I had to repress rampant acrophobia, gambol up a wobbly step ladder, and gracefully balance a fifteen-pound folio while it rained a shower of dead insects over my spick-and-span "power" suit. In a second room adjoining the first, the shelving method had been abandoned altogether. Here the folios were piled on the floor, their spines modestly facing the wall; when stirred from their repose, the bindings with the informative titles disappeared in a cloud of dry rot.

I am grateful to the people who helped me overcome the hazards in gaining access to the past, especially various colleagues. Alden Vaughan is the ideal senior colleague for someone tottering in her first job. He lent me his books, sat by me at the dinners of the Columbia Seminar in Early American History, introduced me to Pat Bonomi and other celebrities, and came to my talk even though he was stricken with ague and the pox. Comrades Foner and Garafola, two sophisticated New Yorkers who took pity on a provincial from Boston ("that toy town"), taught me the names of the strange foods in delicatessens and invited me to sumptuous parties where people of all ages and occupations filled the apartment with the feast of reason and flow of wit. I have written this book so that the comrades will have something fluffy to read to Baby D after the intellectual strain of *Marmalade the Doctor Cat* and *Watch the Pony Grow*. Eric McKitrick plied me with oysters at the faculty club, and smiling with the bland dignity that testified to his superior knowledge disabused me of my erroneous thoughts on George Washington. (Methinks that verily his Lordship be inordinate as to the appetites and that gluttony breeds a dangerous distemper and flatulency of the stomach which must needs put acrimony in the blood.) He talked a lot about bouillabaisse and boasted of his skill at wielding a saucepan, crushing the garlic, and massaging the tender-fleshed fish, but like many professors, it was all talk and no action. Marsha Wright and Walter Metzger took me to operas and concerts, and several funny people kept my spirits up during those times of ennui, despair, and melancholia that so often haunt the untenured professor: Jim Shenton, Jack Garraty, Ainslie Embree (the handsome). Norm Pollack warded off despondency with stories about being an untenured radical Marxist professor at Yale in the sixties, and Gene Rice, with stories of the relics of St. Jerome and the feminization of Columbia's core course, Contemporary Civilization. Gene, like so many of his colleagues, cooks an exquisite meal, and he chivalrously invited me to Thanksgiving dinner after I had left him several notes explaining in detail that I had no place to go. The Midwest has a gourmet cook who rivals the best of New York. Sus Miller prepares banquets on hand-painted Royal Copenhagen plates and plays on the motif of abundance. I have enjoyed being the ward of the Millers and only hope that Doug does not get so fat that he can no longer waddle towards a drop shot.

In my graduate student days, several friends lashed me into productivity. Rachel Klein took me to the library and pointed out the card catalogue; Bill Breitenbach inspired me and his lunchtime congregation with his brilliance; and Jim Essig, who had a calling to write history, proselytized me with missionary zeal. Had the world been kind he would by now be on his fifth book.

For a long time my manuscript just lay around, unable to get up in the mornings year after year. Several people raised an eyebrow at this sloth. Dick (Webfoot) Brown and Kip Pells both read every page of the manuscript and encouraged me to send it off. Others showed more impatience with my argument that the planets had to be in a favorable position for such an ambitious undertaking. Josh Freeman, who was surging ahead with his own gigantic book, beat me to a black and blue pulp. Never a moment went by—on the tennis court when I was preparing a magnificent backhand drive, in his apartment just as I was plunging into a platter of lox—when he would not gratuitously remark that a book couldn't get published unless it was sent to a publisher. Chip Radding took to calling every morning at 6:00 to ask me if this was going to be the day for starting the voyage to the post office.

Several close female friends have helped set the world in the proper perspective as a male plot. I've had many very satisfactory conversations on PMS, fat, and male insensitivity with: Wizzy Whiteside, Freddy Gamble, Puss Schutt, Page Coulter, Betsy Blackmar, Lauissa Brown, and Maureen Flanagan. In a situation that usually calls for introspection, Diane Girling, between debulking and sysplatinum, kept me laughing with an endless stream of whimsical observations on the way of the world. One male friend has pampered me over the years, David Earnest.

I'm not so good at the nitty gritty business of what I believe academics call research, so while others might go to card catalogues and databases, I prefer to consult the living, breathing bibliographies, and I can, without reservation, recommend two: Jeffery Merrick and Michael Undsworth. Jeff (and Jeff is an excellent cook in his own right; in mentioning his academic skills I certainly don't mean to derogate from his more important culinary ones) can produce a hundred index cards on any topic: crime, charivaris, Jesuits, sex—an indispensable friend, and also a reliable one who never failed, whatever meteorological event might be devastating the Village, to take me to La Ripaille for a birthday dinner of some main course and white chocolate mousse smothered with sauce aux framboises. Michael, the reference librarian for history at Michigan State University, took misspelled vague references ("I think his last name might have been Brown, a minister, perhaps, who wrote sometime in the eighteenth century") and wrestled results from ARLIN, STC, OCLC, and other acronymous monsters.

Several people helped with the mechanics of producing a book in the flesh. Albin Jones showed me how to collect statistical data and then processed it for me. Sacdone, my computer buddy, kept my tables from marching off the page, got me out of metas, and taught me how to setf, yput, pick, change, and exit. Kathy Morrissey, my second-base woman, did midnight proofreading; Jean Breitung, our resident herpetologist, and Mary Cary Chipley, manufacturer of jets, promise to read the page proofs. Gregory Yarmesch and Mary Mapes had the exhilarating task of checking citations; they both aged considerably while serving their terms in the microform room. Bill Hixson caught many ugly orthographic blunders and pulled out noxious commas. Two anonymous readers offered excellent advice and saved me from at least some errors. Joanie Withington, my Maryland agent, came up with the title.

My greatest academic debt is to Edmund Morgan, who still reads everything I send him (and I send him every little thing). I like to think of Ed rocking back and forth behind the lectern and stroking its edges, up on his roof mending a hole, behind the coffee pot with a brown paper bag and a bottle of Amontillado at T.A. lunches, arching his eyebrows at a bowl of Indian pudding in Mory's, at the helm of his sailfish, and roaring around Mt. Washington at MACH .82, dipping his wings—always in all ways a verray, parfit gentil knyght.

I have great personal debts, too. Ellen Lee Kennelly gave me a mature lime-green Volvo to putter around to various archives; Franci Wakemen gave me a cottage by the sea to inspire great thoughts; and Aubrey Smith gave me Peter's bed. Mary Hilton (G.G.G.) has over the years stoked me with chocolate chip cookies, cinnamon toast, and cheese soufflé. She also taught me to whistle, lace my skates, ride my bike down the big hill in the cemetary, and catch crabs in the tidal pond behind Big Beach. Obviously without her this book could never have been written.

Perhaps in the course of these acknowledgements I may have been overplaying the prandial motif. I do want to thank one person who definitely cannot cook, my mother. (Her brother, catching her in a rare moment in the ktichen, her hand tentatively on a skillet, a perplexed and affronted look on her face, said that she reminded him of a whore presented with a Bible.) My mother didn't need to hold the family together with puddings and tarts because she read aloud to us hour after hour—Freddy the Detective Pig and Robin Hood to my brother and me, Rex Stout and Dickens to my father (with the usual way-past-bedtime hangers-on). Generally not a patient woman, the Aged P continued to encourage and support me while I pursued a leisurely academic career, testing out first this subject and then that in various settings: Virginia, Cambridge, Melbourne, Berkeley, and exotic New Haven. And all this time, when other people's children were scaling corporate ladders, not by a flicker of an eyelid did she even hint that I might never be educated. Her reward is a history book on funerals and cocks.

I think my ancestors in Virginia and New England deserve recognition for their glorious performance in the American Revolution. The Fairfaxes decided they didn't like equality and went back to England. Ebenezer Withington, a hermit who lived in a hut in Sodom on the shore of Nantasket Bay, discovered a chest of tea floating on the tide. A frugal sort, he swooped it up and stashed the tea away (we strongly believe he chopped up the chest for kindling and saved the nails). But rumors spread. A committee visited him, and he has come down in history as "Old Straddlebug Withington."

And so, gentle reader, I leave this little book to your serious consideration. As far as the exactest care can carry me, I have written it so punctually true that I am hopeful there is none can have any just exception to any part of it, and even though the devil hath in these late and declining times possessed the hearts of many with cursed opinions which do beget a world of error, ruin, and desolation, I shall incessantly pray at his hands, who is the giver of all good things—the god of mercy and peace—that these labors shall prove successful in their operation. In the corrupted currents of this world a guilded hand may often shove by justice and it has been rumored (who will stop the vent of hearing when foul rumor speaks?) that Sheldon Meyer received together with this manuscript a standing cup of scallop shells, one perfuming pot in the form of a cat, and two barrels of figs. If any gross and blind idolaters, fallen away from undoubted truths and wandering daily in vice, should thunder these false calumnies, the end thereof shall be their eternal damnation unless speedy repentance prevent God's judgement, which to wish is godly but to believe is foolish. Meanwhile I shall always pray as I do sincerely desire that by all my endeavors God may be glorified, the truth divine and human vindicated, and the public benefited.

PREFACE

From 1764 to 1776, Americans had to deal with the feeling of dislocation and scatter left by a Parliament that was breaking the previously established rules. Amidst all their bustle of practicality (they formed congresses, produced documents articulating their rights and grievances, established importation and exportation embargoes), they also took measures to alleviate internal tensions and to strengthen themselves as a people. In 1774, the first Continental Congress drew up an official and very specific code of behavior. They banned cockfighting, horse-racing, and the theater, and modified the funeral ceremony. This book will consider the somewhat curious behavior of the Congress and the odd assortment of activities they chose to focus on.

Banned activities, like empty holes, cannot be seen. We can, however, get around that invisibility by roaming through the tracts of moral condemnation that accreted over the years, sometimes centuries, on the activities singled out for purging; by spotting the moral themes that might bear on the political issues; and by dissecting the activities themselves. Cocker manuals, betting odds, bawdy comedies, sentimental tragedies, lewd prints, stark funeral processions: all comment obliquely on the political events of the day and on the character Americans were making for themselves as a people.

Colonists not only abided by the regulations of Congress (they gave up the forbidden activities and modified their funerals), but they also bowed and crooked traditional ceremonies—the funeral and the execution—into mock ceremonies in the service of the political cause and took over the traditional European "skimmington ride"—the ritual by which a community expressed its moral outrage at people who deviated from normal behavior—and produced an American version, tarring and feathering. While the banned activities have to be brought back into visibility for their political significance to be understood, ceremonies, in contrast, were co-opted and refashioned by the patriots for their very visibility. The ceremonies present a text to be read, and the modifications of traditional ceremonies present a conversation between a society at peace and a society in tension. Colonists used ceremonies to make political statements, and the ceremonies themselves, when put to such a use, framed and structured the political issues.

Congress had a political strategy. In regulating behavior, Congress tried to make colonial society homogeneous and cohesive, both horizontally (bonding different colonies together) and vertically (blurring class and gender distinctions). They banned activities and modified ceremonies that splintered social cohesion by stimulating self-absorption (gambling), by encouraging competition (cockfighting and horse-racing), or by emphasizing class divisions (funerals with elaborate display). Congress also identified different sectors of society that might potentially speak in different voices: the poor, women, servants, Tories, gamblers. The poor, women, and servants, all of whom were deemed to have weak wills, were to be insulated from contamination, either moral or political, and incorporated into the political resistance. The deviants—gamblers, spendthrifts, and idlers, whose self-absorption and obsession left no room for political commitment, and Tories, whose political tenets were twisted and warped—were to be transformed into committed patriots or expelled.

This book delves into oddities—the quirks and twitches of the American Revolution (cockfights, horse-races, funerals and executions, real and mock, tragedies and comedies)—and from these oddities, dissected, scrutinized, and injected with significance, ruminates on a national character that emerged in the twelve years of political crisis and eventually freed Americans of their dependence on Britain. The American character was forged in an austere, seemingly arbitrary, morality, slowly fashioned and pieced together between the Sugar Act of 1764 and the Coercive Acts of 1774 and then officially brought together in a code of behavior by the first Continental Congress. This ascetic morality, crystallized in an odd assortment of specificity, put on display and made explicit certain assumptions and values that gave their own hue to the political events and prepared Americans for the establishment of republican governments.

We have long since violated the ethic on which republican government was founded. The virtuous citizenry dedicated to lean austerity—that alleged bulwark of republics—disintegrated shortly after the Revolution into autonomous consumers engulfed in the desire for possessions. Instead of honoring the hard life of cramped gratifications, Americans today revel in materialism. Implicitly, the more you own, the more American you are; and sooner or later in America, all classes, all races, all ages, and both sexes are marked as consumers. We no longer extol the pinched morality of frugality or even the work ethic. Yet while the austere virtue that gave Americans the confidence to establish republican governments has long since dissolved, the great legacy of the American Revolution, republican government, still survives.

Many historians have dealt with virtue and corruption in the American Revolution. Some (Bernard Bailyn, Gordon Wood, and J. G. A. Pocock) have concentrated on the opposition of virtue and corruption as an intellectual and linguistic paradigm that colored the perception Americans had of themselves and the British. Others have focused on the morality itself. Edmund Morgan revealed the similarities between the ethic of the Puritans and the ethic of American revolutionaries. Garry Wills analyzed sentimentalism and Scottish moral philosophy and showed how immersed Jefferson was in these European schools of thought. This book concentrates on the use of morality as a political strategy and is far more oriented towards culture than other books that have dealt with virtue and corruption in the American Revolution. I concentrate on cultural activities that were highlighted during the Revolution, trace their function and structure in eighteenth-century colonial society, and analyze the moral hostility they generated.

European historians like Robert Darnton and Natalie Davis have developed the field of cultural history in sophisticated and analytical ways. Some American historians have dealt with culture in this period (most notably Kenneth Silverman, who surveyed painting, music, literature, and the theater) and a few have related culture to ideology. Timothy Breen has studied the *mentalité* of Virginia tobacco planters and ascribed their crisis of confidence to deteriorating debt relations. Eric Foner placed the artisans of Philadelphia in a culture before analyzing them as a political class. Rhys Issac studied the hostility between the Virginia gentry and Baptists, located it in cultural differences, and related the internal conflict to the imperial crisis. This book, instead of using culture as a means of understanding one class or of distinguishing among classes, concentrates on aspects of eighteenth-century Anglo-American culture that colonists in the period of political crisis could agree on. I deal with a society's self-conscious response to its own culture. I analyze certain activities and ceremonies in depth and probe for connections between political ideology grounded in virtue and behavior organized and controlled by cultural imperatives.

CONTENTS

Illustrations follow page 184

TOWARD A
MORE PERFECT UNION

★ 1 ★

The Declaration of American Independence

On April 19, 1775, the British killed forty-nine colonists and the colonists killed seventy-three British. Two months later in a battle on Breed's Hill in Charlestown, Massachusetts, 124 colonists and 226 British lost their lives. And yet, even though colonists were engaged in a war with Great Britain, they did not declare independence. Instead they sent a petition to King George in which they told him that they found the controversy abhorrent because it violated their affection for him as their king; assured him that colonial breasts retained a tender regard for the kingdom from which they derived their origin; and beseeched him for relief from afflicting fears and jealousies. If only he would prevent the tyrannous legislation of Parliament!

King George, less delicate than his American subjects and less squeamish about the political and psychological implications of armed confrontation, issued a proclamation that declared the Americans in rebellion. That was in August of 1775. In December he approved legislation that required the seizure of American ships on the high seas. And yet the colonists still could not bring themselves to repudiate their king and declare independence. After the first armed confrontation, it took fourteen months of battles, troop maneuvers, parliamentary intransigence, and royal provocations before John Hancock finally pushed a declaration of independence across the table and started to collect the signatures of the Continental Congress. And when they

3

finally did declare independence, they did not indict monarchies, but only George III for letting his parliament—a parliament in which Americans were not represented—tax and pass laws for Americans. Why did Americans take so long to declare independence once the possibility of political reconciliation had evaporated? And why did a people who had vociferously protested during the whole imperial crisis that they were not republicans, who for two years drew back from independence because they were conditioned to feel the pull of allegiance to a king, who even in the final break with Britain did not indict monarchy itself but only King George III,—why did such a people establish without debate, without a pause for reflection, thirteen republics and one confederated republic?

Declaring independence would have been easy had it been merely a political decision. Colonists did not, and knew they never would, recognize Parliament's power to tax and legislate for the colonies; and they must have known that King George would never deny Parliament's sovereignty in any matter. Politically there was no way out except declaring independence, but colonists had emotional reasons for not taking the political step. They shared with the English a common past they did not care to renounce, and they were conditioned to insulate the king from political controversy and to shun any act that might be considered treason. Before the colonists could declare independence, they had to prepare themselves psychologically to think of themselves as a people with an identity of their own.

In many ways the Declaration, as a quasi-sacred document, a national creed memorializing a pinpoint of time, has obscured our appreciation of the difficulties and tensions out of which the Declaration finally emerged. The Declaration did not burst upon the men in the Philadelphia statehouse in spontaneous generation, nor did Jefferson dream it up from a brain teeming with esoteric knowledge and burgeoning with intellectual rarities. Our pride in our eloquent creed and our idolatry of Jefferson, its author, lull us into easy complacency and obscure the intricacies, difficulties, and paradoxes of our past and the real achievements of people working together; people no longer fixed in our national consciousness, but featureless groups drawn together in taverns, town halls, and kitchens—on the docks and in the counting houses. The Declaration of Independence, closely bound in both content and language to the documents that the First Continental Congress had issued two years earlier, culminated a political process. Its terms were shaped by the way American colonists had responded to parliamentary legislation that they deemd unconstitutional.

i

Sometime between six and seven in the evening on December 17, 1773, about 1,000 people assembled at Griffin's Wharf in Boston Harbor. Forty men dressed as Mohawk Indians boarded the brigantine *Beaver,* broke open the hatches, hoisted 111 chests of tea, stove them in, and threw the contents overboard. Meanwhile other groups had boarded the *Eleanor* and the *Dartmouth* and had thrown 228 chests overboard.[1] The nonparticipants watched in silence. As soon as the job was done, the crowd melted away into the darkness.

American colonists did not want tea of the East India Company, which bore a tax, to be landed because they thought that once landed and distributed to stores in cities and towns it would eventually be sold. With each purchase of tea Americans would be paying a tax, and their position against taxation without representation would be corroded. It was easier to cut off the importation of tea at the port cities than to control the sale of tea in stores scattered throughout the cities and countryside. No colony had allowed the distribution of the East India Company's tea. Some had simply turned back the ships. Others had unloaded the tea and stored it in warehouses. In Boston, however, Governor Hutchinson, always eager to define a position and make a righteous stand, refused to send the tea back or to store it. The people of Boston had succeeded in preventing the unloading of the tea, but the governor had the right to confiscate any cargo that was not unloaded within three weeks. Governor Hutchinson planned to confiscate the tea and distribute it to the consignees who would sell it to retailers. The "Mohawk Indians" decided that Boston Harbor was a better place for it.

In 1774, Lord North was the king's chief minister, and he had firm control of the House of Commons. North was not a physically prepossessing man. "Nothing could be more coarse or clumsy or ungracious than his outside. Two large prominent eyes that rolled about to

---

1. Great Britain, Public Record Office, Colonial Office 5 (hereafter cited as PRO, CO5), vol. 133, p. 89.

no purpose (for he was utterly shortsighted), a wide mouth, thick lips, and inflated visage, gave him the air of a blind trumpeter. A deep untunable voice, which, instead of modulating, he enforced with unnecessary pomp, a total neglect of his person, and ignorance of every civil attention, disgusted all who judge by appearance, or withhold their approbation till it is courted."[2]

But North, who had assumed the office of First Lord of the Treasury in 1770 at the age of thirty-eight, had shown a certain political delicacy in the acceptance and refusal of offices and a caution in associating himself with this or that leader at this or that time, which boded well for his success in a political system of personal alliances and factions in constant flux. North may have had rolling eyes and thick lips, and his personal slovenliness may have revolted the fastidious, but "within that rude casket were enclosed many useful talents."[3]

When Lord North heard that on December 17, 1773, some 120 Bostonians had dumped 339 chests of tea into Boston Harbor, he wanted to punish someone. True, the culprits had been disguised as Mohawk Indians and had done the deed after dark, but Lord North was nobody's fool. He knew that 1,500 men who met in Faneuil Hall in Boston on the afternoon of the sixteenth had authorized, at least implicitly, the destruction. He knew that not a single citizen of Boston had attempted to hinder the Mohawk war party—not even the magistrates of the colony. Not that the magistrates sympathized with the mob—indeed, in Lord North's opinion the magistrates of Boston, unlike the magistrates of New York, Philadelphia, and Baltimore, had shown exemplary determination in resisting all attempts to return the tea to England or to store it in a warehouse and prevent its distribution on the market. But the magistrates of the Massachusetts colony obviously no longer had control over the people. Lord North was determined to give them the power they needed to exercise control.

North decided to meet the situation of ineffectual executive power in Massachusetts with practical measures. He would make a few crucial alterations in the charter of Massachusetts, which would free the executive branch from the legislative one. The council might be

2. Horace Walpole, *Memoirs of the Reign of King George the Third*, Denis Le Marchant, ed. (London, 1845) 4:78–79.

3. Ibid., 79.

appointed by the king, for instance, rather than elected by the assembly. The governor might be given power to appoint the sheriffs and the sheriffs given the power to appoint juries. Hitherto, sheriffs and juries had been elected. These changes would free the courts from control of local juries biased against the laws of England and against the officers who had been sent over to enforce the laws. New England towns, too, had shown a tendency to get involved in imperial affairs. They might be limited to a single town meeting a year, which would be restricted to local business. North might arrange for the possibility of changing the venue of a trial. If a trial could be removed at the request of the defendant to another colony away from local hostilities and tensions, or perhaps to England itself, English officials who upheld unpopular laws and occasionally had to use force to do so would be protected from the legal vengeance of the community. But first Lord North and his administration would punish Boston. They would try to bring offenders to trial and they would force the city to pay for the tea by closing the port.

North's plans took form in three Acts that Parliament passed in March and April of 1774 that were known in the colonies (together with a fourth Act on quartering soldiers) as the Coercive Acts: the Boston Port Act, the Massachusetts Government Act, and the Administration of Justice Act. Whatever merits the Acts may or may not have had as policy, they bristled with illegalities. Parliament passed the Boston Port Act without hearing the defense of Bostonians. Furthermore, the Act, in closing the harbor, punished the innocent as well as the guilty. Parliament proceeded as if Boston were a corporation with a corporate will and then punished Boston for a criminal offense, when according to corporation law, corporations could be tried only for civil offenses. The Massachusetts Government Act changed the government of Massachusetts, which had been established by a charter from the king. Legally, the king's solicitor general should have filed a writ of *quo warranto* in a court (Parliament could have acted as a court) and sought to prove that Massachusetts had violated its charter. If Massachusetts lost the case, the charter would have been forfeited at the time of the offense, and the king could issue a new charter with whatever changes he desired. The case, however, was never brought to trial. Instead, Parliament assumed the right to establish whatever government it pleased for Massachusetts, which did not even have representatives in Parliament—an obvious case of arbitrary exercise of power. The Administration of Justice Act, which arranged for the possibility of disregarding vicinage, blatantly mangled due process as it was established in the British constitution.

In passing the Coercive Acts, Parliament located the sovereign power of the British state in Parliament and launched a campaign against established colonial institutions that stood between the sovereign power and individual subjects. The Coercive Acts curtailed the power of a provincial government established by charter, of town governments, and of juries. These local centers of power, British officials thought, diluted loyalty to the king and had to be emasculated. The colonists, for their part, responded to the assault on their legal institutions by forming extralegal collectives—congresses, conventions, and committees—to protect the individual from the power of the British state. By making resistance a community affair and by operating in groups, the colonists frustrated English attempts to fix responsibility on individuals, who could be tried for treason.

The response of the British to the Boston Tea Party and their desire to identify and punish offenders drove American leaders underground and reinforced communal, corporate, anonymous resistance. The Boston Tea Party also exposed the alienation that had grown between the people of Massachusetts and their official colonial leaders appointed by Britain. Thomas Hutchinson spurned conciliation and refused to take measures that might have softened the differences that existed between him and the people of Massachusetts and between the people of Massachusetts and British officials.

Hutchinson was not a timid man. And yet the time for the confiscation of the tea by customs officials found Hutchinson in Milton, far from the scene of action. A man whose house had, ten years earlier, been sacked, stripped, and gutted by a mob angry at the Stamp Act, a man who had often volleyed his disapproval of mob action, sat in his country house on a hill overlooking the marshes saturated in a winter rain, while ten miles away the "Mohawks," unmolested, proceeded on their orderly course of destruction. The absence of a force like Hutchinson from the tension of a frustrated town stands out starkly as either foresight or negligence. Yet Boston did not thank Hutchinson for tactful absence and restraint, nor did the North administration punish him for dereliction.

Why did Hutchinson retire to Milton at the climax of the tea struggle? Perhaps he thought that the Boston leaders, beaten at every turn and twist, would accept defeat; but this is an unlikely explanation for someone as shrewd as Hutchinson and as familiar with mob action. Perhaps he wished to avoid the necessity of calling in troops and at the same time relieve himself of the responsibility of maintaining order; but this is an unlikely explanation for a man who throve on controversy, righteousness, and discipline. Perhaps he wanted to force the issue—to give the people of Boston a chance to prove themselves as violent and irresponsible as he had claimed they were. But however veiled Hutchinson's motives or lack of motives, the response to his absence stands out in the glare of unambiguity. North and his followers stood behind him, while the opposition in England turned on him. What clearer evidence of the alienation of the official colonial leadership from the colonial people than the sight of Barre, Dowdeswell, *et al.*—the members of Parliament who supported Boston and the colonies—turning on the governor, (a colonist, not an Englishman), to vindicate the people of Massachusetts?

The Coercive Acts created two tiers of leadership, one visible and associated with England, and one invisible and associated with the colonies. British legislators forced the leaders of American resistance underground. American resistance, anonymous and corporate, eluded attempts of British leaders to affix responsibility and punish offenders; it also introduced a new concept of leadership. The American style of politics diverged from the British style. In the pool of British politics in the 1760s and early 1770s, human particles coalesced in little clusters, momentary nodules of interest, and then dissolved. Men attached themselves to men, but the attachments were fragile and depended on rewards: of money, of office, of recognition. Because men attained power by letting themselves be used and manipulated, it was not in their interest to blend into the environment. Men of wealth and power tried to attach lesser men to them in a visible orbit. In a world of bargains, deals, and political tit-for-tat, the number of satellites enhanced one's power. Big men and little men alike wanted to stand out, available for offers, ready to be tempted. Personalities were highly visible.

In the colonies, political ideas militated against leadership based on personality and in some ways militated against the very concept of leadership. The colonists in their resistance strove for unanimity. They thought the coercive measures of the British Parliament called for an active investment of effort by everybody. A political movement built on unanimity and universal participation left little room for the play of individuality. In the American political scene, character replaced personality. A cluster of traits—industry, frugality, and charity—smoothed out the ragged terrain of personal idiosyncracy. The style of politics in which leaders did not stand apart from the people but merged with them contrasted with the British style. In Britain, a coterie of politicians, pecking and pecked, lay exposed to news reporters, satirists, and gossipmongers—each cough or tic, each silk cravat or lace ruffle, each royal favor, each liaison, sexual or political, was a stick or twig with which the scrappers would build their nests. The leaders of the empire, their quirks emblazoned on the public consciousness, their foibles enjoyed in coffeehouse gatherings, their features and infirmities the talk of the town, faced the attenuated shadows of Mohawk Indians swarming over the decks and into the hold of the *Beaver,* the *Eleanor,* and the *Dartmouth*—shadows that dissolved into the harbor drizzle, shadows that not one witness, drilled by eager and relentless lawyers and administrators, could conjure up in the flesh. North with his weak larynx and rolling eyes confronted the anonymity and silence of a city, the blankness of a December night in Boston.

ii

The first Continental Congress convened in Philadelphia in September 1774 to deal with the Coercive Acts. The Continental Congress announced in a published memorial that in seeking redress for these grievances they were taking three types of measures, each grounded on different sentiments.[4] They would petition the king for redress of their grievances as an act of loyalty. They were writing an address to their British brethren out of affection, and they had drawn up the Association, which established an economic boycott and proscribed certain activities and whose success depended on fidelity and virtue.

In the Association, Congress set up a trade embargo. After November 30, 1774, colonists would not import any goods that Great Britain or Ireland produced or exported; nor would they import molasses, syrups, panels, coffee, or pimiento from the British West

4. "Memorial to the Inhabitants of the Colonies," in Worthington C. Ford, ed., *Journals of the Continental Congress, 1774–1789,* 1 (Washington, D.C., 1904): 99–100.

Indies; wines from Madeira; or indigo from anywhere. Finally, they would not import East India tea, no matter who the exporters were. In order to secure the effectiveness of the nonimportation measures, colonists would agree not to buy any of these articles. Faced with a nonconsumption agreement, merchants would have no incentive to violate the importation embargo. After September 9, 1775, colonists would not export any goods (except rice, a reluctant concession to South Carolina) to Great Britain, Ireland, or the West Indies.

The First Continental Congress went beyond economic regulations. They also devised a moral program that regulated behavior in very specific ways. Colonists were to give up horse-racing, cockfighting, all gambling, theater, and expensive entertainments of any kind. They also were to cut back on funeral expenses and to bury their dead with propriety stripped of extravagance. Colonists would not wear special mourning clothes other than a black crepe band around the arm or hat for men and a black ribbon or necklace for women, and would not give away gloves or scarves as funeral presents. Someone sitting down to read the journals of the First Continental Congress, convened to take measures in response to the blockade of Boston Harbor, the changes in the Massachusetts charter, and the alterations in due process, might well be startled to come across the Congress' resolve not to attend cockfights or plays, or to give away gloves at funerals, or wear full mourning. Did these men ride for weeks to get to Philadelphia, and were they ushered into the city with fifes, drums, and a military escort, in order to discuss the latest stage productions or talk about the relative merits of bombazine coats and crepe arm bands? Surely such small talk trivialized the great issues. And yet colonists threw themselves into the proposals and took pride in the significance of their regulations.

The specific moral code of Congress is a springboard into the issues generated by the constitutional crisis that precipitated the American Revolution. The theater, funerals, cockfights, and horse-races all had a cultural context, and their cultural contexts annotated the political significance they assumed during the crisis with Great Britain. While each chapter of this book will study the interaction of morality and ideology in a specific cultural arena, the book as a whole will explore the psychological and political consequences of an intercolonial agreement to regulate moral behavior. The very specific moral program emanated from a disciplinarian morality, stood proxy for a whole system of values, operated as a political strategy for involving people in the political cause and for drawing colonists of different regions and classes together, and affected the colonists' perception of themselves as a people. This perception influenced their eventual choice of governments, both state and national.

The First Continental Congress drew on two systems of morality that mingled in the American environment: an ascetic morality of discipline with its roots in American soil, and an aesthetic morality of perception, known as "moral sense philosophy," which blossomed in Scotland, England, and the Continent in the eighteenth century.[5] Elements of both philosophies appeared in the documents of the First Continental Congress, but there does seem to be a pattern of application. The morality of addresses to a people (the people of Great Britain, of the Province of Quebec, of St. John's, Newfoundland, Nova Scotia, East and West Florida) differed from the morality of regulations designed for the colonists themselves. When Congress addressed a people *as* a people they used the language of Scottish moral philosophy, stressing sentiment and kinship. In October 1774, they wrote a letter to their English "brethren" in which they pleaded that the British people, motivated by "magnanimity and justice," would come to the aid of their American "brethren," and that by refusing to re-elect their "wicked Ministers and evil Counsellors," they would restore the "harmony, friendship and fraternal affection between all the Inhabitants of his Majesty's kingdoms."[6] Congress wrote the American people, explaining that "tender affection" held the American people and the British people together in a "social band," that Americans "ardently" wished that the bond might never be dissolved, and that they would never dissolve the bond unless British hostility compelled them to "renounce every regard, but that of self-preservation."[7] Twenty-two months later, Congress, having

---

5. Edmund S. Morgan shows how Puritan attitudes toward work, frugality, and adversity animated the Revolutionary movement in "The Puritan Ethic and the American Revolution," in *The Challenge of the American Revolution* (New York, 1976), 88–138; Garry Wills analyzes Scottish moral philosophy and places it in the intellectual milieu of the eighteenth century in *Inventing America: Jefferson's Declaration of Independence* (New York, 1979).

6. *Journals of Congress* I:90.

7. Ibid., 99–100.

reminded their British "brethren" that Americans had appealed to their "native justice and magnanimity" and "conjured" them by the ties of "common kindred" to disavow Parliament's hostile acts, declared that the British had "been deaf to the voice of justice and of consanguinity" and that Americans had therefore to "acquiesce" in "necessity" and, dissolving the social bond, hold the British like "the rest of mankind, Enemies in War, in Peace Friends."[8] But while Congress addressed peoples in the language of Scottish moral philosophy grounded in sentiment and kinship, when they turned their attention to the colonists whom they were representing and to measures of reform, they applied standards that harked back to their seventeenth-century past.

In 1774, the Congress took a stand: no more horse-racing, no more cockfighting, no more playing cards or rolling dice, no more gaudy dressing, no more theater. When the eye skims lightly over this list, what leaps out is its "shalt not" quality. Congress had put out its own commandments, a bit more specific than those of the Lord, but equally negative. For colonists in 1774, the way to virtue was through discipline. The political crisis encouraged people to concentrate on obligation as the primary criterion of morality. Whereas Scottish moral philosophers minimized the difference between moral discrimination and aesthetic appreciation, Congress, when it devised a program of behavior, forsook the aesthetic nature of morality in favor of its obligatory nature.

The various activities that Congress proscribed were connected to each other in a network of values. A particular activity could engender hostility for different reasons. For example, the theater, it was argued, exposed people to hypocrisy, blasphemy, and sexual profligacy, and also encouraged extravagance and idleness. Or a particular value could account for hostility toward several activities. A belief in thrift would lead people to oppose gambling (cockfighting, horse-racing, cards and dice) and excessive dress. Excessive dress could be displayed at funerals and at the theater. A belief in industry would lead to the condemnation of activities that drew men away from their

8. Garry Wills in *Inventing America* thoroughly explicates Jefferson's use of Scottish moral philosophy in the Declaration of Independence, but he does not relate the Declaration to the documents that previously had issued from the First Continental Congress and had used the same language.

work, like cockfighting, horse-racing, and the theater. In associating ascetic behavior with resistance, Americans mingled politics and morality. Cockfighting, playacting, and horse-racing were bound up with taxation without consent, bribery, and royally appointed judges in a whole pattern of communal values. The particular restrictions that Congress imposed, seemingly so anomalous and arbitrary, worked as a political strategy. Colonists gave their sanction to certain values, related political resistance to moral resistance (the resistance to temptation), projected personal emotions onto a political cause, brought the world of constitutional grievances into everyday life, and extended the reach of resistance to people from all walks of life and all geographic regions.

Congress proceeded with caution in devising the moral program and skirted the periphery of daily life. Had Congress demanded changes of behavior too fundamental or drastic, they might have jeopardized the success of the resistance. Colonists would then perhaps not have been able to make the sacrifice and might have turned against a cause that seemed to undermine their way of life. But the prohibitions of Congress struck mainly at forms of recreation, and forms of recreation that were relatively recent imports into colonial life and were still associated with England. The theater and cockfighting had not assumed an integral place in colonial society. Even horse-racing, which had been part of life in the South since the beginning of the century, changed dramatically in character in the 1750s when English horses were imported and stakes soared. Most colonists could give up these activities with little actual disruption to their lives. Still, they knew they were making a sacrifice, and the act of sacrifice makes people feel good and commits them to the cause for which the sacrifice is made.

The moral program involved people emotionally in the political cause and touched them personally. The funeral regulations prompted individual colonists to think about the political cause at a time when they were in a heightened emotional state. Private decisions—such as the decision not to wear English clothes, not to eat lamb, not to go to the theater—assumed political and moral importance. Since people led their daily lives forever making the little decisions that life always tosses up—what to wear, what to eat, what to do—they were continually aware of the political cause and continually related themselves to it. The moral program, hammered out of the humdrum routines that press upon ordinary people, removed the question of parliamentary sovereignty from the intellectual sphere of arguments to the sphere of everyday life.

The moral program also extended the reach of resistance. The regulations were designed to impinge on the lives of as many people as possible: horse-racing and cockfighting took place in both the city and country in colonies south of New England, but men were more likely to attend cockfights than women. The theater was mainly a city entertainment (although troupes did travel around the countryside) and involved both men and women. The funeral regulations brought New Englanders, who had already successfully banned horse-races, cockfights, and the theater, under the moral umbrella. The New England delegates to the Congress had to guard against giving the impression that New Englanders stood aloof on a pinnacle of purity and were dictating regulations to morally inferior colonies. Taken together, the behavioral proscriptions impinged on the lives of many people, often on a daily basis, and in this way made the political cause constantly present. Men and women, upper and lower classes, country and city people, Southerners and Northerners: all were brought within the fold of resistance.

The morality promulgated by Congress operated on the colonists politically on two levels. First of all, the colonists were setting themselves up as a model. They were demonstrating to themselves and to the world that they were a moral people and that therefore their resistance to England was moral. The world could question the sincerity of a political position when there were strong motives of gain. The moral regulations strengthened, not the sincerity of the colonists, but their perceived sincerity. The moral purity that hedged the political position affected the public assessment of the position.

But moral regulations were not simply a blend of narcissism and propaganda, measures engaged in for self-satisfaction and for the benefit of a gaping world. The regulations the colonists imposed on themselves put them in the proper state of mind to resist what they called enslavement. When colonists talked about slavery in the context of parliamentary taxation and laws, they did not conjure up blacks on the auction block or blacks in the tobacco fields; they meant something quite technical. Slaves were people who could not exercise their will, either because they were not economically independent (they did not own property) or emotionally independent (their passions controlled their will). Colonists did not consider redistributing property, but they did restrict activities that aroused self-centered passions. Even though refraining from an afternoon at the racetrack or an evening at the theater would not make Britain repeal the Coercive Acts, a life pared of frivolities and distractions increased the self-control of colonists and made them virtuous. With virtue coursing through their veins, they would be strong enough to protect their freedom. On a deeper level the process of abiding by the moral code made colonists aware of themselves as a people, a people with a character. The colonists' perception of their character as a people determined what kind of governments they would establish.

iii

Independence did not come in a flash on the road to Damascus. The legislation that issued from Parliament invited corporate resistance, alienated the colonists from their official leaders, and encouraged leaders of the resistance to work anonymously in committees and congresses. Colonists, galvanized by their moral program, focused on a corporate identity. Gradually they came to see themselves as a people distinct from the British, with a character of their own—a character grounded in virtue. According to the accepted political theory of the day, articulated by Montesquieu, a relationship existed between the character (or *genius*) of a people and the government they could sustain. A people motivated by fear would have tyrannies; a people motivated by honor, monarchies; by virtue, republics. Thus virtue had political as well as moral connotations: the virtuous character Americans had defined for themselves prepared them to establish republican government.[9]

9. Several historians have written on the political language of virtue and corruption and on the relationship of virtue to republican governments. For the most intricate and extended treatment of civic virtue and its relation to republicanism, see J. G. A. Pocock, *The Machiavellian Moment: Florentine Political Thought and the Atlantic Tradition* (Princeton, N.J., 1975). Caroline Robbins shows how a group of Englishmen in the eighteenth century adopted republican ideas of virtue to criticize the corruption of government in *The Eighteenth-Century Commonwealthmen: Studies in the Transmission, Development, and Circumstance of English Liberal Thought from the Restoration of Charles II until the War with the Thirteen Colonies* (Cambridge, Mass., 1959). Bernard Bailyn demonstrates that American colonists adopted these same ideas and standards in *The*

In October 1774, when Congress claimed rights guaranteed to all British subjects under the British Constitution, petitioned the king for the redress of their grievances, and addressed the British people as brothers, they did not see themselves as a distinct people and therefore did not repudiate either the king or the British people. Even in 1775, after fighting broke out, although loyalty did corrode, colonists still claimed allegiance to the king; and when in July 1776, fourteen months after the battles of Lexington and Concord, colonists finally did declare independence, they did not indict the monarchical system of government, they merely repudiated George III and the English people. And yet, when each state set up its own government and when Congress drew up the Articles of Confederation, hardly anyone thought of replacing George with an American king. In 1776, American republicanism was not an issue, but a fact.

During the years of political agitation that preceded the outbreak of revolution, Englishmen accused colonists of being republicans, and colonists vociferously denied the charge. Perhaps the colonists were indeed guilty of hypocrisy in 1774 and 1775, cloaking republicanism in ardent protestations of loyalty to the king. But there is another explanation. Perhaps they unconsciously taught themselves to be republicans before they were avowed republicans. In 1774, colonists undertook voluntary ascetic measures to become morally strong and immune from the corruption that would entail slavery. In the process of regulating their behavior morally for the sake of a political cause, they acquired self-esteem as a people. Colonists resisted British legislation in the name of liberty, and in insisting on their political liberty at the same time as they pursued a moral course, colonists saw themselves as worthy of liberty, worthier than their oppressors. The moral program, whose goal was to bind colonists together in a common cause, eventually helped colonists transcend particular grievances and focus on themselves as a people. Colonists

Ideological Origins of the American Revolution (Cambridge, Mass., 1967). Gordon Wood analyzes the transformation of republican government based on the virtue of the people to republican government based on the sovereignty of the people in *The Creation of the American Republic, 1776–1787* (Chapel Hill, N.C., 1969). Edmund S. Morgan shows how political fictions such as the sovereignty of the people and representation can mold reality to conform to fiction in *Inventing the People: The Rise of Popular Sovereignty in England and America* (New York, 1988).

separated government from society and came to believe in the moral superiority of their own society, a superiority that would free them from the necessity of monarchical government.

When colonists resisted encroachments on their liberties, they did not do so as republicans, but in the process of resistance they silently prepared themselves for republican government—not theoretically but psychologically. In abiding by the moral proscriptions of Congress, colonists became not only a virtuous people, but a people focusing on the virtuous life. Colonists could be monarchists while still in the process of learning to be virtuous, but once they proved themselves a virtuous people and were conscious of their virtue, they quite naturally (having decided, because of constitutional grievances and cultural incompatibility, to throw off allegiance to King George and the British people) established republican governments—a classic case of the owl of Minerva spreading her wings at dusk. The republicanism of Americans was not planned. It was not just that Americans did not see themselves as republicans until they were republicans; it was more that they could not see themselves as republicans until they had psychologically prepared themselves.

Historians disagree about the extent of nationalism that existed in 1776. Clearly, many colonial leaders well versed in political philosophy were more interested in forming state governments than in running the Confederation or drawing up a constitution for it; but equally clearly, whatever attachment Americans may have felt to their states, they did have a sense of themselves as a people. The Declaration of Independence acknowledges both national and state identity. First, Congress declared that Americans as a people were no longer bound politically to the British as a people. "When in the Course of human events, it becomes necessary for one people to dissolve the political bands which have connected them with another . . . a decent respect to the opinions of mankind requires that they should declare the causes which impel them to the separation." Second, Congress, once again in the name of "the good People of these Colonies," declared independence for the states. "We . . . solemnly publish and declare, That these United Colonies are, and of Right ought to be FREE AND INDEPENDENT STATES." But while here the Declaration refers to the states in the plural and clearly seems to treat the states as separate, independent governments, the powers the Declaration enumerates—the power to levy war, conclude peace, contract alliances, establish commerce—were in fact allocated to the national government in Congress. However difficult it may be to measure with any accuracy the degree of nationalism in 1776, some things can be stated with certainty: one declaration of independence sufficed for Americans of all the colonies; all the rebelling Americans felt they were no longer British; people from different colonies, feeling they had more in common with each other than with the British, formed a continental army and a continental congress; and all the rebelling Americans felt they were republicans.

Congress could not declare independence until July 1776, in spite of colonial grievances and in spite of the fighting, because it was not until July 1776 that they could be certain that Americans thought of themselves as a people. Having declared independence, Americans woke up to find themselves, as a people, republicans. Had a group of American republicans at any time declared independence, the common cause might well have disintegrated in civil war. But republicanism followed moral cohesion. It was the sense of American identity that finally precipitated the Declaration of Independence, two years after the colonists had defined their political position. Americans as a people declared independence, not Americans as republicans. By the time republican government was adopted in the colonies, it was no longer an issue; the late worm had successfully avoided the early bird.

★ 2 ★

Plays and Politics

i

In 1774, American colonists gave up the theater as part of their program of moral regeneration, a program designed to strengthen the collective will as a bulwark against political enslavement. For centuries men of a religious bent had complained of the sinful effects that plays had on both actors and audience. The Catholic church expressed its disapproval of the acting profession by passing canons that prohibited actors from being buried in consecrated ground or from turning Christian without first renouncing their profession. Church councils and synods condemned all plays (but especially the *Charevarian,* in which actors donned vizards to impersonate devils) and forbade Christian families on pain of excommunication to lend clothes to acting troupes for costumes. In England actors were classified as "Rogues" and were subject to laws regulating poor and disreputable people. Other laws prohibited the selling of satanic vizards and punished profanity on the stage. During the Puritan Commonwealth, of course, plays were outlawed altogether.

Theater was associated with the propagation of vice in general and with foreign vice in particular. When a people lost its sense of purpose or confidence, the theater not infrequently became a victim of xenophobia. Ancient Romans (according to one critic of the theater) feared "that the Entertainments of the Play-house would bring in

20

foreign Vice, and that the old *Roman* Virtue would be lost, and the Spirit of the People Emasculated and softened."[1] Since Romans could not be actors without losing their citizenship, the acting profession was relegated to slaves, who were foreigners. Hence the association of the theater with foreignness was reinforced. The French and the English associated the theater in their countries with Italians, and the American colonists associated the theater in the colonies with the English. In 1697, the French king expelled Italian players from his country, and in 1774, Americans expelled the theater, which was run by English actors and produced English plays, from theirs.

Critics inventoried the evils of the theater from cellar to attic, and concluded that nothing was safe so long as plays were being produced: not religion, industry, chastity, or honesty. "I should be very sorry," announced an upright New York citizen in the newspaper, "that impiety had gained so much ground among us as to support a Play-house upon the ruins of religion."[2] The theater, critics argued, tempted people to forego church for more gripping entertainment and to skip out on their jobs.[3] In going to see plays, people not only wasted time that they might have better spent in industrious occupations, they endangered their souls by turning away from worship. The theater assaulted female virtue. A morally miasmic stench issued from the orchestra pit, where panders and whores congregated, turning the theater into "the best fairs for unchaste bargains." Since innocent women, isolated from the world's depravity, supposedly could not handle the advances of artful seducers versed in the skill of stew houses, "[m]any virgins, who frequented the play-house, made shipwreck of their chastity." "The Devil's Conventicle," "the Synagogue of Satan," "the Chappel of Venus," "a sink of debauchery": a waterfall of epithetic abuse cascaded from the pens of the clergy who saw Satan using the stage to work his will and corrupt people, while righteous citizens in New York and Philadelphia, worried that vice might be unleashed by a resident theater company, took up the hue and cry. And in Carpenters' Hall in the fall of 1774, the congressional delegates, defenders of freedom and arbiters of morality, en-

---

1. *The Conduct of the Stage Considered* (London, 1781), 21–22.

2. *New-York Journal*, 24 December 1767.

3. Edmund S. Morgan, "Puritan Hostility to the Theatre," American Philosophical Society, *Proceedings* 110 (October 1966): 340–47.

closed the hostility toward the theater in their own system of reference and banned the theater as a menace to the common cause of colonial resistance.[4]

Yet, among these delegates, there must surely have been men who had of an evening attended the theater. Hallam's theater company had had seasons in New York City, Philadelphia, Annapolis, and Charleston; and it had toured the small towns of Virginia and Maryland. Some of the delegates had spent time in England and must have found themselves, in the course of ordinary sociability, members of a theater party. Wealthy Virginians and South Carolinians were apt to go to England, and a few jotted down their activities in journals or account books. William Beverley, a Virginia planter, on a trip to England to put his son in school, behaved like a normal tourist. He went to cathedrals, horse-races, and theaters, all on his own initiative. One night, when he was dining out in particular splendor, he found himself carried off by his host to the playhouse at Covent Gardens to see *Conscious Lovers*.[5] But even though some members of Congress might have enjoyed going to plays, they could still have voted to ban the theater as an appropriate response to the political crisis, a decision made not for themselves but in the name of others: the poor, women, servants. The decision might well have had to do less with the experience and tastes of the members than with social and political theories that inhibited them from generalizing on the basis of their own experience and called upon them to protect the dependent—classes of people who, they felt, had no will of their own.

Josiah Quincy, a young Bostonian steeped in Puritan morality and republican virtue, illustrates the prevalent ambivalence towards the theater. In 1778, Quincy, aged twenty-three, made a tour of the colonies. In Philadelphia he went to the playhouse and saw *The Gamester* and *Padlock*. Although he criticized the acting, he found himself greatly attracted to the form of entertainment, which was illegal in his

4. Hugh F. Rankin in *The Theater in Colonial America* (Chapel Hill, N.C., 1960) surveys the theater companies and the reception of the theater from 1716–1774; Kenneth Silverman thoroughly documents the history of the theater from 1763–1789 in *A Cultural History of the American Revolution* (New York, 1976).

5. William Beverley, "Diary," in *Virginia Magazine of History and Biography* 36 (1928): 168.

own colony, Massachusetts. "I was however upon the whole much gratified, and believe if I had stayed in town a month should go to the theatre every acting night."[6] The next year, on a trip to England, Quincy had a chance to gratify his new taste. First he went to *The Beggar's Opera* and concluded, as he had concluded the year before in Philadelphia, that the theater corrupted people. "I am still further satisfied in my opinion that stage is the nursery of vice, and disseminates the seeds of vice far and wide with amazing and baneful success."[7] He then proceeded to attend performances of *The Beaux' Stratagem, Hamlet, The Cobbler, Jane Shore, Comus,* and *Armida.* After each of these assaults on his virtue he usually had some negative remarks. Of *Jane Shore* he said, "no part was performed well but the part by Miss Catley, which being wanton, was done admirably by her"; of the opera *Armida,* "Some parts of the music exquisitely fine: the dancing elegant indeed: but in general, but a poor entertainment for an Englishman."[8] Quincy admitted that the theater held a personal fascination for him. He loved going to plays, even though as a sop to his vibrant conscience he continually noted the poor quality of the performance. Quincy evidently felt himself strong enough to attend a performance and repulse the evil influence, but he remained wary of the corruption the theater might wreak on the morally vulnerable. Although he loved to go to the theater himself, he felt that he should forego this pleasure for the good of society. "[A]s a citizen and friend to the morals and happiness of society I should strive hard against the admission and much more the establishment of a playhouse in any state of which I was a member."[9] The notion of an incompatibility between the theater and moral society prevailed. People with political power accepted this incompatibility, and as citizens made decisions that protected people excluded from the political process and encouraged them to be good citizens.

The delegates to Congress in 1774, in the dawn of the American era, drew up the first list of un-American activities. They tacked skull-and-crossbones on paths that led to corruption; they identified

6. Josiah Quincy, Jr., "Journal," in Massachusetts Historical Society, *Proceedings* 49 (Boston, 1915–1916): 479.

7. Quincy, "London Journal," in *op. cit.* 50 (1916–1917): 439.

8. Ibid., 450, 464.

9. Quincy, "Journal," 479.

specific vices and cordoned them off. The debates and discussions took place behind closed doors, and the members left behind no written records: no explanations, no personal tidbits, no evidence of squabbles. Delegates decided to ban the theater. We do not know who proposed the motion, what individual members thought of it, whether it occasioned a pause for consideration or was swept up in a wave of unanimity as an obvious measure. The debates, if debates there were, are forever behind closed doors, but though we cannot hear the particular opinions of particular men, we can overhear the modulations of the decisions. Individual voices do not rise above the murmur, but the ban speaks for itself, a moral testimony to a political creed. The traditional arguments against the theater as a breeding ground of vice must be located first in the social geography of eighteenth-century America and then in the political geography of a particular crisis.

ii

Hostility toward the theater throve in class- and gender-consciousness. Theater critics couched their arguments in concern for others: the poor, women, and the family; and dealt with the themes of extravagance, dissipation, deceit, and disobedience. During the imperial crisis, leaders incorporated the class-oriented arguments against the theater into the political rhetoric of the time, and devised programs compatible with the rhetoric. Poor people and women, who were not deemed to have independent wills, could not make political decisions, but men of property, who did have independent wills and were therefore capable of making political decisions, could protect the poor and women and prepare them for allegiance to the political cause.

The poor had a role to play in society. They were meant to be industrious and solvent (they should not be poor, that is). If they were going to be poor, they should belong to the "honest," "worthy," "deserving" poor, not to the "idle" poor. The "honest" poor (the old, the crippled, the victims of disaster) were good for society because they stimulated charity. "May we not suppose that the hand of providence has thus unequally dispensed its blessings, to serve as so many calls upon us to act worthy this exalted part of our nature? The poor have a warrant from heaven to draw upon the treasury of the rich, and in the rich man's breast they have a voucher, that gives a force and sanction to their demand."[10] For their part, the poor should respect their betters and obey their masters. For a variety of reasons, the theater was perceived as a threat to the peace and tranquility of idyllic poverty, and, in response to the threat, a coterie of prosperous moralists erected their defense.[11]

The theater, according to the views of the worried non-poor, tempted the poor into an extravagance they could ill afford, an extravagance that ruined not only the spendthrift himself, but his inevitably large family. The children howled for bread while their father gawked at sexual intrigues. Theater-haters, who attended theatrical performances probably to test the depths of depravity available for public consumption, often spotted in the audience a bankrupt tradesman living off charity or a debtor on the brink of imprisonment.[12] These scapegraces sometimes had the audacity to attend with their whole family, thus endangering the minds of their children and wives, as well as depriving their stomachs.

The theater also threatened the poor indirectly, even the "worthy" poor who could resist the temptation to throw away their money on theater tickets. The theater drained money from the well-to-do, money that they should have been giving to the poor. "A fondness for the entertainment of the stage, cannot be gratified without considerable expense. The money thrown away in one night at a play, would purchase wood, provisions and other necessaries, sufficient for a number of poor, to make them pass through the winter with tolerable comfort."[13] According to these critics, money spent on the theater never made its way back into society, but was lost forever. Meanwhile, the people who had denied the deserving poor the eight shillings, five shillings, or three shillings they were paying for a theater ticket were picking up bad habits of extravagance and luxury

---

10. *New-York Journal*, 7 January 1768.

11. Kenneth Silverman reviews the arguments of theater critics that the theater undermined the business ethic, drained money from the community, corrupted industry, and inhibited charity, in "The Economic Debate over the Theater in Revolutionary America," in *The American Revolution and Eighteenth-Century Culture*, Paul J. Korshin, ed. (New York, 1986), 219–39.

12. *New-York Journal*, "Thrifty," 21 January 1768.

13. *New-York Journal*, 7 January 1768.

from the plays themselves. The rich clothes and gaudy finery of the actors set high and expensive sartorial standards and worked the spectators into such an acquisitive fever that they would rush the next day to the tailors, dressmakers, or haberdashers. Their thoughts, having been diverted to fashion, would no longer dwell on the needs of the deserving poor, and charity would wither as private vanity dissipated public spirit.

Those who stood up for the theater against the fusillades of its opponents did not believe in the "vanishing money" theory of economics but advocated the "trickle down" theory. The wealthy had a duty to spend money; expenditures increased employment; and the swirling circulation of pounds, shillings, and pence increased the happiness of all. Adam Ferguson, best known as a Scottish moral philosopher, was also a trickle-down economist.

> The money which the rich expends is paid for the labour of the poor. Different trades live upon the profits of furnishing his cloathing, his table, and his equipage. It is evident how many poor industrious people would starve, if he did not buy the works which they furnish him. The very money he lays out for amusement comes at last into the hands of the poor, and is paid as the price of their labour. A part of it we shall suppose is laid out for the amusements of the Theatre, and the people who receive it there, are so many hands who distribute that money among the industrious poor. Every Player must be cloathed, maintained and lodged: The money which he receives therefor is paid at last to the spinstress, the weaver, the clothier, and other tradesmen who live by furnishing the ordinary necessaries of life.[14]

But according to theater opponents, the trickle-down economists harbored a heterodoxy in their black hearts: they did not make any moral distinction between spending for pleasure and spending for public service. They pictured the rich sustaining the poor indirectly. The poor might engage in activities that did not in themselves directly bear on the public good but that generated income by offering an outlet for the money of the rich. Surely, the objection ran, the rich could invest their money in projects that would tend to the public good and at the same time employ people. Arguing for the theater as

14. Adam Ferguson, *The Morality of Stage-Plays seriously considered* (Edinburgh, 1757), 25.

a means of putting money into circulation merely pandered to the proclivity of the rich for pleasure, luxury, and extravagance. If the point was to alleviate poverty, why not give the money to the deserving poor directly rather than indirectly by a method that lined the pockets of immoral intermediaries, the actors?

Detractors of the theater could dismiss the argument that a theater company, by creating jobs and paying for services, diminished the need for charity, because they thought that charity benefited society. If the poor were helped by some impersonal process, then society itself would suffer from the loss of charity. Charity ennobled the giver and kept the rich responsible. "The very discharge of the offices of benevolence, adds to the internal felicity of our minds."[15] In this sense the rich needed the poor (the worthy poor) for their spiritual well-being. As objects of charity, the worthy poor—children, women, the lame and the halt—provided for the spiritual well-being of the wealthy without threatening their physical well-being. The idle poor were not to be objects of charity; they were to find productive work that enhanced the public good. Society owed nothing to the idle poor.

The theater-wreckers—"[b]raying reverberators," "busy watch tower spies," "jealous reformers of morals"—spiced up the tone of their denunciations by including the argument of the purse, bound to catch public attention when righteousness merely bored. The playhouse, announced one New York critic, would cost the public 6,000 pounds, by which he implied that the actors would leave the city at the end of the season their pockets stuffed with 6,000 pounds of profit. He and later critics with an economic bent talked about the "tax" the theater company levied on the city. In fact, in two months the theater company would have taken in 1,920 pounds, but it would have paid out 1,300 pounds. The company had to pay for the house, costumes, scenery, props, and candles. They also had to pay musicians, a front doorkeeper, a stage doorkeeper, assistant doorkeepers, a bill sticker, a men's dresser, a stagekeeper, a drummer, and a publisher for two sets of bills and for advertisements in the paper. After all these expenses they were left with a profit of 620 pounds, from which they had to pay for lodging, food, and laundry.[16] Opponents of the theater, in talking about the profits of the company, cavalierly neglected to tick off the

15. *New-York Journal,* 7 January 1768.
16. *New-York Gazette; or the Weekly Post-Boy,* 28 December 1761.

liabilities against the assets. They talked about the tax the theater levied on the city and refused to recognize the benefits of circulating money—the profits that "useful" members of society would have made by servicing the theater company: dressmakers, tailors, cobblers, haberdashers, carpenters, painters, merchants.

The foes of the theater had no truck with theories of employment that classified acting as work. They wanted useful people, not money in use; production of worthwhile goods, not monetary circulation. Six years after Hallam's first siege of New York, critics were still calling the amount of money taken at the theater doors a tax. "What an enormous tax do we burthen ourselves with? it is computed at least £300 a week."[17] This particular critic scorned the contention that the money was spent in New York. The exotic and expensive costumes that the actors flaunted obviously came from overseas and tempted young Americans to ape English fashions. "Some pretend the money is spent among ourselves—deceitful reasoning! is not foreign finery their chief expence, and their dresses imitated by our young folks?—Luxury and extravagance is the bane of the age."[18] Money, as he pictured it, flooded out of New York into foreign coffers.

The trickle-down economic theory wrung little esteem from theater critics because they thought that buying and spending destroyed industry and laid waste to virtue. Theatergoers, their appetites whipped up by gaudy theatrical performances, would press towards the shops afterwards to lose themselves in giddy extravagance and luxury. The theater, that temple of pleasure, corrupted both poor and rich. It tempted the poor to leave off their labor and spend what little money they had. Love of pleasure "cuts the sinews of industry. . . . Therefore if this passion spreads among the lower sorts of people, where industry is their only means of subsistence, it must have a fatal effect on them."[19] The poor were not the only victims. The theater also corrupted the rich. On the stage, vice flourished, and theatergoers, in deriving pleasure from this dramatic vice, made themselves responsible for it. "But certainly, if you stand by, and assist Men in their evil Actions, if you make their Vices your Pleasures and Entertainment,

17. *New-York Journal*, "R.S.," 28 January 1768.
18. Ibid.
19. Ibid.

and pay your Money to be so entertained, you make yourself a Partaker of their Sins in a very high degree." Furthermore, by patronizing the theater, the rich were responsible in two ways for ruining the poor: they set a bad example for the poor to emulate, and their patronage kept the theater open, a glittering temptation.[20]

If the theater posed a particular threat to the poor because of their economic vulnerability, it also threatened women because of their physical and mental vulnerability. Given the belief of critics that plays corrupted the audience and wreaked havoc through deception, the people at large had to be convinced that they needed protection. As a way of raising this conviction, critics focused on women, the "weak" who could not protect themselves. Sermons against the theater sometimes took on a chivalric tone. Men were called upon to be knights, to protect women, and to reform the world. An upper-class woman who frequented the theater found herself at a disadvantage when confronting a crusading minister. He would claim that because of her correct and proper upbringing she would be defenseless against the onslaught of obscenity and lewdness wafting from the stage. Having never been exposed to obscenity or lewdness, she would not be able to recognize them for what they were (evil), and therefore, with no defenses, would be vulnerable to corruption. If she boldly answered that of course she could recognize obscenity and lewdness—even prurience, lechery, and salacious advances—then she convicted herself of indiscreet living. Where did a proper young woman pick up this knowledge unless she were slipping out occasionally and hitting the hot spots—or, of course, unless she were attending the theater, that school for scandal?

> The Customs of Education, and the Laws of Decency, are so very cautious, and reserv'd in regard to Women: I say so very reserv'd that 'tis almost a Fault for them to understand they are ill Used. They can't discover their Disgust without disadvantage, nor Blush without disservice to their Modesty. To appear with any skill in such Cant, looks as if they had fallen upon ill Conversation; or managed their Curiosity amiss.[21]

20. William Law, "The absolute Unlawfulness of Stage Entertainments fully demonstrated," in *The Works of the Reverend William Law, A.M.* 2 (London, 1762): 11; *New-York Gazette; or Weekly Post-Boy,* 1 February 1768.

21. Jeremy Collier, *A Short View of the Immorality and Profaneness of the English Stage,* second edition (London, 1698), 7–8.

Moralists picked their way through arguments that seem to people of a different age elitist, sexist, and prim. But given the accepted notion that the poor and women had weak wills, and given the subject matter of the plays being produced, critics of the theater, operating within the confines of their intellectual and moral world, had legitimate fears. Environmental in their approach, they argued that exposure to vice made vice familiar, and familiarity weakened the barrier of modesty. As Pope put it:

> The Fair sate panting at a *Courtier's Play,*
> And not a mask went *un-improv'd* away:
> The modest Fan was lifted up no more,
> And Virgins *smil'd* at what they *blush'd* before—[22]

Constant exposure to sex and infidelity would make all people—but particularly women—unchaste and unfaithful.

The outrageous immorality of eighteenth-century English theater seemed to substantiate the arguments of theater critics. English comedies concentrated on the relationship between the sexes. Life in England was presented as sexual intrigue laced with gambling, extravagance, dandyism, and political corruption. Critics wanted to ban the theater because they thought that corrupt plays would corrupt the audience. Ironically, the very plays that the critics worked so hard to ban presented American audiences with a view of English life that they could readily identify as corrupt and from which they could dissociate themselves when the political crisis polarized virtuous Americans and corrupt Englishmen. English plays portrayed England as a country of sexual looseness and political degradation.

In eighteenth-century English comedies, the perversion of human relationships undermined institutions: the family, marriage, and even government. "Happy families are all alike; every unhappy family is unhappy in its own way," Tolstoy pronounced, but he could not have had in mind the eighteenth-century English family as it was presented on the stage. On the stage all families were unhappy, and all were unhappy in the same way and for the same reason. Infidelity pervaded every relationship. Wives cuckolded husbands; husbands cheated on

---

22. Alexander Pope, "Essay on Criticism," in *The Twickenhan Edition of the Poems of Alexander Pope,* John Butt, ed. (London, 1950): Vol. 1, p. 299, ll. 540–544.

wives; men and women, whatever their marital status, devoted their lives to intrigue and to making people look like fools; children disobeyed and tricked their parents or guardians; parents, their eyes glittering with gold, forced children into profitable but unpalatable marriages. Not a lovely crew. Playwrights spread before their audiences a display of rakes, thieves, sharpers, libidinous old men, whores, dupes, and "chattering crop-eared coxcombs." Antagonists of the theater feared that these far-from-wholesome plays were undermining the institution of marriage in the colonies. One went so far as to claim that having a theater company in town led to a decline in the marriage rate, that index of the moral and economic health of a society. "The judicious Montesquieu observes, that the sure sign of a place thriving is frequent marriages, formerly the people here married young, for they could easily support a family; is this now the case? no, rather how few marriages are now among us."[23] He and other critics argued from economy. Plays wasted money that should support families. Without money, families would disintegrate in destitution, and prospective couples would not undertake to get married.

The display of cuckoldry and intrigue dished up for English and colonial audiences jeopardized marriage as an ideal. Many comedies elaborated on the theme of ensnarement. Either the man or the woman wished to escape matrimony and had to be tricked into it. "Matrimony!" jeers a woman to a man who has just confessed his matrimonial intentions. "[H]a! ha! ha! What Crimes have you committed against the God of Love, that he should revenge 'em so severely to stamp Husband upon your Forehead?"[24] Love and marriage did not go together on the eighteenth-century stage. Love thrived outside marriage in assignations, intrigues, innuendoes, and impersonations. "Let the World see we are Lovers after Wedlock; 'twill be a Novelty," says one heroine to her fiancé.[25] Rope ladders and balconies accommodated ardent lovers; disguises deceived suspicious spouses, parents, and guardians; closets and chimneys concealed paramours. Everyone spent most of his or her time deceiving others and skirting the truth. On those occasional moments when people spoke directly, they made a jest of fidelity.

23. *New-York Journal,* "R.S.," 28 January 1768.

24. Mrs. Centlivre, *Busie Body* (London, 1709) Act I, scene i, p. 11.

25. *Busie Body,* Act IV, scene v, p. 52.

Lady Lurewell: Shall I be free with you, Sir *Harry?*

Sir Harry: With all my Heart Madam, so I may be free with you.

Lady Lurewell: Then, plainly, Sir, I shall beg the favour to see you some other time, for at this very Minute I have two Lovers in the House.

Sir Harry: Then to be as plain, I must be gone this Minute, for I must see another Mistress within these two Hours.[26]

If unmarried girls had all the fun, why did anyone ever saddle herself with a husband? Indeed, dalliance and intrigue seem to have served as an eighteenth-century equivalent of a career: an occupation in which a woman could employ her wit, and that would distract from the boredom of an underemployed and routine life. But then, matrimony did not put an end to dalliance and intrigue; only the victims changed. Husbands took the place of parents as dupes. And often marriage made a woman freer.

Lord Townly: How, Madam! Is any Woman under less Restraint after Marriage than before it?

Lady Townly: O! my Lord! my Lord! They are quite different Creatures! Wives have infinite Liberties in Life, that would be terrible in an unmarried Woman to take.

Lord Townly: Name One.

Lady Townly: Fifty, if you please—To begin, then, in the morning—a married Woman may have Men at her Toilet, invite them to Dinner, appoint them a party, in the Stage-box at the Play; engross the Conversation there; call them by their Christian names; talk lowder than the Players;—from thence . . . clatter again to this End of the town, break, with the Morning, into an Assembly, crowd to the Hazard Table, throw a familiar Levant upon some sharp lurching man of Quality, and if he demands his Money, turn it off with a loud Laugh, and cry—you'll owe it him, to vex him![27]

The plays that were popular in the eighteenth century seemed to lend credence to the dire assessment of theater critics that the theater

26. George Farquhar, *Constant Couple,* in *The Works of George Farquhar* 1 (New York, 1988): 204, Act IV, scene ii, ll. 61–68.

27. John Vanbrugh and Colley Cibber, *The Provoked Husband* (London, 1728), Act I, scene i, pp. 3–4.

undermined social values. Vice on the stage might have served as a didactic technique for getting across morality if the bad were pitted against the good. Then an audience of young innocents, predisposed toward virtue, might identify with the good and reject the bad. But searching through the comedies of the eighteenth century it is hard to find any good or sympathetic people to identify with. Role models, that is, were in short supply. One critic complained that plays instilled bad values by depicting children disobeying their parents. But surely the audience, appalled by disobedience, would sympathize with the parents, and the virtue of obedience could be proselytized by the back door. Perhaps. But cast an eye on these models of parenthood. Take the cases of Isabinda and Charles and Miranda and Sir George Airy. Isabinda and Charles are in love and would like to get married, but obstacles present themselves in the form of Sir Jealous Traffick, father of Isabinda, and Sir Francis Gripe, father of Charles. Sir Jealous, charmed by the Spanish treatment of women, wants his daughter to wear a veil and not to speak to men in public. In pursuit of this ideal, he has arranged for her to marry a Spaniard and, while waiting for the Spaniard to arrive, has taken the precaution of locking his daughter up. Sir Francis Gripe is even less lovely. Suffering from a rampant case of avarice and lust, he is a wrecker of happy marriages *par excellence*. He blocks Charles' marriage not only by disinheriting him but by refusing to relinquish the fortune that Charles has inherited from his uncle. Furthermore, he is an old lecher. Although "nothing but bones rattling in a leathern bag," he plans to marry one of his young wards, Miranda (who is forced to intrigue in order to get him to release her fortune, which he holds in trust). "Od! I'm all of a fire," Sir Francis says, referring to his passion for Miranda. She responds in an aside, "'Tis a wonder the dry Stubble does not blaze."[28] Guardian of a bevy of wealthy wards, Sir Francis has quite a marriage racket going. Since he controls the estates of his wards, who cannot marry without his consent at least until a certain age, he raffles them off to the highest bidder.

Many plays made a mockery of virtue. Sir Harry Wildair, a good-humored rake who refuses to be baited out of his good humor, berates a potential mistress who has just scornfully turned down fifty

---

28. *Busie Body*, Act III, scene v, p. 36.

guineas and given it as her opinion that her virtue should quell all Sir Harry's lascivious thoughts.

> *Sir Harry:* But pray Madam be pleas'd to consider what is this same Vertue that you make such a mighty Noise about—Can your Vertue bespeak you a front Row in the Boxes. No, for the players can't live upon Vertue. Can your Vertue keep you a Coach and Six, no, no, your Vertuous Woman walk a foot—Can your Vertue hire you a pue in a Church? Why, the very Sexton will tell you, no. Can your Vertue stake for you at Piquet, no. Then what business has a Woman with Vertue?—Come, come, Madam, I offer'd you fifty Guineas,—there's a hundred. . . .

[She refuses and tells him that only cowards dare affront a woman.]

> *Sir Harry:* Affront! S'death, Madam, a hundred Guinea's will set up [a bank] at Basset, a hundred Guinea's will furnish out your Lodgings with China; a hundred Guinea's will give you an Air of Quality; a hundred Guinea's will buy you a rich Escriture for your Billet *deux,* or a fine Common-Prayer Book for your Vertue. . . .[29]

In the end Sir Harry realizes that he has affronted a virtuous woman (he had been tricked into believing her otherwise), and that he will have to propose marriage or challenge the cozener to a duel. He chooses marriage, the more courageous course, as evidence of his valor. But the audience never sees Sir Harry and Angelica in matrimonial bliss. Instead the audience has been exposed to the life of plays, assemblies, basset and piquet, masquerades and the accoutrements of fashion: sartorial elegance, jewelry, equipage. They do not see a particular incident; they see a way of life.

In the process of ridiculing matrimony, the English comedies of the eighteenth century presented a sexual maze. Men dressed up as women to gain access to their mistresses; women in the role of mistress or wife sought control over men; and men, in making women the chief object of their existence, subsided into effeminacy. Beaux pranced and strutted to draw attention to themselves, decked out in finery and heavily perfumed. Whenever confronted with an awkward situation, they skittered away, mocking the manly virtues of courage

---

29. *Constant Couple,* Act V, scene i, ll. 108–28.

and honesty. Sir Harry Wildair, the affable rake, on being challenged to a duel of honor as a gentleman, laughed off the challenge.

> A Gentleman! Why there agen now. A Gentleman! I tell you once more, Colonel, that I am a Baronet, and have eight thousand Pounds a year. I can dance, sing, ride, fence, understand the Languages. Now, I can't conceive how running you through the Body should contribute one Jot more to my Gentility. But pray Colonel, I had forgot to ask you: What's the Quarrel?[30]

Gentlemen were distinguished from beaux by their adherence to the code of honor. Whatever their gambling, drinking, and sexual habits, they were no cowards.

> *Wife:* O! Mr. *Constable,* here's a Rogue that has murder'd my Husband, and robb'd him of his Cloathes.
>
> *Constable:* Murder and robbery! then he must be a Gentleman. Hands off there, he must not be abus'd—Give an Account of your self: Are you a Gentleman?
>
> *Clincher, sen.:* No, Sir, I am a Beau.
>
> *Constable:* Then you have kill'd no body, I'm perswaded. How came you by these Cloathes, Sir?[31]

Comedies presented a life in which the concentration on women weakened men and made them effeminate and unfit to carry on the affairs of the country. The whole country seemed to be sucked into a vortex of sexuality. Through the steam and vapors of concupiscence, intrigue, and innuendo, Parliament glistened in the background. It was presented as the arena for controlling relationships between men and women. One character is spending half his estate to get into Parliament so that he can pass a law requiring Englishwomen to wear veils and not converse in public with men. Another wants to pass a law regulating the amount that mistresses can demand from their lovers. "I have no mind to meddle in State Affairs; but these Women will make me a Parliament Man, spight of my Teeth, on

---

30. Ibid., Act IV, scene i, p. 197, ll. 29–34.
31. Ibid., p. 198, ll. 84–91.

purpose to bring in a Bill against their Extortion."[32] Here was the world turned topsy-turvy. Private dalliance was mirrored in public affairs, and the resources of Parliament were to be used to control women—not to wipe out prostitution, but to make the exploitation of women a bit easier. Parliament was brought down to the level of petty family squabbles.

Sir Francis Wronghead of Bumper-Hall is a case in point. By a timely bribe to the sheriff who sent in the election returns, Sir Francis carried the borough of Guzzledown and came to London to retrieve his private affairs by being a Parliament man. His wife, a veritable jade, runs riot as soon as she finds herself in the rich London soil. First she spends 100 pounds in one morning on toys, trinkets, and clothes, and pooh-poohs her husband's objections to this extravagance. "My dear, do you think I came hither to live out of the fashion? why, the greatest distinction of a fine lady, in this town, is in the variety of pretty Things that she no Occasion for."[33] The Wrongheads, who are made to look like fools, may inspire the audience with disgust for their folly and extravagance. But meanwhile the British election system in all its corruption has been publicized and the dignity of Parliament denigrated.

When colonists banned the theater in 1774, they did so to protect colonial virtue: the virtue of the poor, the virtue of women, the virtue of Christians. The concept of Christian virtue differed from that of republican virtue. The emphasis of the colonists in banning the theater was on Christian virtue: protection of female chastity, the family, and life conforming to moral principles (work, thrift, and honesty). But English comedies also portrayed male dalliance and foppishness and lent credence to the argument that the theater rendered whole populations "effeminate." One critic somberly noted the fate of classical Athenians. "The theater had a very considerable share in sinking the Athenians into effeminacy and indolence."[34] The virtue that the Athenians lost was not, needless to say, Christian virtue. Classical virtue, the virtue of the Athenians, Romans, and Florentine republicans, was more directly associated with *vir* (man). In arguing that the theater turned men into women and made a

32. Ibid., Act v, scene i, p. 213, ll. 134–36.

33. *The Provoked Husband,* Act IV, scene i, p. 65.

34. Philander, "Votaries of the Theater," *New-York Journal,* 4 February 1768.

people unfit to defend their lives and property, polemicists introduced republican virtue into the debate. Men were virtuous when they owned property, bore arms with which they could defend their property, and participated in the political process. Since colonists owned property and guns and were protesting their right to legislate for themselves, it made sense for them to reject plays that portrayed men whose virtue was dissolved in effeminacy.[35]

Members of Congress, in drawing up a list of prohibited activities, very deliberately focused on English activities: horse-racing, cock-fighting, and the theater. They seem to have been constructing an English way of life from which colonists could dissociate themselves. Colonists, whether or not they had actually seen the plays that were staged in New York, Philadelphia, and the Southern towns, could readily identify them as English. Not only were the plays English, but the actors themselves were English. Those colonists who had actually attended the theater or had read the plays that were available in print would have carried away with them a particularly sordid view of English life that could easily assume propagandistic value in a political conflict that was defined in terms of virtue and corruption.

iii

Criticism of the theater reflected the elitism and sexism of the time. Educated men saw themselves controlling the depravity of lower classes and protecting the virtue of women. When demonstrating the evil effects of the theater on the poor, they dwelt on the economic theory that the theater drained money from the colonies and dissipated it; when demonstrating the evil effects of the theater on women, they had only to point to the plays themselves, which displayed sexual promiscuity and intrigue, the breakdown of the family, and the reversal of gender roles. The ban of the theater in 1774 in response to the Coercive Acts, by tapping this reservoir of elitist and

35. J. G. A. Pocock, in *The Machiavellian Moment: Florentine Political Thought and the Atlantic Tradition* (Princeton, N.J., 1975), discusses republican virtue. Edmund S. Morgan shows how republican thinkers in seventeenth-century England emphasized widespread distribution of property as the foundation of individual independence, and individual independence as the bulwark against government corruption in *Inventing the People: The Rise of Popular Sovereignty in England and America* (New York, 1988).

sexist criticism, drew all classes and both sexes together in a common political cause.

Virtue worked as a political equalizer. Anyone who behaved virtuously, whether or not his or her capacity to make political decisions was recognized by society, could qualify as a patriot. The ban on the theater, a political statement taken in the name of the poor and women, tacitly proclaimed the capacity for patriotism of these two politically incapacitated groups. Conversely, people of whatever class or gender who did not behave appropriately rendered themselves unfit for patriotism. While the moral program extended an invitation to everyone to join the political cause, it also excluded those who violated certain values. Theatergoers were one such excluded group. Theater critics maintained that people who attended the theater could become obsessed, slaves to their passions. According to political theorists, madmen and slaves were outside the political process, unsuitable material for patriotic resistance to tyranny. Madmen and slaves each undermined the political cause in their own way.

During the imperial crisis, the language of theater criticism merged with the language of political protest. The two languages worked together to identify patriots and to stigmatize outsiders—people beyond the pale of patriotism. An observer of the emotional fracas of 1774 engendered by the Boston Tea Party and the Coercive Acts can find connections between hostility towards the theater and hostility towards Parliamentary Acts in the rag-and-bone shop of words. People (madmen, slaves, criminals), virtues (charity, industry, frugality), and vices (selfishness, idleness, extravagance, deceit) jostle each other in both language clusters. We can try to order this linguistic clutter and construct an ecological system of relationships by asking questions: what attitudes were madmen and slaves thought to have towards virtue and vice; how did certain virtues bolster political resistance and certain vices undermine it, and how did the execution of criminals—an officially sanctioned drama—define the proper attitude for the public to take toward vice and sin?

A madman had no attitude towards virtue and vice (which is not to say that he was not living a life of vice, only that he would not have been able to evaluate the morality of his acts). He had no mental resources left over from his obsessions to spend on virtue and vice, and if he had tried to consider a moral issue he would have failed, because obsessions would bereave him of judgement. Opponents of the theater were a shrewd lot. With here a reference to madness, there to passion, there to obsession, they worked up a case against theatergoers. A man, they said, dropping into the theater to spend a pleasant evening laughing at the nosiness of Marplot or the nocturnal sprees of Sir John Brute emerged as a madman: his speech disordered, his eyes glazed, his mind jerking along in impulsive movements. Transformed by the theater, this crazed man who lived only for pleasure was just as lost to society and his family, just as oblivious to duty, just as incapable of work as a gambler.

By what legerdemain did the critics turn a theatergoer into an addict? By presenting the theater as a palace of pleasure. Going to the theater was pleasurable; in pursuing pleasure a man lost control over his reason; and, presto! he became addicted. By this line of reasoning, the theater as a palace of pleasure where passion dissolved reason became the equivalent of a gambling den, cockpit, racetrack, tavern, or whorehouse. In vain were the protests that the theater did not shred the fabric of society the way these other diversions did.

> By these [taverns, whorehouses, etc.] Servants and Apprentices are induced to embezzle their Masters Property, to neglect their Business, and ruin themselves—In these internal stews & Gaming Houses, many a man is tempted to Spend at Night, all he earn'd in the Day . . . and to conclude his Frolick, goes home and Abuses his Wife or Family, who perhaps are perishing for Want of those Necessaries which the Tavern, and not the Play House has deprived them of.[36]

—Exactly the case with the theater, was the answer. True, men did not go to the theater to gamble, drink, or whore, but from the havoc wreaked on their peace of mind they might just as well have spent the evening gambling, drinking, and whoring. And indeed, the claim was, men often did top off an evening at the theater with a visit to the tavern and the stews. Thus the theater was smuggled into the syndrome of obsession. Obsession, whether induced by the theater or by gambling, undermined the specific virtues on which colonists were grounding their resistance—charity, industry, frugality—and, by destroying the will, turned free people into slaves.

The architects of colonial resistance to Britain rejected the theater

36. *New-York Mercury,* 28 December 1761.

because, for them, charity, industry, and slavery had a specific political context. In 1774, the colonists came together as a people on a wave of charity. In blockading Boston Harbor as a punishment for the Tea Party, Britain very obligingly created a city of martyrs, a city in need of outside help for its very survival. This drastic measure of Britain's effectively eliminated any opposition to the patriot cause by shifting attention from the legal issue of responsibility for destruction of private property to the humanitarian issue of people in need of food and fuel. Colonists, whatever their opinion of the Boston Tea Party may have been, could hardly let a city starve or object to donations raised to help people in need.

Bostonians made psychological hay of their martyrdom. In poignant and piteous howls dutifully published in all the newspapers, they bewailed their suffering and dramatized the cruelty of the British. The response to their appeal for help was electrifying. Provincial conventions passed resolutions recommending liberal contributions and appointing committees in each county to collect supplies for Boston. "We think ourselves called upon, by every principle of humanity and brotherly affection, to extend the utmost and speediest relief to our distressed fellow-subjects in the town of *Boston*," announced the Virginia convention; while other provincial conventions issued similar expressions of benevolence.[37] Notices publicizing Boston's plight and calling for help were sent out from the capital cities to all the countries; subscriptions were instituted; and the liberality of donors was published in the papers. The effusion of charity that bound the colonies together surprised the British, who had assumed that their measure against Boston would split the colonies. William Gage, the commander-in-chief of the British forces in the colonies, wrote from Boston to the Earl of Dartmouth, the secretary of state for the colonies, "this Province is supported and abetted by others beyond the conception of most people, and foreseen by none."[38]

The highly publicized suffering of Boston elicited a highly publicized charitable response from all the colonies. Giving made people

---

37. *American Archives,* Peter Ford, ed., 4th series (Washington, 1837) I:688 (hereafter, *AA*).

38. Ibid., 805.

feel good, and in giving they became committed to the cause. Boston kept the spirit alive by publishing again and again its thanks for this or that donation. "The Christian sympathy and generosity of our friends through the Continent cannot fail to inspire the inhabitants of this town with patience, resignation, and firmness, while we trust in the Supreme Ruler of the universe, that he will graciously hear our cries."[39] Colonists rallied to the common cause under the banner of charity. Charity for the suffering people of Boston aroused colonists emotionally and gave them a chance to participate personally in a common cause. Provincial legislatures, local committees of correspondence, newspaper publishers, ministers: all encouraged colonists to give liberally to Boston; and colonists, in responding to this plea, identified with Boston's suffering and committed themselves to passive resistance to Britain. Charity for Boston transformed a political debate into an emotional cause.

The Continental Congress wished to sustain the emotion that had been aroused by Boston's suffering. They did not want to jeopardize a political position held together by generosity and gratitude. With charity-mongers hawking their product at every opportunity in 1774 and 1775, anyone trying to peddle the theater would have had a hard time of it. At last the fifteen years of activity by theater-detractors bore fruit. They had trained the public to believe that the theater had certain evil social effects, and these effects were seen as particularly destructive in the political context of 1774. Focusing on the suffering of the Bostonians at the hands of the British, colonists saw a need for charity on a massive scale if the colonies were not to be divided and then crushed. But they had been told that the theater diverted money from charitable causes and made theatergoers insensitive to the needs of others. In 1768, a rumor had flown around New York that a man had offered fifty pounds for a box at the theater. An opponent of the theater used the rumor to illustrate the antisocial effects of the theater.

The fact is hardly credible, but if it is true, it affords the strongest argument that can be urged to prove the mischievous tendency of a theatre. It would seem from this that people were grown mad after plays: And if they really tend to promote such a spirit of dissipation and

39. Ibid., 728.

extravagance, it is very certain they will proportionably diminish our charity. Rather let it be said that we are distinguished by our benevolence and humanity, than by our luxurious pleasures.[40]

In the emotional world of 1774, held together by giving and gratitude, a world in which need and suffering were dramatized for political purposes, spending money on personal pleasures was incongruous and unpatriotic. Although eight shillings, five shillings, or three shillings, the price of theater tickets, was not a fortune, in the circumstances any such selfish spending seemed unwarranted and extravagant. When people in one city did not have food or fuel, people in other cities should not support frivolous activities dedicated to pleasure.

The pursuit of pleasure wasted money that should have gone to worthy causes and turned people into selfish debauchees insensitive to the suffering of others; it also wasted time that should have been devoted to work. The colonists came together as a people on a wave of charity, but it was carefully controlled charity, charity that fitted into a complex of ideas about work and the public good. Bostonians were aware of the danger of receiving massive donations. Anxious to avoid the stigma of living in idleness off the labor of others and to avoid corrupting the poor of their own city, they devised a program for using the charitable donations to employ laborers who had been thrown out of work by the closing of the harbor. Bostonians had to depend on charity, but they did not have to live in idleness. The committee appointed to receive the donations used the money to lay out a brickyard that would employ about eighty men; to buy wool, cotton, and flax to distribute to spinners; to erect looms for weavers; to buy leather for shoemakers, hemp for rope makers, nails for blacksmiths. By working, Bostonians proved themselves worthy of the charity of their neighbors.

The Boston committee for handling donations not only advertised their work projects, they stressed the public nature of the projects. The unemployed were put to work re-laying the pavement, making dikes, and cleaning docks (but only the docks owned by the city, not those belonging to merchants).

40. *New-York Journal*, 7 January 1768.

These were all publick concernes and of no advantage to any individual, any further than as a member of the community to which he or she belonged. Not a single wharf, dock, dyke, or pavement, belonging to any individual, was ordered to be made or repaired.[41]

People donating money or goods to Boston could be sure that they were not enriching a few private citizens. Loyalists tried to sow dissension by hinting at corruption, but the Boston committee kept records, open to public inspection, of all their transactions. "It may not be improper to observe that the Committee have opened a regular set of books, in which they record all their proceedings, and give credit to the several Provinces, towns, and particular persons from whom they receive any donation."[42]

The charity that held colonists together in an emotional web of giving and gratitude was not dissociated from work. The colonies raised money for the relief of Boston, but also for manufacturing and agricultural projects that would keep money in the colonies, employ the poor, encourage emigration from Europe, and, by decreasing American dependence on imports, erect a partial barrier against luxury and vice. In the context of a national endeavor to raise money for Boston and for manufacturing and agricultural projects that would benefit the public, no place existed for the theater, which, in the popular imagination, drained money away from worthy causes, enticed people away from work, and encouraged them to pander to selfish pleasures when they should have been devoting themselves to public needs engendered by the political crisis.

Watching plays could turn into an obsession, and obsessed people, deaf to claims of charity, did not make good patriots. The theater also bred slaves, and slaves did not make good patriots either. The theater enslaved people by arousing passion, which overwhelmed reason. With reason unable to direct the will, the will was at the mercy of passion. It was therefore not free, and people who did not have free wills were slaves. Banning the theater, an activity that weakened the will, fitted into the colonial program of resistance to parliamentary legislation, because colonists thought of the Coercive Acts of 1774 as a program of enslavement. The Coercive Acts made colonists into

41. *AA,* I:740–44.
42. Ibid., 785.

slaves by weakening their will and made the executive into a master by strengthening his. While the colonists lost "control" over their lives, liberty, and property, the governor and his council could act "at pleasure" and "gratify" their "passions and interest." For the colonists, the legislation issuing from Parliament was not simply unconstitutional; it was an aggressive assault on their freedom, as conceived in terms of eighteenth-century psychology.

The Coercive Acts weakened the will of colonists in several ways. In the Massachusetts Government Act, Parliament extended the executive's power of appointment and reduced the power of the people to express their will in elections. Previously, the twenty-eight councilors (who served as councilors of the governor and also as the upper house of the legislature) had been elected annually by the lower house; according to the terms of the Act they were now to be appointed by the king and were to hold their office at his pleasure. Furthermore, the number of councilors holding office at any time could fluctuate from twelve to thirty-six. Opponents of the Act saw the extension of executive power as part of a process of enslavement—strengthening the will of the rulers and undermining the will of the people exercised in the lower house of elected representatives. "The power given to the Crown of occasionally increasing or lessening the number of the Council, on the report of Governors, and at the pleasure of Ministers, must make these Governors and Ministers masters of every question in that Assembly; and by destroying its freedom of deliberation, will wholly annihilate its use."[43]

The same Act drastically extended the governor's power of judicial appointment. The governor could appoint and remove at will judges, commissioners of oyer and terminer, the attorney general, provosts, marshals, justices of the peace, and sheriffs. (Only the chief justice and the judges of the superior court, once appointed, could not be dismissed without cause.) The power of appointment and dismissal gave the governor control over the courts. Formerly grand juries had been elected, nominated, or appointed by the freeholders and inhabitants of the towns. Now they were to be summoned and returned by the sheriffs of the counties, who were appointed by the governor and could be dismissed at will by him. (In England the

43. Ibid., 94.

sheriff, once appointed, could not be dismissed even by the king.) Opponents of the Act saw the governor using the sheriff, whom he controlled, to crush juries and break the will of the people.

> The Governor and Council thus entrusted with powers with which the British constitution has not trusted his Majesty and his Privy Council, have the means of returning such a Jury, in each particular cause, as may best suit with the gratification of their passions and interests. The lives, liberties and properties of the subject are put into their hands without controul; and the invaluable right of trial by Jury, is turned into a snare for the People, who have hitherto looked upon it as their main security against licentiousness of power.[44]

The Boston Port Act also included measures that would enslave the colonists in the sense of weakening their will. This Act closed Boston Harbor for an indefinite period at the will of the king and council and gave the people of Boston no definite way to end the blockade. The king was allowed to reopen the harbor once restitution for the tea was made. But he did not have to. The Act made slaves of the people of Boston by putting them at the mercy of the king and removing them from the protection of the law. "The legal condition of the subject (standing untainted by conviction for treason or felony) ought never to depend upon the arbitrary will of any person whatsoever."[45] The words reverberating through the protests—"power," "control," "mastery"—all were matters of the will, of who could exercise his will over whom. The Coercive Acts expanded the areas in which the executive, appointed by the Crown, could exercise his will, and contracted the area in which the people could exercise theirs. In restricting elections, reducing the power of representative assemblies, increasing royal appointive power, undermining due process, and threatening the independence of juries, the Coercive Acts loosened restrictions placed on the will of rulers and sapped the initiative of the people. If rulers could impose their will arbitrarily on the people, then the people were slaves.

It was in this context of political crisis that colonists condemned

44. Ibid.
45. Ibid., 95.

the theater. Their interpretation of enslavement as a mental process led them to condemn activities that weakened the will. In viewing plays, spectators became victims of passion, and in becoming victims of passion, their will deteriorated and left them ripe for enslavement. Because colonists saw enslavement as a mental process—the loss of will—and the Coercive Acts as a program of enslavement, then banning the theater, which weakened the will by arousing passion, made sense as one precaution against political suicide in the crisis.

For fifteen years, colonists—from New England, New York, Philadelphia—had voiced protests against the theater. These protests, which belonged to a long tradition of hostility to the theater in the Western world, antedated the political discontent of the American colonies and in that sense were independent of it. But because colonists cast their political protest in moral language, lining up the forces of virtue against the forces of corruption, moral indignation against the theater was smoothly incorporated into the greater moral constellation that set American colonists off from the British as a people. By 1774, going to the theater was perceived as a violation of colonial political goals. The general arguments that the theater took money away from the poor, that people who spent money on the theater would not donate to charity, that acting was not work because it produced nothing that benefited the public, that the theater aroused passions that destroyed the will, suddenly became urgent and specifically relevant in 1774, when Parliament passed legislation that attacked institutions through which colonists could exercise their will, when industry and frugality reduced dependence on foreign imports, and when charity served as a political stratagem for binding colonists together in the common cause of resisting rule by Parliament.

★ ★ ★

A mad flea, a slavish fly—that leaves the criminal flitch of bacon. Attendance at plays turned people into madmen and slaves. Occasionally critics of the theater referred to acting as a crime.

> Much has been said at this censorious Time
> To prove the Business of the Stage a Crime.[46]

46. *New-York Mercury,* 11 January 1762.

And occasionally critics argued or intimated that attendance at plays turned people into criminals (although this argument did not really take hold until the nineteenth century). In the eighteenth century, crime and theater were locked in a subtler but deadlier embrace. Critics of the theater argued that the audience was encouraged to take an inappropriate attitude towards vice and that this inappropriate attitude threatened the social order. No police force protected society. State and religious authorities, sensitive to any potentially disruptive attitudes and activities, worked hard to maintain order by psychological means. Ironically, even as critics voiced disapproval of the theater as morally and therefore socially subversive, authorities turned execution, one of the bulwarks of social order, into a drama. Executions, however, unlike plays, were designed to instill in spectators the proper attitude toward crime and toward vice, which lay at the root of crime. The war of the theater was waged over the bodies of the poor, servants, women, and children—people with weak wills susceptible of perversion, but not yet perverted. But the official treatment of condemned criminals in colonial America casts its own lurid light on attitudes toward the theater. The route to the intellectual and psychological sources of the rejection of the theater as a vehicle of moral inspiration winds its way through the underworld of colonial crime and ends on the scaffold in New England, where spectators and the criminal himself acquired the proper attitude towards crime, vice, and sin.

★ 3 ★

The Stage and the Scaffold: Comedies

In 1774, Congress made an explicit decision to moralize politics. The decision involved more than labeling certain behavior immoral and politically subversive; the decision necessitated a judgement about methods of moral education. Congress had not only to define the values of a society they were trying to unify in resistance to British tyranny, but also to devise the means of inculcating these values in individual members of society and of removing obstacles to this inculcation. The delegates who spent hours together in Carpenters' Hall, day after day, planning a course of action that would draw together people from disparate regions, classes, and occupations, had been exposed to two moral philosophies with a different slant. Some moralists were concerned with the social validity of occupations and the spirit in which these occupations were pursued. Having a low opinion of human nature, they thought people would succumb to temptations unless they were kept under control. These moralists talked about industry and frugality. They wanted people to keep busy so that they would have no time to be distracted by vice, and they wanted people to use the fruits of their labors for the public good. We shall call this cluster of concerns and attitudes the "morality of discipline" or "ascetic morality." Other moralists concentrated on emotional physiology. They talked about the moral sense, affecting acts, and benevolence. They wanted people to be open to the experiences of life, because they believed that people had the capacity to

48

recognize good motives in good acts and the inclination to imitate the good acts of others and to incorporate good motives that would guide their own future behavior. We shall call this cluster the "morality of perception" or "aesthetic morality."

For the most part the two moralities coincided in relative peace or mutual neglect, with people wandering in and out of both, unconsciously using the vocabulary now of one, now of the other, according to the constraints of a particular situation. But in the debate over the theater the moral views collided. Here the issue was moral education. People who might agree on what acts were virtuous and what acts were vicious might disagree on how to disseminate virtue and eradicate vice. In attacks and counterattacks, the moral legions battled, not over the nature of virtue and vice, but over the nature of humans and the mechanics of moral improvement. People who believed in the depravity of human nature and in discipline as the means of curbing this depravity did not approve of the theater; people who believed in the essential goodness of human nature and in an innate moral sense that was inspired by good and repulsed by evil did approve of the theater.

Congress had to choose between two systems of moral education based on two different premises. In choosing the morality of discipline over the morality of perception, they succeeded in simplifying moral issues, in bifurcating the world into good and evil and thereby making moral choices seem obvious. A morality based on perception bogs down in subjectivity, and the quest for moral certitude and stability is whelmed in a maelstrom of volatile feelings and sentiments. Congress did away with the uncertainty and instability of a morality based on perception and instead marked out a clear choice (sometimes out of trivialities) between good and evil, a choice that solidified values and purged the subjective opinions that always swarm around any moral judgements emerging from feeling and sentiment. But while the morality of discipline had its advantages as political strategy, Congress did sacrifice a vehicle of moral education (the theater) that in many ways would have served the cause.

In the eighteenth-century, plays, both comedies and tragedies, were often considered studies of virtue and vice. Comedies exposed vice; tragedies showed its awful consequences. Congress rejected both comedies and tragedies. They did not draw a distinction between plays that turned morality into a laughing matter and plays that could have bolstered a political cause swaddled in virtue; they simply banned the theater. Comedies were filled with rogues and hypocrites whose exploitation of people infected society and endangered its health. Audiences laughed at these rogues and hypocrites, and playwrights let them off scot-free. Tragedies told the story of great men who paid a great price for great mistakes. Sandwiched between the fictional characters of comedies and tragedies were the rogues of the real world who ended their lives on a scaffold. These rogues, similar in so many ways to the rogues of comedies, were expected to perform the lead in a tragic moral drama—the execution. The condemned men served as a fulcrum of reality between two fictitious extremes. Their fate reveals why neither the rogues of comedies nor the heroes of tragedies could contribute to the moral movement of the American Revolution.

i

The theater did have its advocates, moral philosophers who thought that suitable plays could stimulate virtue. In eighteenth-century Britain, the morality of perception rested on the notion that people possessed a moral sense by which they discerned moral values independently of the expressed will of God or of the state. Essentially good by nature, people absorbed morality by watching the actions of those around them. The third Earl of Shaftesbury (1671–1713), for example, believed that the moral sense was innate, but that moral concepts were not. Custom and education influenced people in the development of their notion of what was right and wrong. Frances Hutcheson (1694–1746), a professor of moral philosophy at Glasgow, built up a theory of the moral sense based on Locke's theory that people have no innate ideas but instead receive simple ideas from the world though the senses. To the senses of vision, touch, hearing, taste, and smell, Hutcheson added a moral sense, just as passive as the other senses and just as dependent on stimulation from outside sources. Through the moral sense, people perceived benevolence and depravity—the motives behind acts. According to Hutcheson, an act that a person witnessed struck her or his moral sense and elicited feelings of pleasure, if the act helped other people; or of pain, if it hurt other people. Then, with the help of reason, the observer inferred the character of the agent from the act. "The object of this sense [the moral sense] is not any external motion or action, but the inward affections and dispositions, which by reasoning we infer from the actions observed."[1]

Moral philosophers of this aesthetic school—Scottish moral philosophy—did not condemn the theater. Plays, which represented human action, fitted nicely into their theory of moral philosophy. Actions on the stage aroused the emotions of spectators, and the emotions corresponded to a judgement of the moral nature of the acts: virtuous acts aroused pleasure; vicious acts, indignation. In responding emotionally, the spectator developed a finely honed moral sensibility. As one moral philosopher put it, "When we see an audience therefore in tears for an object of compassion, when we find them affected with the generous sentiments which come from a virtuous character, deeply engaged in wishes for the success of the good, and for the disappointment of the wicked; it would scarcely occur that such an audience could be better employed in an hour of leisure."[2] Through the moral sense, a person became capable of approving or disapproving of different types of actions and of inferring from actions the affections or disposition of the agent. Hence plays were useful in concentrating morally significant action on a stage and making it visible to large numbers of people.

Let us apply moral sense philosophy to a particular play. Here is the plot of *Douglas,* a tragedy that gained considerable repute and was often performed in the colonies. As the wife of Lord Randolph is strolling outside her castle through the woods, whose melancholy gloom accords with her soul's sadness, it occurs to her to break sixteen years of silence and confide all the details of a lurid past to her maid. Sixteen years ago, she reveals, she secretly married the son of the Scottish chief with whom her father (another Scottish chief) was feuding. Shortly after the secret marriage, the two families donned their war kilts, and in the ensuing battle her husband was killed. Knowing that her family would not be pleased with the clandestine marriage, she delivered her baby in secrecy, a boy whom she sent away on a ship with a nurse. But a storm blew up, and neither the nurse nor the child was heard of again—both drowned, according to

1. Francis Hutcheson, *A System of Moral Philosophy* (London, 1755) 1:97.

2. Adam Ferguson, *The Morality of Stage-Plays seriously considered* (Edinburgh, 1757), 18.

the pessimistic mother. Later she married Lord Randolph, a kind man for whom she had respect and affection but not love. After Lady Randolph has exhumed her past for the benefit of the audience, the play moves right along. Lord Randolph, her husband, prepares to go to war with invading Danes; Glenalvon, his heir, confides in the audience his plot to have Lord Randolph murdered and to seize Lady Randolph, whom he had earlier tried to rape (an event unknown to any, since Lady Randolph virtuously kept the secret); and young Douglas, the supposedly drowned baby, now a grown shepherd lad, appears in time to save Lord Randolph from being murdered. His first plot foiled, Glenalvon, who, it would seem, has chosen Iago as his role model, tells Lord Randolph to observe that his wife has fallen in love with the mysterious young shepherd boy (Douglas). In fact, Lady Randolph has identified her son and is carrying on a strictly maternal relationship with him. In a bloody grand finale, everybody meets in the woods one night. Lord Randolph tries to kill young Douglas; Glenalvon attacks from behind; Douglas kills Glenalvon but is himself mortally wounded and dies in his mother's arms. Lord Randolph reappears out of the darkness and says he is sorry about the mix-up (mistaking Douglas for a lover and not realizing he was a son), but Lady Randolph, inconsolable, throws herself off a precipice—all in iambic pentameter.

As a tragedy the play fails to sound an immortal chord, since the hero who is brought down undergoes no psychological struggle, initiates no action, and is consequently devoid of interest. He does not contribute to his fate, either consciously or unconsciously. But as a sentimental melodrama the play has moral value. Glenalvon is indisputably evil. Not only does he go in for rape and murder; he works his will through deception and pretended virtue. But lest he deceive the audience, the conscientious playwright has Lady Randolph identify him for what he is in the first scene.

> Subtle and shrewd, he offers to mankind
> An artificial image of himself:
> And he with ease can vary to the taste
> Of different men, its features.[3]

3. John Home, *Douglas* (London, 1757), Act I, scene i., p. 9.

The play has a villain who arouses moral indignation. The play also has a hero. Douglas, brought up in poverty as a shepherd, exhibits nobleness of heart, fidelity to his stepfather and his newfound mother, and bravery. As a noble hero, Douglas excites in a morally impressionable audience an admiration of virtue. Lord Randolph, a good man with the fatal flaw of jealousy, acts as a warning, and Lady Randolph, a mother who finds her son only to lose him, arouses compassion. Adam Ferguson, a Scottish moral philosopher, claimed that *Douglas* improved the minds of spectators by intensifying their aversion to wickedness and engaging their hearts in behalf of virtue. "The designs of one person [Glenalvon] are painted in such colors of hateful depravity, as to become a necessary object of detestation. The mistakes of another [Lord Randolph] awaken our caution, and become a lesson of prudence. The generous and elevated mind of a third [Douglas], warm and exalt our sentiments; and that person, on whom the chief distress of the story falls [Lady Randolph], moves to compassion, and proves at last a warning against rash and fatal despair."[4]

Suitable plays warmed the hearts of moral sense philosophers, who believed that people apprehended moral qualities in concrete instances. Morality consisted of case studies, not abstract principles. These moral philosophers emphasized emotions (sentiments), bypassed the old-fashioned morality built on the notion that reason apprehended principles that could guide conduct, and touted the moral sense, which received impressions from the actions of others.

Scottish moral philosophers did not argue for a direct correlation between stage events and life events. They believed in the educational value of exposure to virtuous acts, whether real or fictitious. They did not think a person had to wait for a similar situation to crop up in real life before the experience of seeing a tragedy could take its moral effect, because it was less the witnessing of a virtuous act than the experience of having emotions aroused that made a person more inclined towards benevolence. In watching *Douglas* there was no real moral to be ingested, but having once felt compassion for the suffering of others, one would be more sensitive to suffering in the real world. "They . . . who were the readiest to shed tears, for the distresses represented in the Tragedy of *Douglas,* have been the most

4. Ferguson, 11.

forward in compassion to the poor, and in liberal designs for their relief."[5]

Adherents of the stage in the colonies took up the sentimental defense in the theater debates of the 1760s, and actors spouted similar arguments in prologues and epilogues. They championed specific experience over general rules ("For gloomy Minds through Ignorance may rail, / Yet bold Examples strike, where languid Precepts fail") and emotion over reason ("Reason we hear, and cooly may approve; / But all's inactive till the Passions move") and in general reassured the audience that in coming to plays they were nourishing their moral sense, not endangering their souls.[6] But these pleas for the morality of entertainment were swamped by newspaper attacks on the theater that drew on arguments accreted over centuries of hostility. These were the arguments that the Continental Congress had ears for.

Congress made its decision about the theater in the dusk: on one side, the sunshine of human benevolence; on the other, the midnight of human depravity. In banning the theater, Congress chose the rock-bound path of distrust and fear that twisted down into the dark corruption of human nature. In this realm of uncompromising black-ness, there was no place for the visual clues that guide behavior on the sunlit surface—the kind act and the good motive. Control, not the stimulation of benevolent acts, would keep people in moral step in a world in which the visibility of virtue could not compensate for the visibility of vice. Congress did not simply define values that would strengthen the resistance movement; they promoted one system of moral education and rejected another. The rejection of a system seemingly appropriate in many ways to fostering values that would have bolstered the political cause stimulates speculation on the reasons for and consequences of the rejection.

ii

John Dryden, drawing on Aristotle's *Poetics*, made a distinction between comedy and tragedy that relieved comedy of all moral burdens. Tragedies, in which great men stumbled from one crime to

---

5. Ferguson, 26.
6. *New-York Mercury*, 11 January 1762.

another until Clotho or Lachesis or Atropos did them in, presented the workings of justice in all its relentless majesty. Men suffered for their character defects and misdeeds, whether committed knowingly or unknowingly; they did not skip off the stage scot-free, kicking their heels. (The habit actors had of kicking their heels on making an exit considerably annoyed critics of the stage, as did histrionic "strutting.") Comedies, however, dealt with "low" people, and bringing low people to justice, according to the Aristotelian Dryden, could not inspire fear, awe, or pity in the audience. Far better to let the audience get a good laugh at the folly of the world. This sort of argument, in which aesthetic goals replaced moral ones, tweaked clerical detractors of the stage. "It seems then *Executions* are only for *Greatness,* and *Quality,*" complained one critic. "*Justice* is not to strike much *lower* than a *Prince. Private People* may do what they *please.*"[7]

But in real life, as everyone knew, people who were executed came primarily from the lower classes. Mariners, runaway apprentices, the footloose unemployed—these were the men who dangled before the public in prerevolutionary America. Runaway apprentices cut themselves off from the community. They might wander around the countryside as day laborers, or join a traveling show, or enlist in the army and go off on one of the military campaigns that were always available in the 1750s, or sign up on a whaling ship or a privateer. But if these jobs failed, they might turn to crime. Most men who were sentenced to be hanged for crimes (other than murder) did not belong to a community. They were transients, immigrants, sailors, or racial outsiders: Indians or blacks. Many condemned people dealt more in deception and fraud than in violence. Counterfeiters, thieves, and burglars were hanged, not for an isolated offense, but for the persistence of their assault on the credulous and gullible, for the accumulation of deceit; they were hanged by magistrates exasperated at the endless, wearing, rubbing friction on the bonds of trust that held society together.[8]

7. Jeremy Collier, *A Short View of the immorality and Profaneness of the English Stage* (London, 1698), 155; John Dryden, *An Evening's Love, or the Mock-Astrologer* (London, 1671), "Preface," [vii].

8. Jean-Christophe Agnew argues that the deception inherent in the representational art of the theater undermined the ordered social hierarchy in much the same way that market relationships undermined it. *Worlds Apart: The Market and the Theater in Anglo-American Thought, 1550–1750* (New York, 1986).

Many people who were executed had tried to make their way in the world through deception. So, too, did the rogues of comedies. But characters in plays not only deceived other characters, they deceived the audience; the playwright himself could deceive the audience and could even betray the characters he created; and actors could betray the playwrights by misrepresenting characters. Deceptions and betrayals were built into the structure of representational art. Theater critics showed how deception operated on several levels and had several victims.

Critics presented the spectators as victims—victims of the playwrights and actors who colluded to trick the audience and take them for a tumble. Playwrights deceived the audience by not speaking to them directly. Even in the prologue, when actors were meant to leave off acting and be real people, when they were to point out to the audience the moral of the play and guide them towards the proper response, they still played a part and even offended the audience with obscenities. Surely here, when all acting was meant to be set aside and the playwrights were speaking their own thoughts, decency could be maintained.

> Now here properly speaking the *Actors* quit the *Stage,* and remove from Fiction into Life. Here they converse with the *Boxes,* and *Pit,* and address directly to the Audience. . . . But here we have Lewdness without Shame or Example: Here the *Poet* exceeds himself. Here are such Strains as would turn the Stomach of our ordinary Debauchee, and be almost nauseous in the *Stews.*[9]

Playwrights, in throwing away the opportunity of dealing directly with the audience (the purpose of the prologue), perverted the prologue from moral edification to lurid pornography.

Playwrights not only betrayed the audience, they betrayed the very characters they created and to whom they had a responsibility. By making their characters do evil deeds or blaspheme, playwrights condemned them to perdition and sullied their reputation. Jeremy Collier, a clergyman who eyed the theater with considerable hostility, lamented the dirty trick that Shakespeare played on Ophelia, when, after depriving her of her wits, he had her lapse into bawdy

---

9. Collier, *Short View,* 13.

language. Euripides, an honorable playwright, had protected Phaedra even in her madness by preserving the regularity and decorum of her language.

> Had *Shakespeare* secur'd this point [linguistic decorum] for his young Virgin *Ophelia*, the *Play* had been better contriv'd. Since he was resolv'd to drown the Lady like a Kitten, he should have set her a swimming a little sooner. To keep her alive only to sully her Reputation; and discover the Rankness of her Breath was very Cruel.[10]

Bad language had a bad influence on the audience, but it also injured the reputation of the characters, who had a life of their own.

Let us say the playwright was a good, honest fellow who truly wanted to improve his audience. He packed his play with morality, created sympathetic virtuous people, made vicious people appear foolish and punished them for their vice, and sandwiched all the action between a straightforward prologue and epilogue, both of which pointed out the moral and guided the audience to the proper response. Still all was for naught, because actors could thwart the best intentions of the most moral of playwrights. Standing between the audience and the moral of the play, actors could distract the attention of the audience.

> Now amidst a mixed audience at a Play-house, I believe it will be found that the *actors* engaged more of their attention than the *author* of a play. The principal thing regarded is, whether the actor performs his part well; the plaudit is oftener given to him than to the author of the play. The manner and appearance of the *one* strikes the imagination with a pleasing and agreeable surprise, while the character of the *other* lies in a great measure concealed from the vulgar eye.[11]

The performance could stand in the way of the message or change it.

Actors were seen as hypocrites and were condemned for teaching the techniques of hypocrisy. The word *hypocrisy* comes from the Greek word *hypokrisi,* "playing a part on the stage." Hypocrisy operated on three levels. Actors feigned to be what they were not and to feel what they did not feel, in order to convince the audience of the

10. Ibid., 10.
11. *New-York Journal,* 31 December 1767.

reality of a make-believe world. The audience, in watching a play, would pick up the techniques of acting and the idea of deception, and in real life would simulate characters and feelings in order to deceive. And in the plays themselves, tragedies and comedies alike, many characters were hypocrites who tried to deceive other characters: Iago, Glenalvon, Stuckley, Vizard, Alderman Smuggler, Colonel Fainwell, and many others. Lady Lurewell in *The Constant Couple* has two lovers, one of whom sums up her character. "You're all Lyes. First your heart is false, your Eyes are double; one Look belyes another: And then your Tongue does contradict them all.—Madam, I see a little Devil just now hammering out a Lye in your Pericranium."[12] Deception made marriages meaningless and undermined the family, but deception ran deeper and undermined morality itself, the mortar that held society together.

Representational art created layers of deception, and the stage abounded with cozeners, scoundrels, villains, and tricksters: friends betrayed friends; husbands and wives vied with each other in hoodwinking duels; servants tricked masters; poor men pretended to be rich to ensnare rich brides; women pretended to be men to test their husbands or lovers; men dressed up as women to gain access to their mistresses. The deceptions and disguises, the betrayal of trust, the breaking of contracts and vows, and the personal nature of hypocrisy—all tied the plays that were being produced on stage with the underworld of crime.

In real life, thieves and counterfeiters whose lives ended in a noose left behind them in print a dizzying career of petty crimes of deception. Once a runaway apprentice dipped into small-scale theft—here a handkerchief, there a knee buckle—the momentum would soon increase as the thief learned how easy and relatively safe it was to deceive the unwary. With no police force, sophisticated methods of crime detection, or effective institutions of incarceration, society—dependent on recognizing the thief—described him in the papers, whipped him in public view (sometimes he was whipped all around the town or city), placed him in the glare of a pillory, and branded him on the forehead (taking off his disguise on the one hand and

12. Farquhar, *The Constant Couple,* in *The Works of George Farquhar* 1 (New York, 1988): Act III, scene iii, ll. 46–49.

marking him on the other); while the wily thief for his part depended on disguise, trickery, and deceit.

Francis Burdett Personel, a criminal who was eventually executed for murder, duped the gullible from Baltimore to Pittsburgh and even took in whole communities. Personel, an Irishman, stuck out four years of his term as an indentured servant in Maryland before he decided that he had had enough. Stealing an ax and some clothes from his master, he ran away ("I travelled that night but slowly my shoes being bad," he later recalled in jail) and settled down to a career of "borrowing" and deception. He borrowed a fancy coat, hat, and "other necessities," and being so well dressed was able to set up as a schoolteacher in Virginia. He promised a widow he would marry her, and on her faith in the promise borrowed a mare, bridle, and saddle, and away he rode. "Thus," he concluded, "you may see I have been a hypocrite."[13]

Crime during this period was often intimate: one person deceived another face to face. If a cozener failed in his hoodwinking attempt and was caught with the goods, the victim might merely demand retribution and perhaps a trifle more and the affair would never come to trial.[14] Occasionally complaints or pleas surfaced in the newspapers. "It would undoubtedly be highly serviceable to the public," wrote one man concerned about the vulnerability of naïve and trusting people, "if such Accounts, and exact Descriptions of the Persons of all convicted Rogues were published by Authority in every Government."[15] Newspapers did try to protect the public. They warned when counterfeit money was in circulation and printed instructions for detecting false coins by flaws in the design or inaccuracy in the weight. They printed notice after notice from masters offering rewards for the capture and return of runaway servants. Since runaway servants often turned to thieving to support themselves, it was to everyone's advantage (except the servants') for them to be identified and returned. Clothes could conceal identity when they were used as

---

13. *An Authentic and Particular Account of the life of Francis Burdett Personel, written by himself, who was executed at New-York, September 10th, 1773; in the Twenty-sixth Year of his Age, for the Murder of Mr. Robert White* (New York, 1773), 8.

14. See for example, *A brief Account of the Life and abominable Thefts of the notorious Isaac Frazier* (New London, Conn., 1768), 5, 6, 8, *et passim*.

15. *Massachusetts Gazette* and *Boston News-Letter*, 12 January 1764.

disguise, but clothes could also serve as marks of identity, especially in a society in which they were expensive and could not be readily replaced.

Notices offering rewards for the capture and return of runaway servants smothered the reader with sartorial details and textile specificity. Colonists expected a nicety of identification from their compatriots, who were to notice not just the item of clothing, its condition, and its color, but its fabric: ratteen, oznabrig, light frieze, shalloon, etc. They asked people to pick out a pair of black ribbed stockings hurrying away among the crowds or a hat with worsted binding as it bobbed its way through the marketplace. It was a society accustomed to detailed observation and trained to identify and classify people by appearance. A master trying to reclaim a servant who had run away several times and knew how to write counterfeit passes told people exactly what to look for.

> [He took with him] a brown Linsey Woolsey Jacket, with dark Stripes in the back Parts of it, and lined with Lindsey of Sheep's gray; gray Yarn Stockings, new Shoes, carved white metal Buckles: He also stole and took with him, an ash colour'd Drab Coat, lined before with Shalloon of the same Colour; a Wool Hat half wore, a new flag Silk Handkerchief, a reddish brown Country Stuff Jacket, lined with brown Shalloon; light Mohair Buttons, three Shirts of No [8?] Hundred in a Linnen Bag, and many other things not known.[16]

But the notice ended on a note of despair, a warning to the public and a baleful admission of futility. "N.B. Perhaps he may change his Name and Cloaths."

Crime—the crime of deception, not violence—was akin to the intrigues and disguises of comedies. The criminals of the marketplaces and dockyards, the wandering hypocrites who leeched onto widows or duped country communities, resembled their cousins, the knaves and rogues of the stage who in comedies kicked their heels and took advantage of human foibles and weaknesses.

Critics of the theater condemned comedies for flouting justice by publicizing unpunished crime. They accused playwrights of creating vicious monsters and then rewarding them with the fat of the land.

16. *New-York Gazette; or the Weekly Post-Boy,* 11 March 1754.

Did the plays in fact abound with vicious knaves and villains and lascivious old men who climbed to fortune and happiness over the bodies of entrapped heiresses and ruined dupes? Many a knave and villain and lascivious old man tried to make this ascent, but at the fall of the curtain in the fifth act, were they destined to live happily and richly forever after by an irresponsible playwright? Ask Vizard (*The Constant Couple*) what he thought about his lot, or Count Basset (*The Provoked Husband*), or Lord Foppington (*The Careless Husband*), or Obadiah Prim (*A Bold Stroke for a Wife*), or Captain Brazen (*The Recruiting Officer*), or Tattle (*Love for Love*). So was all right with the world and God in his moral heaven? Well, yes and no. While the vicious in comedies did not in general secure the rich heiress or succeed in cheating a dupe out of his inheritance, neither were they consigned to misery. They did not sit in the stocks, pay a fine, or lose their fortune. Their punishment, such as it was, usually amounted to nothing more than the failure of their schemes (although sometimes they found themselves married to a less than desirable partner). Possible failure might have appeared to the morally critical as a somewhat weak deterrent to schemes of enrichment. But even humiliating failure might have served some moral purpose had it not been all over so quickly. In the end the virtuous might triumph and the vicious fall, but, except for that final moment, wags, coxcombs, intriguers, and rakes held sway and entertained the audience with their philosophy for nine-tenths of the play—the moral ending slipping in almost unnoticed and certainly unprepared for, a mere nod to convention at the expense of aesthetics and truth to character.[17]

Comedies in which vice went unpunished could be seen to undermine the state-supported drama, the richly ceremonial and morally orchestrated execution of criminals, who, for the most part, came from the lower classes. In this macabre drama the wages of sin were

---

17. *The Provoked Husband,* for example, has a particularly unconvincing and irrelevant ending that could hardly have made much of an impact on the audience. Vanbrugh wrote the play in 1705, but left it unfinished. Twenty-three years later, Colley Cibber came along and gave it a platitudinous ending in which a witty, headstrong woman, whose chief delight is in defying her husband's objections to her style of life, suddenly submits and drenches the audience in a shower of self-accusatory remorse. This hybrid play is not a freak in the eighteenth-century menagerie; several playwrights and actors doctored plays they considered extreme in their lewdness and ribaldry. It is open to question how effective this moral medicine was.

death, not ridicule, a moral demonstrated with a certain definitude; and the major role was not usually played by merchants or gentry. In executions, rogues similar to the rogues of the comedies had to assume the part of tragic heroes. The authorities who staged executions engineered this reversal of roles by working hard to create the moral ambience of a tragic drama.

iii

Magistrates and ministers staged quite a performance for the moral edification of those who might be tempted to rob, counterfeit, or murder. The Sunday before the execution, the prisoner often appeared in church (at his own request, the minister would announce) to hear a last sermon (although sometimes a sermon was preached at the execution). Sitting in chains apart from the congregation, he would by virtue of his impending and certain death lend piquancy to a sermon on Luke 23:43 (Christ's words to the thief on the cross, "Today shalt thou be with me in paradise"), or Romans 6:23 ("For the wages of sin is death, but the gift of God is eternal life though Jesus Christ our Lord"). Sometimes the condemned man even went to two churches to take in two sermons. On the day of the execution, people left off work to watch the prisoner walk from the jail to the place of execution. Here a minister might deliver a sermon, the condemned man might make a last speech of repentance and warning, or an official might read a statement made by the condemned man. Sometimes, in an attempt to prolong the solemnity and awfulness of the execution, a minister might preach another execution sermon the Sunday after the execution.

Execution sermons followed a pattern. Perhaps the minister would address the prisoner by name or merely as "Unhappy man" or "Unhappy object" as a way of introducing him to the congregation, but he would then break out with an explication of the biblical text for an hour or so with no specific reference to the present situation. He would conclude by applying the text first to the condemned man and then to the congregation. Here the minister had to maneuver with care. In his professional capacity as a minister he wanted to work the condemned man into a state of conviction, to demonstrate to him his depravity and the hopelessness of his situation. "And the solemn day is now come," one minister informed a condemned man (in case the fact had escaped his attention), "—and preparation is made for your execution. The grave has opened its mouth to receive you, and you will presently be laid in it. . . . O what an awful situation is this!"[18] Another minister pointed out to another condemned man that he had no hope of escape. He was well guarded and the fatal instruments of death were ready. "You have but a very few moments to breathe in this world. . . . Your coffin and your grave, your last lodging are open ready to receive you."[19] Ministers thought they were doing the right thing with their Christian taunting. Only if the condemned man could be brought to a sense of his own guilt and hopeless condition would he turn to Christ for help, and only if a man turned to Christ would he be saved.

If the condemned man played his part well, he could become a member of society by dying on its behalf. "And thus those Men whose Lives are no longer of any use in the World, are made of some Service to it by their *Deaths*."[20] In order to be of service to the world, the condemned man was expected to shoulder full blame for his actions by absolving all others: his tender mother, the judges, the jury, the informers, the state officials, and society itself. He had to perform two duties, confess and repent.

Prisoner confessions, destined to be published, bulge with crimes, petty thefts bursting the seams. The feats of particularization and the piling up of evidence to the point of absurdity also suggest fear and compulsion in the confessor—a fear of leaving unconfessed any tidbit or scrap of criminality and a compulsion to damn himself down to the last drop. Arthur, the Negro hanged for rape, listed his thefts relentlessly: here two dollars, there five dollars, a comb from one person, a quantity of flour from another, a razor, some cider brandy, a pair of shoes, bread, meat, rum, stockings—from a farmer, a goose; from a widow, a kettle to boil the goose in. At Weston, some butter; at Waltham, some chocolates and rum; at Watertown, a brass kettle.[21]

18. Thaddeus Maccarty, *Mr. Maccarty's Sermon on the Day of the Execution of William Linsey* (Boston, 1770), 25.

19. Samson Occam, *A sermon preached at the Execution of Moses Paul, An Indian, who was Executed at New Haven for the Murder of Mr. Moses Cook* (Boston, 1773), 15.

20. *A short Account of the Life and Character of John Campbell, Now under Sentence of Death, for Robbery, and to be executed this 29th of December, 1769* (New York, 1769), 1.

21. *The Life and dying Speech of Arthur a Negro Man* (Boston, 1768), 1.

Sometimes a criminal, after listing a thousand and one crimes, would pause apologetically to excuse himself if he had inadvertently left out any stray theft that might have eluded a weak memory. Isaac Frazier, a notorious thief, ticked off forty-seven specific robberies and burglaries (date, place, victim, items stolen), but at last, admitting defeat, he had to conclude with a nebulous generalization. "I acknowledge myself to have been guilty of almost an innumerable number of other thefts, but have forgot the order of time in which they were committed."[22] A man who has spent his life deceiving others suddenly wanted everything out in the open *exactly* as it happened. Truth was to stand exposed in all its nakedness.

Sometimes the desire for the whole truth encompassed a desire for nothing *but* the truth, and the prisoner would vigorously deny some false accusation that had been laid against him. One man insisted that despite a life of crime that, he realized, justified his execution, he wanted it in the record that he did not swear, that he had never committed murder, and that he did not drink to excess.[23] No errors were to exist in the final account book. "I must confess," said a pirate demurely, "that I was not guilty of Murder, nor of striking Men as others were: But of all other Sins I was guilty, for which, I ask God Pardon."[24] A man sentenced to die for counterfeiting, a crime that he freely admitted, denied that he had stolen cloth, a crime he had earlier been convicted of and for which he had been pilloried and fined. He also denied stealing horses. He was a counterfeiter, yes; but a thief? no. "It has been rumoured, that in the *Jerseys* I had been concerned in stealing of horses; but declare myself innocent of the accusation:—*the command in my heart was,* THOU SHALT NOT STEAL; which I always kept."[25] Condemned men purged themselves of lying, deceit, and hypocrisy by insisting on the accuracy and completeness of minutiae. The ideal prisoner was convinced of his own depravity, but to take on the depravity of others would expose him to the sin of

22. *Isaac Frazier,* 15.

23. Ibid, 16.

24. *An Account of the Pirates, with divers of their Speeches, Letters etc. . . . who were Executed at Newport . . . July 19th, 1723* (reprint, n.p., 1769), [12].

25. *The life and confession of Herman Rosencrantz; executed in the City of Philadelphia on the 5th Day of May 1770, for Counterfeiting and Uttering the Bills of Credit of the Province of Pennsylvania* (Philadelphia, 1770), 9.

hypocrisy, which he had been wallowing in all his life but from which now he was attempting to emerge. By confessing thoroughly and accurately, he cleansed himself of deception; when he reached the scaffold, he was no longer the rogue of comedies.

Criminals were expected not only to confess but to repent. Repentance bound all the characters in the drama: the criminal, his family, his victims, the families of his victims, the ministers, and the state officials; and repentance drew the audience in, too. Without repentance, the drama as a moral lesson fell flat. A resentful, defiant victim would arouse, not compassion, but vengeance, a destructive emotion that could lead to violence; a victim who denied guilt as well as contrition might arouse the spectators to hostility towards the authorities. Bryan Sheehen denied to the end that he had raped Abial Hollowell. He "insisted that his lying with her, which he owned, was by mutual agreement."[26] Because of his stout denial, many people entertained doubts of the woman and thought that Bryan should not be hanged. Ministers, state officials, and newspaper editors all encouraged the prisoner to leave behind in print a trail of self-condemnation. Confession and repentance justified the state and made the execution drama moral.

The eighteenth-century colonial execution was meant to reinforce communal values. Although executions were conducted in the name of justice, justice was not enough. A murderer could be dragged kicking and screaming up to the scaffold and duly hanged and the demands of justice be satisfied; but eighteenth-century authorities did not want their criminals dragged to the place of execution kicking and screaming. A prisoner's resentment suggested unfairness in the system. A prisoner's remorse and gratitude reinforced the morality and even charity of the system. One account reported the capture and imprisonment of pirates as an act of mercy, for which the pirates were grateful. "Thus far had they gone from God! But when they were brought into Prison, they quickly seemed thankful to God for his Mercy in bringing them thither. And they set and kept up something of daily Religion."[27] Authorities were represented as reluctant

26. James Diman, *A Sermon, Preached at Salem, January 16, 1772. Being the day on which Bryan Sheehen was Executed, for committing a Rape, on the body of Abial Hollowell . . . of Marblehead* (Salem, Mass., 1772), 23.

27. *Account of the Pirates*, [13–14].

to inflict capital punishment. They delayed the execution until prisoners were ripe for salvation. "A whole year passed after he was found guilty, before his sentence. . . . There was mercy to his soul, in affording him a year to consider his latter end, and prepare for it."[28] Many prisoners thanked the authorities for being so merciful. As one said, "Certainly, if I had been put to death at that time, I should have been a lost soul, for my conscience was a hell to me, and witnessed against me."[29] Indeed, the authorities sometimes were portrayed as so bent on being merciful that the execution itself was reduced to a minor but necessary unpleasantness forced upon them in their pursuit of moral reformation.

In order to produce a moral drama, authorities had to control and channel the emotions of spectators. Confession and repentance affected the attitude of the public both toward the authorities who performed the execution and toward the prisoner himself. In condemning himself, the prisoner relieved the spectators of the burden of condemning him and left them free to be compassionate. Ministers urged their flock to identify with the sinner. "Let me exhort and intreat all who may attend the execution of this poor condemned criminal, to lay to heart such an affecting sight, and to behave with decency and seriousness on such a solemn occasion."[30] The criminal's repentance allowed the spectators to separate the crimes from the man: they could condemn the crimes while pitying the man. A minister watching a satisfactory execution in which all the forms were observed expressed his contentment. "Tenderness to a poor wretch, with a just indignation against his enormous villanies, seemed to govern the whole affair."[31] The public repentance of a man who was about to die exposed people to communal values that drew them together.

In executions, the lowly rogues were turned into tragic heroes who suffered for their crimes and were dissociated from the rogues of the comedies. In comedies, the lowly rogues did not suffer greatly

---

28. Aaron Hutchinson, *Iniquity purged by Mercy and Truth a Sermon Preached at Grafton, October 23d, 1768. Being the Sabbath after the Execution of Arthur, A Negro Man at Worcester, aged about 21. For a RAPE.* (Boston, 1769), 16–19.

29. Personel, 11.

30. Andrew Eliot, *A Sermon preached on the Lord's-Day before the Execution of Levi Ames* (Boston, 1773), 30.

31. Hutchinson, 19.

for their misdeeds; they remained rogues and they remained comic. Ideal criminals, on the other hand, paid double dues to society: they apologized and died. The ideal repentant criminal, as the protagonist of the execution drama, "performed" his death, but he could not "act" it, since all emotions, feelings, and actions had to be real. His death was staged and dramatic, but it also actually happened.

*   *   *

The distinction between plays and executions was the distinction between literary text and social ceremony. Authorities could reject the one while milking the other for all its potential drama because of their attitude towards reality and creation. Plays, if they were to have moral value, had to depict vice as well as virtue. For the father to forgive the prodigal son, the son had to be prodigal; for no one to cast the first stone, a woman had to be condemned as an adulteress. Playwrights, if they were to inculcate morality, had to create crime and sin to highlight virtue. Theater critics did not argue that plays presented a false world; they argued that plays presented a vicious world and often an unjust one. Even though the real world might be vicious and unjust, too, playwrights were responsible for gratuitous vice and injustice. Playwrights denied the responsibility of creation. They only mirrored the world the way it was, they claimed; the responsibility for vice and injustice lay in the way of the world. "I desire," said William Congreve, "that it may not be imputed to the Perswasion or private Sentiments of the Author, if at any time one of these vicious Characters in any of his Plays shall behave himself foolishly, or immorally in Word or Deed. I hope I am not unreasonable; it were very hard that a painter should be believ'd to resemble all the ugly Faces that he draws."[32] If people wanted more virtuous plays, they would first have to reform the world, which was the stuff plays were made on. "Corruption of Manners," said one advocate of the theater, "is not to be attributed to the licentiousness of the Drama."[33] Plays did not corrupt society; corrupt society corrupted plays.

Opponents of the stage rejected both the reality and the fantasy of

32. William Congreve, *Amendments of Mr. Collier's False and Imperfect Citations* (London, July 1698), 9.

33. John Dennis, *The Usefulness of the Stage* (London, 1698), 23.

life depicted on the stage. They took the vice of plays at face value as real vice, and Congress in banning the theater seems to have concurred with this judgement. If vice was vice, whatever its locality, it would make no sense to restrict certain activities on the grounds of their illegitimacy and then give people an opportunity to derive vicarious enjoyment from these illegitimate activities by going to a play; to scour the world of gaming, for example, and then allow it to flourish on the stage. But opponents also condemned the fantastical element of action on the stage—its unreality, which they associated with hypocrisy and deception. Actors, after all, only pretended. Ambivalence towards reality also haunted the public executions of the eighteenth century. A criminal was put to death because of his crimes, but the reality of his crimes detracted from the moral value of his death as a performance. Ministers in their sermons modulated the sordid details of the crimes into generic sins: greed, lust, deceit. The execution presented a mirror image of the comedy. Comedies were rejected because they were too real (sin, crime, and vice were made visible) and not just (the guilty were not punished). Executions were acceptable as a moral performance because they masked reality (the visibility of penitence replaced the visibility of crime) and they publicized justice and reality (the criminals were punished and really died).

Comedies, in which people escaped punishment because they were lowly, undermined the drama of justice, in which the guilty (usually people from the lower classes) paid the price for what they did. Ironically, however, executions as they were staged in the colonies conformed to the tragedies of the stage. Spectators at an execution witnessed the awful results of crime (which, decked out in sermons and confessions, appeared more as sin), but in praying for the salvation of a penitent sinner, they relieved themselves of the guilt of condemnation. Their hearts melted in the great pot of compassion. Similarly, the theater audience, in feeling compassion for the heroes of tragedies who suffered and paid for wrongs with their lives, were having a moral experience. Why then did many magistrates and ministers, the very people who refined the execution ceremony, condemn all plays, tragedies as well as comedies, and why in 1774 did Congress accept this condemnation and ban the theater?

★ 4 ★

The Stage and the Scaffold: Tragedies

IN MANY WAYS, tragedies and executions offered the same opportunities for moral reformation. In tragedies, the compassion of the spectators was aroused by the suffering of people who came to the realization of their own corruption. *Othello,* for example, fitted into colonial attitudes towards vice and crime. Othello's crime, the murder of Desdemona, resulted from his sin, jealousy. Othello, in discovering Desdemona's innocence, came to a realization of his own guilt. He accused himself, thereby winning the sympathy and compassion of the audience (who are prone anyway to take the side of Othello because of Iago's evil) and then acknowledged the justice of any punishment he might suffer in this world or the next.

> Whip me, ye devils,
> From the possession of this heavenly sight!
> Blow me about in winds! roast me in sulphur!
> Wash me in steep-down gulfs of liquid fire!
> O Desdemon! Desdemon! dead! Oh! Oh![1]

His repentance for his deed did not free him from responsibility and punishment (in this case, self-inflicted punishment). Othello's psy-

1. *Othello,* in *The Pelican Shakespeare,* Alfred Harbage, ed. (Baltimore, Md., 1958), Act V, scene ii, ll. 277–82.

chological response conformed to colonial notions of criminal propriety. When Othello saw what he had done, he felt guilty because of the ruin entailed on others. The ideal real-life criminal was also expected to feel guilty because of what he had done to others: his tender mother, his victims, his victims' relations, trusting society, and, most important, Christ. In hurting others the criminal had sinned against Christ, who commanded people to love their neighbors as they loved themselves. Criminals had put themselves before all others; in repenting, they were to put all others before themselves.

The architects of public justice—the judges who condemned the criminal, the magistrates who executed him, and the ministers who tried to save him and instruct the community—in employing histrionic techniques to turn executions into dramas, implicitly accepted the thesis of moral sense philosophers that aesthetic works, especially tragedies, could elevate an audience to moral heights. They repeatedly referred to the execution as an "affecting" scene. In the case of the state drama, an act of justice had replaced an act of benevolence as the stimulant of the moral sense. And yet, in the process of the drama, justice was actually transformed into benevolence in a subtle metamorphosis: the authorities saving the criminal spiritually even while breaking his physical neck; the criminal repenting and thus doing the right thing by all the young people who had turned out to watch him die; and the spectators, melted by the criminal's repentance, forgiving him for crimes perpetrated against society, praying for his salvation, and spiritually joining him in his walk to the gallows.

It is easy to see why the Continental Congress would have banned comedies in the political crisis. It is less easy to see why they refused to use tragedies as a means of propagating moral values and inspiring allegiance to the cause. *The Gamester,* for example, portrayed the drastic effects of gambling, and *Cato* glorified republican virtue impregnable against corruption. If execution, an acceptable moral drama, had educational value because rogues were transformed into penitent sinners who paid the price for their sin and because the audience identified with the criminal as a sinner and had compassion for him, then surely tragedies also could provide a moral experience for the audience. The protagonists and the villains of tragedies suffered for their sins and crimes, and the audience became emotionally involved in the suffering on the stage and responded to it with sympathy and compassion, not with detachment and ridicule. Yet packed with morality as they might have been, tragedies, like comedies, failed the moral test in 1774. Why did the whirlwind of hostility buffet tragedies that conformed in so many ways to the rites of execution, the state-sanctioned drama that reinforced social values?

Crucial distinctions set tragedies apart from executions. Executions sought to transcend the individual experience and turn it into a social experience. Tragedies did not relinquish their hold on individuals. Great men were destroyed or destroyed themselves, but they remained great, and they remained intact as individuals. The exclusion of tragedies from a resistance movement grounded in morality defined the political goals of the movement and the morality that Congress was promulgating, and illuminated the paradoxical role of leaders in a society that had come to fear power and was confronting its corrupting effects by engineering a moral revolution of the people. The moral strength of the many was to oppose the corrupt power of the few. What place could there be in this paradigm for leaders who were aligned with the moral people? People who identified with the American cause would face the problem of how to support that cause and direct it without being corrupted by power and without compromising the virtue of the people.

i

Tragedies and executions both addressed a subject of importance in Revolutionary America: how acts of individuals impinged on society. In the imperial crisis, political concepts propelled Americans toward conforming to a public moral code. The emphasis on conformity and unanimity turned nonconformists into deviants and diminished opportunities for would-be leaders who stood apart from the people. A central theme of tragedies and executions—a theme literary dramas handled quite differently from the social drama engineered by the state—greatly concerned Americans resisting what they defined as tyranny.

Tragedies focused on deeds and character, while the execution drama focused on a spiritual state divorced from deeds and character. Tragic heroes performed deeds and commented on the significance of their deeds; and they did so as individuals absorbed in the uniqueness of their own particular situation. Because they did not withdraw from their own personality, they presented no generalized experience; because they did not renounce their deeds and turn to Christ, they offered no spiritual guidance. Tragedies limned a moral system built on deeds, oriented towards life, and represented by heroes. Execution drama nullified deeds, directed attention to the life to come, and reduced all men to the common denominator of sinner. Both tragedies and executions pushed to the fore the moral value of acts, but the former focused on the acts themselves, while the latter transformed them into generic sins. When Congress banned tragedies as well as comedies, they evaluated the significance of acts in a moral, and, in 1774, when morality was called to the assistance of politics, in a political scheme.

Ministers turned executions into dramas, but they went one step further and turned these dramas into a form of public worship. As a consequence of this transformation, deeds were relegated to a forgotten, because forgiven, past that was no longer important in the context of the spiritual drama. From the time of his sentencing until the time of his execution, the prisoner was transformed from a criminal into a sinner. Murders, thefts, counterfeiting, and rapes receded into the past while all attention focused on the condemned man's struggle to attain the proper attitude towards sin, to loathe himself for his own corruption. With each execution a battle for a soul, the execution slid from retribution to spiritual event. Ministers, right in the thick of the salvational fray, took up the part of spiritual advocate. The criminal may have lost his case in the civil courts, but he still had a chance in the spiritual court, which judged, not deeds committed, but attitudes towards deeds, the doer, and Christ. Therefore, alongside the last speeches and confessions, sermons and more sermons issued from the presses to put executions in the proper context.

Ministers in their sermons spiritualized executions, and in the process of spiritualization, pushed the crime or crimes for which a man was condemned to die into the background and masked them with the disembodied language of the church. Even as ministers moralized about the execution, they protected the ears of their listeners by speaking in the language of Old Testament prophets, not of newspaper reporters. A minister delivering a sermon before an execution reprimanded the prisoner for his attacks on female chastity, but hastened to say, "the nature of the subject forbids me to enlarge, lest I should put that modesty to the blush, which is the ornament of both sexs."[2] Executions were to be pure, not sordid. With genealogical sleight of hand, ministers dismissed altogether the origin of the execution in crime. The guts of murdered victims, raped and brutalized vaginas, counterfeit bills, and daring robberies did not spill from the pages of execution sermons, which instead were demurely garbed in the same old tried and true sins. A bloodless list—idleness, drunkenness, uncleanness, lying, stealing, profanity—supplanted the facts of the case. By emphasizing generic sins over specific crimes, ministers eased the confession narrative of criminals into a theological context.

Confession narratives, with their emphasis on statistical thoroughness, represented the stage of conviction in the morphology of conversion. Before a man could be open to receive saving grace, he had to come to a realization of his own utter depravity, the helplessness of his condition, and his complete dependence on Christ. In confessions, therefore, which spiritually prepared the criminal for conversion, crimes were enumerated; but in execution sermons, sins replaced even threadbare facts that might have stirred the sordid reaches of the imagination. Ministers, who wanted to arouse compassion without passion, saw no need to spread out the crimes of condemned people for public consumption and every reason to cloak courtroom facts in church proprieties. They focused on the coming execution, not on the past deeds. In the shadow of the scaffold, repentance and forgiveness were to take root. Ministers turned the execution into a form of public worship; they molded the experience of the criminal, convicted of specific crimes, into a generic experience of the struggle for salvation; and in so doing, dissolved the individuality of the criminal and obliterated the crimes themselves.

But while ministers tiptoed around crime and modestly skirted its squalid details, playwrights sloshed in the mud. They did not refer to betrayal; they showed a mother betraying her son or a subject betraying his king. Cuckolding, gaming, swearing, killing: all took place in full view. Austere moralists who sought an Archimedean point outside the world from which to have leverage on the world did not find that point in plays—not even in tragedies—which offered no relief from the sordidness of reality, no moral evaluation, no Christian

2. Samuel Stillman, *Two Sermons Occasioned by the Condemnation and Execution of Levi Ames* (Boston, 1773), 51.

utopia. Spectators, they thought, would founder in the details of daily intercourse and intrigue. Unlike parables (which also dealt in the events and happenings of the world), tragedies had no moral platform from which to view the story.

Adam Ferguson, the Scottish devotee of the tragedy, shrugged off the absence of moral platforms. For him, the difference between plays and parables did not strike at the heart of morality, because he thought of morality as a continuous process of evaluation.

> In a Parable, we wait for the moral till the story is concluded, when the whole appears to have been an illustration of some moral precept; in a good Tragedy, we have a continued moral from beginning to end; the characters, the sentiments, and the observations, which come from the persons who speak, are calculated to move and instruct us; and we are deeply engaged by such representations, because we take part with amiable characters, and become anxious about the event.[4]

But moral philosophers in the disciplinarian mold, who did not share the optimistic view of human nature held by Scottish moral philosophers in the aesthetic mold, doubted that spectators, cut loose from an explicitly articulated lesson, could bear the strain of restructuring raw experience along a moral axis. Gripped by the immediacy of events and awash in passions, spectators would succumb to moral oblivion at best; at worst they would feel the tug of vice.

Tragedies dealt with the specifics of life, character, and deeds. Ministers presiding over executions turned their backs on deeds (the crimes that brought the prisoner to the gallows) and even on character. The ministers and the crowd that clustered around the condemned man were not interested in his character; they cared only about his spiritual state. But tragedies focused attention on action and forced the audience to evaluate the characters on the basis of their acts. When Hamlet was dying, he did not think about salvation and damnation; he worried about his reputation. If people were ignorant of the facts of the case, they might misinterpret his deeds and misjudge his character. "What a wounded name, things standing thus unknown, shall live behind me!"[5] Hamlet wanted people to

4. Ferguson, 7–8.

5. *Hamlet,* in *The Pelican Shakespeare,* Willard Farnham, ed. (Baltimore, Md., 1957), Act V, scene ii, ll. 333–34.

know the truth about him as a living man. In his distress at the prospect of leaving behind a trail of dishonor, he turned to his friend Horatio and begged him to inform the world of the facts, to lay out the evidence so that people could judge him accurately and honestly. This was the service that the living could perform for the dead, to tell the story of their lives. "Horatio, I am dead; / Thou livest; report me and my cause aright / To the unsatisfied." And a moment later, "If thou didst ever hold me in thy heart, / Absent thee from felicity awhile, / And in this harsh world draw thy breath in pain, / To tell my story."[6] When a man was condemned to die, the ministers told his story—but only the last sentence, the part about conversion. The story Horatio told of Hamlet was quite a different story. When Fortinbras, straight from his conquest of Poland, viewed the Danish ground strewn with noble and royal bodies, Horatio fulfilled his obligation to his friend.

> And let me speak to th' yet unknowing world
> How these things came about. So shall you hear
> Of carnal, bloody, and unnatural acts,
> Of accidental judgments, casual slaughters,
> Of deaths put on by cunning and forced cause.[7]

And Fortinbras answered, "Let us haste to hear it and call the noblest to the audience." The deeds and acts of Hamlet will be passed under review, and on the grounds of the evidence the living will sit in judgement on his life, not on his death.

Shakespeare's tragedies dramatize the rebirth of social order, not the rebirth of the dying hero. The death of men who had threatened the social order either by losing control of themselves (protagonists like Othello, Macbeth, and King Lear) or by manipulating others to commit violent acts (villains such as Iago and Edmund) restores the balance and stability of society. Albany, Cassio, Fortinbras, Malcolm, et al. emerge from the shambles, issue orders in a burst of efficiency, and save the state from chaos. Hamlet, before he dies, names Fortinbras as his successor, so that the transmission of power will run smoothly. "I do prophesy th' election lights / On

6. Ibid., Act V, scene ii, ll. 327–29; ibid., ll. 335–338.

7. Ibid., ll. 368–372.

Fortinbras. He has my dying voice."[8] And Malcolm, restored to the throne of Scotland, raises his loyal thanes to earls and calls back his "exil'd friends abroad / That fled the snares of watchful tyranny."[9] Macbeth's death is submerged in plans for the coming coronation. The state is saved; the villains punished; and justice takes its course. But unlike the protagonists of the execution dramas, the characters in tragedies who fall victim to justice or retribution do not change. Shylock may become a Christian, but he hardly undergoes a conversion experience, and of the dying heroes nothing can be said except, "the rest is silence." The essence of tragedies was not moral reform, but human experience; not the character of society, but the character of individuals who brought down the state.

The decision to ban the theater, an activity that aroused private emotions, viewed in the context of attitudes towards the execution, a ceremony that aroused public consciousness, tells something of the colonists' needs in 1774. Executions as stage productions merged moral discrimination with aesthetic appreciation, but while an execution might be transformed into a drama, ultimately it served an identifiable social end. The execution took place, not to provide an aesthetically spiritual experience for the spectators (this may have been a desirable and sought-after end, but it could not justify the event), but to protect society, whose survival depended on conformity to the law. In spiritualizing the execution, authorities tried to annex the idea of virtue to justice. But through the aesthetic and spiritual mists that enveloped the event, the scaffold loomed starkly as a witness to law and the consequences of transgression. A man may or may not have been saved by Christ, but he was definitely executed. No matter how softened by Christian compassion and benevolence, the message that the execution sent forth, the message that justified the punishment, was: lawlessness incapacitates people for society. Executions shored up the law, a system of rules that people entered into together in order to maintain society. Criminals undermined the habitual trust people had to have in one another's allegiance to the law in order for society to remain intact.

Plays did not serve an identifiable social end. They offered a me-

8. Ibid., ll. 344–45.

9. *Macbeth*, in *The Pelican Shakespeare,* Alfred Harbage, ed. (Baltimore, 1956), Act V, scene viii, ll. 66–67.

dium for a private experience. Members of the audience related to the characters on stage, but they did not relate to each other. In contrast, people who witnessed an execution identified with each other. They, as a group, were different from the condemned man, and the meaning of the public execution lay in this difference. On a spiritual level they could identify with the condemned man (he was a sinner and they were all sinners), but on a social level they could not. They were members of society who abided by its laws; he had refused membership by breaking laws and jeopardizing society. An execution was an action taken on behalf of a group for the public good; and people who benefited from this collective good that criminals threatened attended executions as a public statement, an affirmation of community.

In the surge of political events in 1774, the morality that swept the colonies was a morality based on social values, not private emotions; on behavior, not deeds. Congress was concerned to render people fit members of society. They were interested in behavior and conduct, but more specifically, in behavior and conduct in society. The activities they banned were antisocial activities that isolated people in their emotions (gambling) or enveloped them in a mist of private perceptions (plays). In devising a moral program that could be used politically to draw people together and give them an identity as a people, Congress implicitly rejected private morality based on individual perception, instinct, and sentiment and explicitly chose public morality based on injunctions and proscriptions that applied to everyone. This impersonal, austere morality, oriented toward abnegation and behavior and insulated from deeds and heroism, helped make resistance corporate and anonymous—not the project of a few great men.

In 1774, colonists did not polarize leaders and society. Quite the contrary; they were engaged in an endeavor to have society speak for itself. Throughout the imperial debate, Americans, oppressed by acts of Parliament, were concerned to locate political authority and define its limits. Americans denied Parliament's authority while maintaining allegiance to a king who vigorously upheld Parliament's authority. Their claim of inviolable attachment to their sovereign hobbled political action. They could not, without committing treason, publicly establish their own leaders in opposition to the king and his appointees. Instead, they tried to avoid treason by resorting to anonymous corporate resistance. Their resistance came from below and depended on unanimity. As Benjamin Franklin said, "We must all hang together, or assuredly we shall all hang separately." Americans stressed their unanimity and also their character as a people. They extolled their freedom, strength, and virtue, and denounced slavery, vassalage, and corruption. When the people became active in politics, a new theoretical relationship developed between leaders and society, a relationship based on character. Leaders were not to rule people or act upon them. Society and its leaders were to share the same character; they were expressions of each other.

The political crisis and the ideology that emerged from it discouraged the performance of deeds for personal glory. Congress, by passing economic and moral regulations, helped make the people themselves a protagonist in the conflict. After independence, Americans did not crown a new king who would stand for the state in opposition to the people. Instead, they erected a confederation of republican governments. How were things to get done in a government where power could not be concentrated? How were leaders to operate in a system that stressed the power of the people?

The political crisis called for leadership, but the ideology that developed during resistance muted individuality, fostered communitarianism, and atomized power. Leaders had to dissociate their decisions and acts from their own personal will and make them in the name of the people. In the political arena, a corporate body, Congress, made decisions, but for a war to be prosecuted successfully, a general had to be in control. Washington had the problem of exercising enough power to win the war, but not enough to threaten the state. In the diplomatic arena, too, the paradox of republican leadership was dramatized. Diplomacy carried on by diplomatic missions diluted the power of individuals but proved ineffective as personal animosities rent the seams of commissions. The two chief American diplomats, Franklin and Adams, treated the problem of republican diplomacy in different ways—the one succeeding as a diplomat, the other as a republican.

ii

In 1774, Congress turned Hamlet, Othello, and Macbeth out of doors, along with lesser heroes like Douglas, Beverley, and even Cato, that arch-defier of imperial tyranny. Tragic heroes stood out from the rest of mankind and eventually were humbled "by those very Acts of Heroism which rather distinguished an ambitious than a virtuous Impulse."[10] Spectacular deeds, not everyday behavior, defined the tragic hero. Congress banished heroes as well as rogues. Tragedies, while they might stimulate the moral sense, did not offer appropriate role models. Americans, as republicans, had to wrest their victory from the British in anonymity; they were not to admire heroes who set themselves apart from the community and drew attention to their individuality. When Americans spoke, they spoke as one people in congressional petitions, declarations, and requisitions; and when they emerged from the fighting, they emerged as a confederation of republics.

In the imperial crisis, Americans directed their energy to forging a strong community that could resist corruption. Political concepts propelled them towards conformity to a public moral code that standardized behavior. With the emphasis on corporate action and corporate morality, individual leaders hesitated to act like leaders in the traditional sense, i.e., to set themselves apart from the people. After the Declaration of Independence, the leaders of America in politics, in the army, and in diplomacy had to confront limitations that republican ideology put on the exercise of power. Unlike Hamlet, Lear, and Macbeth, American leaders did not stand for the state; they served the state.

Three men who served the American republic illustrate the constraints republican ideology placed on leadership and the differences between heroes and republican leaders: George Washington, Benjamin Franklin, and John Adams. Only George Washington approached the status of hero, but unlike Hamlet or Aeneas (another founder of a country), Washington did not want to be remembered for his deeds. He wanted to be remembered for his character, a character based on behavior, or, as he would have put it, on conduct. An act of glory, in his code, did not count for as much as an act of restraint. In the years when the ineffectiveness of Congress made conducting the war increasingly difficult for Washington, he consistently refused to take civil power into his own hands. And at the end of the war, he furled his personality together with his military glory and chose the obscurity of private life, cultivating his wheat and breeding his asses,

10. *South-Carolina GAZETTE,* "Humorist No. III," 8 January–15 January 1754.

over the glory of kingship. When a colonel in the army suggested to Washington that he put on a crown and rule a people drifting apart in the absence of a strong central government, Washington fired off his response: "[Y]ou could not have found a person to whom your schemes are more disagreeable."[11]

Garry Wills, in a suggestive biography, shows that Washington tried to exert political power by dramatically staging his resignation of military power. Having first made it clear that he would not seek or accept political power, Washington could then throw his prestige behind a plea for stronger central government. Wills seems to suggest that Washington resigned in order to gain power.[12] Edmund Morgan, on the other hand, suggests that Washington was driven by a desire for honor.[13] If so, Washington would have resigned because he knew it was the duty of a republican general to resign and refuse political power. Washington tried to make his life conform to republican models because he treasured his reputation and because he believed in republicanism and all the values it entailed. That he gained political influence (rather than power) by resigning would be, according to this interpretation, the concomitant benefit of an act undertaken for other motives.

Many people have commented on Washington's immense concern for his reputation. Washington cared deeply about what people thought of him. In the early years he worked hard to earn a reputation, and in the later years, having earned it, he worked hard to preserve it.[14] When faced with decisions—big decisions like whether to attend the Philadelphia convention or whether to accept the presidency, and little decisions like whether to resign from the Society of the Cincinnati—he weighed the probable consequences his decision would have on his reputation, which he dreaded endangering. But

11. *The Writings of George Washington,* 24 John C. Fitzpatrick, ed. (Washington, 1938): 272 (hereafter cited as *Writings*). Quotation in Edmund S. Morgan, *The Genius of George Washington* (Washington, D.C., 1980), 13.

12. Garry Wills, *Cincinnatus: George Washington and the Enlightenment* (New York, 1984), 3–25.

13. Edmund S. Morgan, *The Meaning of Independence: John Adams, George Washington, and Thomas Jefferson* (Charlottesville, Va., 1976), 29–55.

14. For the early years, see Paul K. Longmore, *The Invention of George Washington* (Berkeley, Calif., 1988).

Washington's relationship to the people—the people of Virginia, the soldiers in his army, Americans—had another side. He cared about *their* honor, *their* reputation, *their* character. For his officers to have honor, *they* had to decide not to overthrow government. Washington refused to take credit for their decision because his aggrandizement would derogate from the virtue of their decision. For a republic to survive, the people themselves had to be virtuous in order to guard against tyranny; they could not simply rely on the honor of a leader. The paradox for a republican leader was that republican citizens could not simply be led; they differed from subjects in a monarchy. Today, we find the notion that a people has a character illusive, even dangerous. The concept is, after all, homogenizing and can be used to exclude individuals for reasons of race, religion, ethnicity, etc. But Washington and others in the eighteenth century found the concept neither illusive nor dangerous. It was the foundation of their political philosophy. In the political theory of the eighteenth century, the character of a people determined the type of government they would establish. In republics, the responsibility for success shifted from leaders to the people themselves, who had to maintain and exercise virtue. Ironically, the concept that the success of republican government depended on the virtue of the people drastically curtailed the initiative of republican leaders and muted their personality.

The relationship between Washington and his country lacks drama because the two are so closely identified. The people were virtuous; their leader was virtuous. Washington's virtue entitled him to the respect of a virtuous people, but it could not substitute for their virtue. Washington was not one of the people—he was not, that is, a democratic leader—but the character he built for himself, and the character Americans as a people were expected to have in order to sustain republican government, merged. As the leader of a republican government, Washington had a tendency to conceal rather than to obtrude his personality. The very nature of republican government discouraged personal aggrandizement. No Virgil sang of the man Washington, because the man Washington was inaccessible. Washington ducked behind republican principles and conformed to expectations; he did not aim at the spectacular.

The drama of tragedies and epics often lay in the conflict between the claims of the state and the actions of individuals in power driven by personal emotions and goals. Macbeth, Hamlet, and Lear all had personalities, and they all expressed their individual wills. They either created a situation that then consumed them or responded to problems that entangled them personally. Their private lives clashed with public responsibilities, and both they and the state were destroyed. The drama of the *Iliad* is concentrated in Book Twenty-four when Achilles, having rejoined the war and accepted its code and the responsibilities and fate of a warrior, responds to the suffering of Priam and learns what it is to be human. The drama of the *Aeneid* is concentrated in Book Four when Aeneas succumbs to personal passion and abandons his duty to his people. Washington's life does not dramatize the tension between the private and the public; right from the beginning Washington identified himself with the public, and he did so by repressing his individuality. Unknowable, inaccessible, Washington conformed to republican expectations and served his country well, both as a general and as a president. He has become a symbol, but he declined the role of a hero.

Republicanism put constraints on leaders. In the political arena, decisions had to be made by the representatives of the people. A strong leader, if he wished to remain a republican, could not simply have taken over and defined the course of the Revolution. In the military arena, the chief of the armed forces, if he wished to remain a republican, always had to defer to civil authority. During the American Revolution, the leaders, both civil and military, did remain republicans. No civil leader took over Congress, which continued throughout the war to act as a body politic. Congress became weaker and weaker as powerful thinkers, men who had pushed the colonies towards independence and would later take part in the federal government, retired to their states or went abroad as diplomats. Nonetheless, no civilian succumbed to the temptation to seize power and fill the void, and the military did not overrun government because George Washington was the commander-in-chief. Diplomacy during the Revolution presented its own challenges to men trying to make deals and win the support of monarchies while adhering to republican principles.

George Washington, arguably the most republican of the Founding Fathers in that he had the greatest opportunity to take over the Revolution and, in view of the increasing incompetence and weakness of Congress, the greatest provocation to do so, illustrates the constraints that republicanism put on military and political leadership. Benjamin

Franklin, arguably the least republican of the Founding Fathers, illustrates the conflict between republicanism and diplomacy. Franklin served his republic brilliantly as a diplomat, but perhaps he was able to do so because he was relatively untrammeled by republican virtues and scruples.

Benjamin Franklin is the most colorful of the Founding Fathers. We can attach a personality to him and conjure images: a poor boy entering Philadelphia all alone, his pockets stuffed with shirts and socks, a puffy roll under each arm and a third in his mouth; an inquisitive and intrepid scientist at the end of a kite; a diplomat with a beaver hat surrounded by fashionable French ladies. Benjamin Franklin was, in truth, an image maker, a self-promoter, and a publicity man. How strongly did he adhere to principles? He did not at first recognize the Stamp Act as unconstitutional and in fact had used his influence in England to get a friend appointed as a stamp distributor. Even when the unpopularity of the Act was borne in upon him, he did not seem to grasp the constitutional principles behind the protest. In front of a committee of Parliament he attempted to "explain" the American position; in fact, to explain it away by making a distinction that Americans themselves were not making between internal and external taxes. Americans, according to Franklin, did not object to all taxes, only to internal taxes. Import duties (that is, external taxes) Americans recognized as the lawful domain of Parliament. In fact, Americans recognized Parliament's authority to set import duties to regulate trade, but not to raise revenue. They objected to all parliamentary taxes, both internal and external, because they did not have representatives in Parliament. Whether Franklin put reconciliation above principle or whether he really did not see the fallacy of the distinction he was making, he contributed to the misunderstanding between British and Americans in the early years of the constitutional crisis.[15]

Washington could be a republican and a general simply by keeping the military subordinate to the government. Franklin in a sense faced

15. For a discussion of external and internal taxes, see Edmund S. Morgan, "Colonial Ideas of Parliamentary Power, 1764–1766," in *The Challenge of the American Revolution* (New York, 1976), 3–42. For Franklin's examination in the House of Commons, see Edmund S. Morgan, ed., *Prologue to Revolution: Sources and Documents on the Stamp Act Crisis, 1764–1766* (Chapel Hill, N.C., 1959), 143–46.

a more difficult problem than Washington, a problem perhaps insoluble—to reconcile diplomacy with republicanism—insoluble because many of the talents required for successful diplomacy stood in contradiction to the ideal republican character. Luckily for the future of the United States, Franklin, while he preached republican virtues, did not regulate his own life according to these virtues. Franklin's ability to create images and personae that hid rather than reflected his own character, while it was not the kind of activity that austere republicans engaged in, let alone approved of, enhanced his effectiveness as a diplomat. While republicans condemned the theater, Franklin came close to being a character in a play—not a tragic hero, but a comic, highly successful contriver. Franklin made the world into a theater and acted in it with great aplomb.

In his autobiography, which he started writing in 1771, Franklin created a persona who slowly and painfully learned the value of certain virtues—industry, frugality, and honesty—the same virtues that political philosophers thought sustained republics. Franklin stressed the importance of appearances. His persona pushed a wheelbarrow filled with the paper he had just bought through the streets of Philadelphia to demonstrate his frugality and industry. He dressed plainly, avoided places of "idle diversion," and never went fishing or hunting. "In order to secure my Credit and Character as a Tradesman, I took care not only to be in *Reality* Industrious and frugal, but to avoid all *Appearances* of the Contrary."[16] Franklin stressed appearances because he was interested in the usefulness of virtue. The conversion of his persona from a profligate, deceiving youth who spent money entrusted to him, who colluded with a friend to deceive his friend's wife, who dissipated his salary at places of amusement—the conversion of this youth to an industrious printer who through his industry achieved material prosperity and, ultimately, independence was designed to inspire youths to follow a similar course. Franklin's goal was in a sense republican. He envisioned a strong country of prosperous citizens who in their prosperity would be independent. He did not advocate the virtues because they were good in themselves, but neither, in spite of the contempt he earned later from Mark Twain and D. H. Lawrence, did he advocate material prosper-

16. Benjamin Franklin, *Benjamin Franklin's Autobiography*, J. A. Leo Lemay and P. M. Zall, eds. (New York, 1986), 54.

ity because it was good in itself. His ultimate goal was the establishment of a strong, healthy country, and he was willing to use propaganda to further this goal. In *Benjamin Franklin's Autobiography,* Franklin equated his persona with the colonies. It has even been suggested that he chose to have his persona concentrate on thirteen virtues to underscore the connection.[17]

Franklin never brought his autobiography up to date. Franklin the persona in *Autobiography* clashed with the historical Franklin. On returning to England in 1757, Franklin had taken up with a mistress and resumed his friendship with the weak and deceiving James Ralph, and years later in France he led a richly sybaritic life. In real life, the successful Franklin did not feel constrained by the ethic of frugality and industry he touted so highly in *Autobiography.*[18]

Twenty years after his sojourn in England, Franklin was in Paris as the ambassador from the United States, and here his tranquility was marred by the arrival in 1778 of John Adams, the most fiercely republican of all the Founders. The clash between John Adams and Benjamin Franklin reveals the anomaly of Franklin and the tension between republican principles and effective diplomacy and between republican principles and acting. John Adams embodied republican principles. Like Franklin, Adams wrote an autobiography, but unlike Franklin, he was not artful. His purpose was not didactic. While Franklin was less concerned with the truth about himself than with the creation of a persona for didactic purposes, Adams related historical events as they impinged on him and were filtered through his personality. Adams differed from Franklin in the way he conceived of his relationship to the republic. Adams identified with the republic in the sense that he strove to achieve virtues that he thought were republican: industry, frugality, and honesty (but not, like Franklin, conciliation). He strove to achieve those virtues because the virtues were republican. They were, that is, an end in themselves. But Adams did not think of his life history as representing the collective history of the republic. Adams served the republic—but though known as vain and self-righteous (in contrast to Franklin, who was not so known), he would never have

---

17. Michael T. Gilmore, "Franklin and the Shaping of American Ideology," in Brian M. Barbour, ed., *Benjamin Franklin: A Collection of Critical Essays* (Englewood Cliffs, N.J., 1979), 105–24, at p. 114–115.

18. Ibid., 119–20.

had the presumption (again, ironically, in contrast to Franklin) to equate the republic with himself.

Adams descended on the diplomatic scene in a whirlwind of righteousness. He was immediately struck by the decadence, luxury, and corruption of French society. Shortly after his arrival in France, he was invited to a dinner party where a female guest accosted him with sexual innuendoes and puns. Afterwards Adams smugly summed up the incident in his autobiography: "if such a[re] the manners of Women of Rank, Fashion and Reputation [in] France, they can never support a Republican Government nor be reconciled with it. We must therefore take great care not to import them into America."[19] Adams felt sorry for the French, whose decadence barred them from a republican Elysium.

But the French were not the greatest of Adams' problems; chief among the trials that jangled his nerves and affronted his sensibilities was Benjamin Franklin. Franklin's behavior, which did not comport with Adams' notion of behavior proper for a republican, rankled Adams, who described with disgust Franklin's daily routine. While Adams, up at dawn, read diplomatic dispatches and drafted replies before breakfast, Franklin rose late and immediately after breakfast received a throng of visitors—not diplomats intent on doing the business of the state, but philosophers, academics, economists, and women and children. Franklin, *déshabillé* and without a wig, told stories and drew attention to his "simplicity" until it was time to get dressed for dinner. The French dined between one and two o'clock, and Franklin was almost always invited out to dinner. After dinner he might talk with philosophers or go to a play, but most often he had tea with the ladies, listened to music, or attended card parties (Franklin himself played chess or checkers). Franklin was so involved with these "Agreable and important Occupations," Adams sniped, that Adams and Arthur Lee, the third member of the American diplomatic commission, could not gain access to him. When Lee and Adams had drawn up papers and had had them copied, they often had to wait several days before Franklin found the time to sign them. Adams, who was always included in the dinner invitations to Frank-

19. L. H. Butterfield et al., eds., *Diary and Autobiography of John Adams* (Cambridge, Mass., 1961) 4:37.

lin, eventually decided to decline so that he would have time to "do the Business of the mission."[20]

Adams' description of Franklin has often been used to ridicule Adams for his jealousy, his spleen, and his prudishness. But the description also reveals the distaste of a republican for a display of values and behavior that flouted republican principles. Specifically, Franklin went to plays, drank tea, and attended card parties—all activities that Americans had banned. Generally, Franklin reveled in indolence and put off work. Industry and frugality, the values on which Americans based their resistance and self-definition, were conspicuously absent from Franklin's French routine. But Adams' hostility may also have sprung from an innate distrust of the dramatic performance, a distrust of people who played a part.

In *Autobiography,* Franklin had created a persona for didactic purposes. In France, years later, Franklin created another persona, this time in real life, not in a book: the persona of a public man, the American diplomat. It was perhaps this *persona* that Adams mistrusted. He would have mistrusted it because it *was* a persona, and he would have found it distasteful because it was calculated to appeal to the high-class, sophisticated—yet frivolous and decadent—society of Paris. The society of Paris was anything but virtuous and anything but republican. Part of Adams' frustration with and bitterness towards Franklin in the years when they were serving as diplomats should be seen in ideological and not merely personal terms. Franklin was using "simplicity" and "Americanisms" (like his hat and country proverbs) to entertain the French. In that sense he was debasing republican virtues. And Franklin was playing a role. In that sense he was violating the virtue of honesty.

Diplomacy, oriented toward results, and republicanism, grounded in virtue, did not go together. Successful diplomacy operates outside the realm of principle and morality. Many Americans of the newly established republic did not, however, seem to recognize this incompatibility. French diplomats told Americans they were in the war only for America's sake, and many members of Congress, full of the importance of their republican experiment, seem to have believed French protestations of altruism. Adams and Franklin did not. Ad-

20. Ibid., 118–19.

ams' reluctance to depend on the French stemmed from principle. Adams did not think the French, who were dissolute and extravagant, who had loose morals and wallowed in luxury, were worthy of being allies of the Americans. He feared lest they corrupt Americans, whose strength lay in their virtue.[21] Franklin did not take French protestations at face value because he recognized them for what they were, diplomatic cunning and maneuvering. But unlike Adams, Franklin felt no distaste for diplomacy; he loved it, and he excelled in it. It allowed him the full play of his talent for creating a persona that could achieve results. He was both an actor in a play and the director of the play. Paradoxically, while his credentials as a republican, when placed under scrutiny, might be suspect (the persona he created for himself was republican, but it was a persona), he made an excellent diplomat for the American republic.

Today, Franklin is the most accessible of the Founders because he is not obscured behind the veil of republicanism. Washington even in his lifetime became a symbol. He lived his life according to models; he kept his personality subordinate to principles. Like all symbols, he was an abstraction. Later, as myths enveloped him, he became, not a personality, but a morality lesson. Adams' personality occasionally does break through in his bouts of jealousy or anger, but when it does, it serves only to trivialize him. Adams truthfully confided his weaknesses and foibles to his diary, and Americans have latched onto these human weaknesses and dismissed the man as unworthy of national respect. But of all the Founders, a coruscating personality attaches only to Franklin. Never mind that the created personality might conceal the character; Americans over the years have done Franklin the honor (or sometimes the dishonor) to accept him as he presented himself. But the very creation of a personality, the ability and desire to sell an image, sets Franklin apart from the republicans of the eighteenth century. In some ways Franklin is closer to the time when Americans could put an actor in the White House or respond to two-minute sound bites of candidates posing in front of the flag than to the time of statesmen whose character was defined not by deeds, not by personalities and images, but by character and conduct, by the continual adherence day after undramatic day to republican principles and expectations.

21. Morgan, *Meaning of Independence*, 18–20.

The hero performed deeds and talked about the deeds he had performed. These deeds were the core of his character. Without them he would be forgotten, and being remembered was everything to the hero. He clung to his personal identity and marketed it to posterity.

The condemned criminal who conformed to the will of civil and church authority gave up his past. He renounced his deeds and demanded of people that they remember him for his struggle for salvation. A repentant criminal who stood on the scaffold bore witness to the truth, but the truth he bore witness to was not his own truth, but Christ's. His final act was to renounce his own will and submit himself to the will of Christ.

The republican leader also bore witness to a truth that was separate from his own identity. He did not, like the condemned man, renounce his past, but he did refrain from deeds that served only to enhance his personal glory and instead sought honor in conformity to principles that discouraged personal aggrandizement. Because behavior (or conduct) formed the basis of his character, he could not rely on deeds to aggrandize him. Like the condemned man, the republican leader renounced his own will, but instead of submitting to the will of Christ, he submitted to the will of the people as expressed by their representatives.

Time extinguishes the penitent criminals and makes personal the impersonal republicans by garnishing them with myths. Heroes are remembered because their names are synonymous with their deeds. They live their lives as an expression of their will and they die as a result of their self-expression. But while the world remembers heroes, it gives little thought to the state they so often bring down with them and leave in shambles. George Washington has never been made the hero of a play or epic. In his life, before he was transformed into myth, Washington was a quintessential republican. By his personal restraint, his refusal to use the army to control Congress, and his refusal to see himself, a powerful general, as the answer to political inefficiencies, Washington preserved the state. In averting a military coup when the random ineptitude of civil government pressed the patience of the army to the limit, he told his officers, who wanted to resort to force, that virtue lay in *not* acting. If they wanted honor (albeit impersonal honor), they should hold back. "You will give one more distinguished proof of unexampled patriotism and patient virtue, rising superior to the pressure of the most complicated sufferings; And you will, by the dignity of your Conduct, afford occasion for Posterity to say, when speaking of the glorious example you have exhibited to Mankind, 'had this day been wanting, the World had never seen the last stage of perfection to which human nature is capable of attaining.' "[22] By perfection Washington meant republican government, a way of life made possible by the character and conduct of all men, not just heroes.

*   *   *

In 1774, the first Continental Congress ignored the softer, modulated voices of moral aesthetes and heeded the shriller tones of disciplinarians. Colonists may have been reading Hutcheson and his cohorts; they may have cried over *Pamela* and followed Lawrence Sterne on his sentimental journey; they may have appealed to Englishmen as their brothers; but when they thought about what kind of people they wanted to be and how they should behave in order to realize this ideal, they decided to give up horse-racing, cockfighting, elaborate funerals, and the theater. Congress, in promulgating specific rules of behavior biased toward restraint and abnegation, adopted the attitude of moral disciplinarians towards virtue and vice. Of course, all moral philosophers, not just disciplinarians, were, like Calvin Coolidge's minister, against sin; but they approached the problem of behavior in different ways. Disciplinarians rejected the sentimentalist belief that artistic imitations of life could inspire spectators to live a virtuous life and came down in favor of rules and proscriptions. Examples might be an effective way of teaching, but they had to be examples from real life. Fake examples (life on the stage) would produce fake responses—hypocrites inspiring hypocrisy.

Most political revolutions do not step out in the world naked, but issue forth garbed in some moral attire. An individual alone in his own concerns would have come to the problem of morality with a blurred and divided mind, asking nothing of it in general, but accepting principles—benevolence, industry, frugality—on a day-to-day basis as the occasion dictated. But in 1774, the delegates, acting as a congress, had to create an intercolonial morality and had to ask something particular of this morality: that it draw people from all colonies together in resistance. Behind the bald statement that "colo-

---

22. Washington, *Writings* 26:222–27.

nists will no longer attend plays" lay a litter of attitudes and beliefs that had been sorted into two piles: one to be discarded as inappropriate to the crisis of 1774, and the other to be used politically to coalesce a people and bring them to a sense of their own identity. The rubbish heap of tragedies and comedies, the discarded refuse of sentiment, affection, and benevolence, bear witness, not only to the moral values of the colonists in 1774, but to the strategy they devised for inculcating these moral values and for using a cohesive moral community, visibly bound together by moral regulations, as a bulwark against political oppression. Congress did not simply define appropriate values, they promoted one system of moral education and rejected another.

The claims and counterclaims in regard to the moral value of plays, having been bandied around for centuries, finally pall. If any debate on the subject took place in Congress it must surely have ebbed into a fatigued exchange of anticipated arguments. But while the reasons for banning the theater are tainted with the stale air that envelops any longstanding controversy, the decision, once made, shaped the character Americans were creating for themselves as a people. When colonists banished heroes and established a code of behavior that each and every member of society was expected to abide by without taking credit for being exceptional, they edged their way towards a republican ideal. Since colonists did not see the crisis of 1774 in terms of the destructive power of one man, they did not look for a great man to save them. Colonists interpreted the political situation as a crisis of the people, not a crisis of leadership. The solution did not lie in liquidating victims or looking for a savior, a Fortinbras or a Malcolm—in fact, saviors were dangerous because they relieved the people from responsibility for the state of society. The solution lay in a moral reformation that included everyone. Morality, like land ownership and guns, had to be widely distributed in order to protect liberty.

★ 5 ★

Funerals and Politics

In those early days in October 1774, delegates, trickling to Philadelphia from the North and the South, milled around while waiting for Congress to convene, wearily took stock of each other, and recorded impressions in diaries and letters. Everyone knew the New England delegates were "warm," even "hot," and yet despite this agreement among the psychological meteorologists, everyone—those reluctant to commit all the colonies to resistance solely on account of Boston and those fired up to take a constitutional stand—had to admit that New Englanders were conducting themselves with propriety. Moderation tempered their arguments; sobriety regulated their pace. Joseph Galloway, a conservative delegate from Pennsylvania who opposed any assault on Parliament's sovereignty, admitted that Bostonians were "in their Behavior and Conversation very modest." Galloway, however, detected a superficiality in this somber decorum. Bostonians may have been modest, "yet they are not so much so as not to throw out Hints, which, like Straws and Feathers, tell us from which Point of the Compass the wind comes."[1] Others, more sympathetic to the plight of Boston and Massachusetts, took a less cynical view of New Englanders. Caesar Rodney, from New Jersey, stood in awe of the Virginia delegates. "More Sensible, fine fellows

1. *Letters of the Delegates to Congress, 1774–1789,* Paul H. Smith, ed. (Washington, 1976), I:24 (hereafter cited as *LD*).

you'd Never Wish to See." And how did the Bostonians measure up to these sensible Virginians? "[T]he Bostonians who (we know) have been Condemned by Many for their Violence, are Moderate men, When Compared to Virginia, South Carolina and Rhode Island."[2]

There could be no doubt about it; the New Englanders were on their best behavior. They knew their reputation as hotheaded zealots, extremists, and republicans, and they were not going to let this reputation sabotage intercolonial resistance to parliamentary tyranny if they could possibly help it. They would lie low and let others do the controversial proposing. On the first day of Congress it was Thomas Lynch of South Carolina, not any New Englander, who outmaneuvered the conservative Galloway and arranged for Congress to meet in Carpenters' Hall rather than in the Pennsylvania State House. It was Lynch who proposed Charles Thompson, an ardent Son of Liberty who had not been elected to Congress, as secretary.[3] And the next day, when Congress convened in Carpenters' Hall, Samuel Adams, a Congregationalist from Boston whose reputation for radical politics had spread throughout the colonies, was on his feet, not with violent measures of resistance, but with the proposal that Jacob Duché, an Anglican clergyman, should open the Congress with prayers—a move Adams found "prudent," as he confided to a friend.[4] George Reed from Delaware confirmed Adams' evaluation. Reed told John Adams "what a masterly stroke of Policy" it was. He assured Adams that proposing prayers by Duché had had a very good effect. "The Sentiments of People here, are growing more and more favourable every day."[5] It was Samuel Ward, a Baptist from Rhode Island, who moved that Congress offer thanks to Duché for his service. And it was Ward and Thomas Cushing, a Congregationalist from Boston, who were appointed to draw up the thanks.[6] Clearly the New Englanders were doing things right. Clearly they were exercising the greatest care not to offend the other delegates. Clearly they would not want to jeopardize these political gains.

---

2. Ibid., 58.

3. Ibid., 25.

4. Ibid., 35, 55.

5. Ibid., 60.

6. Ibid., 35.

Now imagine, a month later, the delegates discussing the program of moral proscriptions—the sacrifices, the tests of commitment that Congress would recommend for the colonists. The people of South Carolina, Virginia, Maryland, and New York raced horses. New Englanders did not. These same people who gambled on horses gambled on cocks. New Englanders did not. Theater companies had succeeded in New York, Philadelphia, Annapolis, Williamsburg, and Charleston. In Providence, Newport, and Boston, they had not. When it came to using morality as a political strategy, New Englanders must have been in a bit of a quandary. They would hardly have wanted to jeopardize the political solidarity they had been at such pains to construct by standing aloof in moral superiority. If they wanted to avoid jarring their colleagues, they would have to come up with some sacrifice of their own to show their commitment to the cause. As it happens, they had one program of moral improvement ready-made. For the past ten years they had been linking sartorial restraint at funerals with morality and political resistance. Although we do not know who proposed what in the First Continental Congress, it is quite probable that New Englanders were behind the funeral regulations that Congress agreed to recommend to all colonists: ". . . on the death of any relation or friend, none of us, or any of our families, will go into any further mourning dress, than a black crape or ribbon on the arm or hat, for gentlemen, and a black ribbon and necklace for ladies, and we will discontinue the giving of gloves and scarves at funerals." We do know that Congress adopted funeral regulations that New Englanders had already succeeded in linking to the political cause.

i

In 1764 and 1765, when Parliament passed legislation taxing the American colonists, New Englanders took actions intended to make their resistance visible in a nonviolent way. In 1764, Parliament passed the Sugar Act. According to the terms of the Sugar Act, import duties were placed on sugar, wine, coffee, and many materials: silk, calico, linen, and French lawn. These import duties were designed not only to regulate trade, but to raise revenue. Although the colonists recognized Parliament's right to regulate trade for the benefit of the Empire, they did not recognize Parliament's right to raise revenue by imposing import duties. Such a measure constituted taxation, and people could be taxed only with their consent, given by themselves or by their representatives. Since the colonists had elected no representatives to Parliament, they had not consented to the Sugar Act, and the Sugar Act, to the extent that it imposed taxes on the colonies, was unconstitutional.

In response to the Sugar Act, colonists took two kinds of measures: measures of industry and measures of frugality.[7] Forming societies for promoting arts (i.e., manufactures), agriculture, and economy, they offered prizes to whoever could make the most linen, weave the greatest number of stockings, tan the best twenty hides of bend leather (the stoutest kind of leather made from the back and flank of the cow or ox and used for soles of boots and shoes), make the best 100 pairs of women's shoes, dress the best 100 skins for breeches, make the best 100 pairs of beaverskin gloves, etc. The incentives for home production of such items were coupled with encouragement of frugality, especially abstention from buying British imports. Groups of people gathered together and publicized agreements to behave in conspicuous ways that would reinforce the colonies' political stand. Fire companies announced that members would not eat mutton, in order to preserve the sheep for their wool. Students at Yale agreed not to drink foreign liquor.[8]

When colonists first started changing their behavior in response to British legislation, their motives were not purely constitutional. The colonists viewed the consequences of the Sugar Act from a pragmatic point of view as well as from a constitutional one. They feared economic disaster. In the context of rising prices, colonists drew a distinction between necessities and luxuries. Anything that was not necessary became a luxury. Instead of taking a stand against luxury itself, colonists sometimes objected to the Sugar Act on the grounds that import duties made objects of luxury economically unavailable to American colonists. Taxation necessitated frugality.

In 1765, a year after passing the Sugar Act, Parliament passed the

---

7. For a discussion of the Sugar Act and the colonial response to it, see Edmund S. Morgan and Helen M. Morgan, *The Stamp Act Crisis* (New York, 1962), 30–58.

8. *Massachusetts Gazette and Boston News-Letter,* 6 December 1764, 3 January 1765, 30 November 1764, 5 July 1764; *Pennsylvania Gazette,* 28 February 1765, 7 March 1765.

Stamp Act, whose sole and unambiguous purpose was to tax the colonists. The act did not levy import duties, which could be interpreted as a means of regulating trade and not of raising revenue. Instead, the Stamp Act set up taxes on newspapers, almanacs, certain legal documents, playing cards, and dice. Since taxes on domestic items could have nothing to do with regulation of trade, the taxes of the Stamp Act could be interpreted only as taxes. But even after the passage of the Stamp Act, far more threatening constitutionally than the Sugar Act, not all colonists fastened their attention on the domestic taxes; some still harped on the import duties of the Sugar Act. And not all colonists identified luxury as a moral evil that had to be extirpated from colonial society to ensure political survival. Editorialists once again emphasized the dispensability of luxury items, not their corrupting power, and pointed out that repressive economic measures would render the colonists unable to afford luxury imports.[9] Colonists praised industry, but again, they did not at first link industry with frugality as twin forces opposing corrupting luxury. Sometimes, indeed, they lauded industry as a means of procuring luxuries.

Little by little, however, frugality entered the public consciousness as a virtue in itself and not just as a means of putting economic pressure on England. Abstention was touted as moral and healthy. According to one author, the decision of the Yale students not to drink imported liquor "will not only greatly diminish the expences of Education but prove, as may be presumed, very favourable to the Health and Improvement of the Students."[10] As frugality became an absolute virtue divorced from political circumstances, so did consumption of luxuries become a vice regardless of the provenance of the luxuries.

When New Englanders established a program of public frugality to protest the Sugar and Stamp Acts, they included funeral regulations in their program. Bostonians, who had a history of public concern with funerals, were the first to associate burial practices with a political cause. In the summer of 1764, some of the principal merchants of Boston met and resolved to take a public stand on decorum of dress. They would eschew lace, ruffles, and all "su-

9. *Boston Post-Boy*, 1 July 1765.

10. *Massachusetts Gazette and Boston News-Letter*, 30 November 1764.

perfluities" of dress, and among superfluities of dress they included special mourning clothes that people were accustomed to buy to express their regard for a deceased relative or friend. Token symbols, they decided, could replace the expensive suits of mourning. Instead of dressing all in black, mourners could tie a piece of black crepe around their hat or arm.[11]

In September, Bostonians proposed another funeral regulation. It was the custom for the family of the deceased to give gloves to family friends and important mourners. Gloves could vary in quality according to the status of the recipient (the élite received leather; the plebeians, chamois) and in color according to the status of the deceased (virgins were commemorated with white, for example; children, with lavender). The Boston reformers did not forego the custom of giving away gloves, but they stipulated that the gloves should be made in the colonies and not imported from England. They had two concerns: to keep money from leaving the colony and to pare away useless expenditures. Colonial glovers were encouraged to make gloves that could be used after the funeral, not special funeral gloves "that are seldom drawn on a second time."[12] The gloves should be suitable to the New England climate and should bear some mark, such as a pine tree or a bow and arrow, that would distinguish them from English gloves. Such gloves would sell for two shillings to six shillings.

In the political crisis, the élite set the new style for funerals, and newspaper essayists, quick to make psychological hay in a status-conscious society, applauded them. "While this Town is bless'd with Gentlemen of Fortune, to exhibit Examples of Frugality, we have no Reason to fear that Luxury will ever be our Ruin."[13] The élite, by associating luxury with corruption and frugality with virtue, were protecting the people not only from penury but also from immorality. "Happy will it be for this Community, when all the former Extravagancies of Mourning Habit, so destructive not only to the Purses of the People, but even to their Morals too, should be totally abolished."[14]

11. *Massachusetts Gazette and Boston News-Letter,* 30 August 1764.

12. *Massachusetts Gazette and Boston News-Letter,* 27 September 1764.

13. Ibid.

14. Ibid.

The people of Boston were asked to follow a moral banner. But the restrictions on mourning clothes and funeral presents also fitted into the political and economic resistance of colonists to British legislation. The Sugar Act taxed textiles imported from Great Britain: silk, bengal, calico, cambric, French lawn. By doing away with special mourning clothes, colonists could cut back on textile importation and in this way keep more money in the colonies. In the summer of 1765, it was estimated that the new style of funeral had saved Boston 10,000 pounds in one year.[15] Colonial abstention would also inflict heavy losses on English merchants and manufacturers, who would then, it was hoped, lobby in Parliament for repeal of the legislation that had angered the colonists. English glovers were already in trouble because foreign gloves were flooding the English market. Colonists were aware of the economic plight of English glovers, whose discontent was reported in colonial papers. In April 1765, Bostonians could read in the newspaper that the journeyman glovers in London intended to petition Parliament to block the importation of foreign gloves, which had "reduced several hundred families . . . to great distress."[16] Colonists must have felt assured that the reduction of colonial demand for English gloves could only put more strain on a declining business, increase unemployment, and lead to social unrest in England.

The first funeral without mourning dress to receive publicity was that of Mr. Ellis Callender, the son of a Baptist minister. Behind the bier trooped a long line of relatives, none of whom wore mourning clothes. The chief mourner appeared in his everyday clothes, with a simple piece of black crepe tied around his arm. The chief mourner's wife, the nearest relation to the deceased, displayed her sartorial restraint by wearing "no other token of Mourning than a black Bonnet, Gloves, Ribbons, and Handkerchief."[17] The new style caught on, thanks to the publicity it received in the papers. In the last week of September, three more Boston families and one Charlestown family buried their dead without decking themselves in mourning dress. On October 8, two Boston papers confidently reported that "The Practice of putting on Mourning at Funerals is already almost

15. *Boston Post-Boy,* 1 July 1765.

16. *Boston Post-Boy,* 1 April 1765.

17. *Massachusetts Gazette and Boston News-Letter,* 20 September 1764.

abolished in this Town."[18] As the new style spread, Bostonians gloated over their success in setting the example. "The New Regulation of Funerals is now establish'd in this Town; and we hear that it is highly approved of and conformed unto in divers Parts of the Country."[19] Neighboring towns sent word of their approval and reported funerals without mourning dress: Roxbury, Marblehead, Dorchester, Concord, Cambridge, and Newburyport.[20] By 1765, funerals without mourning dress had also taken place outside Massachusetts in Newport, New York City, and Portsmouth.[21] In January 1766, a Pennsylvania paper announced that Henry Harrison, an alderman of Philadelphia and former mayor, had been buried in "the new mode."[22]

The publicity attendant on simple funerals subsided with the repeal of the Stamp Act in March 1766. But in 1767, Parliament passed the Townshend Acts, one of which set taxes on certain imports to the colonies: paint, lead, paper, glass, and tea. Since these taxes were designed to raise revenue and not to regulate trade, the colonists considered the Townshend taxes just as unconstitutional as the stamp tax and organized resistance along similar lines. Once again New Englanders raised the cry of funerals in the new mode as a way of demonstrating publicly a determination to resist. But this time towns took the initiative and organized resistance movements, although the choice of whether to abide by town recommendations still remained with the individual. On October 28, 1767, the Boston town meeting decided to encourage colonial manufacturing and frugality by drawing up and circulating a subscription. People who signed the subscription made a contract with each other not to import certain items (for example, loaf sugar, gloves, apparel) and to encourage the use and consumption of goods made in the colonies. Included among the articles of agreement was a resolution

18. *Boston Post-Boy* and *Massachusetts Gazette and Boston News-Letter,* 8 October 1764.

19. *Massachusetts Gazette and Boston News-Letter,* 1 November 1764.

20. *Boston Post-Boy,* 29 October 1764, 14 January 1765, 21 January 1765; *Massachusetts Gazette and Boston News-Letter,* 15 November 1764.

21. *Boston Post-Boy,* 21 January 1765, 25 February 1765; *Massachusetts Gazette and Boston News-Letter,* 1 November 1764, 18 December 1764.

22. *Pennsylvania Journal,* 8 January 1766.

pertaining to funerals. "And we further Agree strictly to adhere to the late Regulation respecting Funerals, and will not use any Gloves but what are Manufactured here, nor procure any new Garments upon such an Occasion but what shall be absolutely necessary."[23]

Once again neighboring towns sent notices to the Boston papers that they had taken similar measures of economy.[24] And neighboring colonies were swept up in the swirl of activity. A New York paper publicized the spread of measures of frugality and industry throughout the New England colonies.[25] People from Rhode Island and Connecticut participated in the movement. In November 1767, the Providence town meeting drew up a subscription, slightly more comprehensive than Boston's, in which the signers promised, among other things, to forebear "the Use of black or Mourning Apparel, Gloves and Liquors, at Funerals."[26] The people of Newport joined the movement. They passed the usual restrictions but added rings to the list of undesirable items.[27] In New London, Connecticut, people coupled extravagant funerals with the lavish entertainments given on the election of officers to the militia. Both were to be discouraged.[28]

No set procedure that would be susceptible of failure existed for promulgating the funeral regulations. Success depended on towns, on newspapers, on churches, on estate executors, and even on testators. Different towns operated in different ways. The Boston town meeting arranged to publish its votes and resolutions, to circulate copies among the freeholders of Boston, and to send copies to the selectmen of all towns in Massachusetts so that they would be inspired to encourage similar measures in their towns. Newspapers announced that the subscription rolls for Boston had been placed in the town clerk's hands and that the selectmen "strongly recommend this Measure to Persons of all Ranks, as the most honorable and

23. *Boston Town Records, 1758–1764,* 28 October 1767, p. 224; *Massachusetts Gazette and Boston News-Letter,* 5 November 1767.

24. *Boston Gazette,* 2 November 1767, 21 December 1767, Supplement.

25. *Boston Gazette,* 18 January 1768, from the *New York Journal.*

26. *Boston Gazette,* 7 December 1767.

27. *Boston Gazette,* 14 December 1767.

28. *Boston Gazette,* 25 January 1768.

effectual way of giving a public Testimony of their Love to their Country, and of endeavouring to save it from ruin."[29]

In Newport a group of private citizens took the initiative and instigated town proceedings. They sent a proposal to the town council "for encouraging Industry, Frugality, and our own Manufactures." The town council called a town meeting and reported favorably on the proposal. The town then voted to "take all prudential and legal measures to encourage the produce and manufacture of this Colony, and to lessen the use of Superfluities," and as one such prudent measure, resolved on frugal funerals. The town clerk drew up a number of subscription papers detailing the town's resolutions, and the town meeting appointed a committee to get the signatures of the inhabitants of Newport. The town meeting also arranged to have the resolutions published and sent to the town councils of all the towns in Rhode Island as a suggestion of measures they might take. Not all towns passed funeral recommendations or proposals for encouraging industry and frugality. One town actually voted against such a proposal. In this case the dissenting citizens drew up their own subscription and circulated it without the town's backing.[30]

Although many towns did take measures to curtail funeral extravagance, they did not modify the way they buried the poor. Towns were to give poor people a decent burial. Towns paid for the linen in which the corpse was laid out, the coffin, transportation of the coffin to the grave, digging the grave, and tolling the bell. As payment for service rendered, towns usually gave a pair of gloves to the minister and the women—usually poor women—who laid out the body. The glove transaction was mercenary. The Watertown selectmen specified that the two women who laid out an Indian squaw were to receive "A Pair, of Gloves or the Value of them, for that Service."[31] Funeral regulations spawned by the political crisis were designed to eliminate waste—expenditures for useless items. As a token response to the spirit in which these regulations were made, towns could have substituted cash payments for gloves. But in fact, the poor continued to be given useless objects for burying the poor. In the case of charity funerals, respect for decency and tradition triumphed over distaste

29. *Massachusetts Gazette and Boston News-Letter,* 26 November 1767.

30. William Lincoln, *The History of Worcester* (Worcester, Mass., 1837) 72–73.

31. *Watertown Records* (Newton, Mass., 1928) for June 1756, 5:177–78.

for waste. In Watertown the selectmen continued to pay for services with gloves, not money. The funerals of Lydia Warren and Mary Priest in 1766 and of Samuel Collidge in 1767 did not differ from the funerals for poor people given by the town in the 1750s.[32] In 1773, Needham spent thirteen shillings and three farthings for gloves for the funeral of a poor man.[33] Since people participating in the funerals of the poor received inexpensive gloves, this expenditure probably means that the town bought around thirteen pairs of gloves for the funeral. Perhaps because funeral reform was initially associated with curtailment of extravagance, and curtailment of extravagance was urged for the sake of the poor, no one thought of making charity funerals for poor people into a political statement.

Either the town or the church was responsible for burying the minister. (If the town and the parish were synonymous, the town paid; if not, the church paid.) Again, some towns and churches showed little inclination to apply the regulations to their own corporate undertakings. In 1768, for example, Hamilton Parish in Ipswich, Massachusetts, gave a pair of white leather gloves to all the ministers who attended their minister's funeral—eighteen pairs of gloves in all.[34] Although it is possible that the gloves were American-made, there is no indication that they were. And white gloves, because of their uselessness, were just the sort of gloves that funeral reformers complained about. Other churches, however, were more politically conscious. In June 1769, the congregation of the Old South Church of Boston, in making arrangements for the funeral of their senior pastor, Joseph Sewall, voted "to adhere strictly to the Regulations of not wearing Mourning; and also voted to desire those who attend the Funeral, to conform to the said Regulations."[35]

Towns and churches could take a stand on funeral reform, but the success of the movement ultimately depended on individuals: on executors and testators. In some cases executors received specific instructions in the will. After the summer of 1764 a scattering of

---

32. *Watertown Records*, V:177, 178, 183, 203, 206, 208, 304, 307, 319, 320.

33. "Needham Town Records," 22 February 1773, Vol. III, p. 44. See also 27 March 1767.

34. Joseph Felt, *A History of Ipswich, Essex, and Hamilton* (Cambridge, Mass., 1884), 199.

35. *Massachusetts Gazette and Boston News-Letter*, 29 June 1769.

people when making their wills broke away from the standard form—"My body I bequeath to the earth from whence it came to be decently interred at the discretion of my executor"—and stressed the importance of frugality. A Boston printer told his executor to bury him "agreeable to the prudent Method now practiced." A Boston merchant desired his wife and children not to purchase any new clothes for the funeral, "that they may be examples of that œconomy so much desired respecting funerals." A gentleman from Dedham looked forward to the good example he was going to set. He directed his executors to "observe the new Method respecting my Interment being desirous of doing all in my Power towards establishing so Useful a Regulation." Others strictly forbade unnecessary expenses or stipulated a decent burial "without any great formality or expense." One put a ceiling of four pounds on the total funeral cost.[36]

But even without specific instructions, executors were prompted by local leaders to conduct funerals in the new mode. The "upper sort" not only initiated the funeral movement, but by their example encouraged the "lower sort" to adopt the same methods of frugality. Newspapers urged town selectmen and people of reputation to encourage bereaved families to conduct funerals in the new mode, and recommended that clergymen endeavor to introduce the practice in their parishes. "The Inculcations of so respectable a Body, upon this Subject, would have great Weight."[37] Community leaders attended funerals conducted in the new mode to make public their approval of the frugality and to protect the relatives from accusations of stinginess. In Portsmouth the principal ladies and gentlemen of the town attended the funeral of Mrs. King, the wife of a merchant, to show their respect, not only to the deceased, "but also the truly laudable,

36. Samuel Draper, Will, 4 February 1767, Suffolk County, Massachusetts, Probate Records, Vol. 66, p. 128; William Whitwell, Will, 8 January 1774, Suffolk County, Vol. 74, p. 413; Isaac Bullard, Will, 5 February 1770, Suffolk County, Vol. 69, p. 69; Samuel Pierce, Will, 7 October 1768, Suffolk County, Vol. 67, p. 174; James Noble, Will, 13 December 1769, Suffolk County, Vol. 74, p. 283; Hannah Gay, Will, 30 September 1769, Suffolk County, Vol. 70, p. 152. Other people from Suffolk County mentioned frugal burials in wills they wrote after the summer of 1764: James Griffon (Vol. 65, p. 11); John Steel (Vol. 67, p. 157); Powers Marriot (Vol. 67, p. 236); David Wheeler (Vol. 69, p. 311); James White (Vol. 70, p. 338); Margaret Steel, (Vol. 72, p. 414); Joseph Fisher (Vol. 74).

37. *Massachusetts Gazette and Boston News-Letter*, 15 November 1764.

and lately introduced Custom of burying the Dead, without extravagant and expensive Charges arising from the purchasing [of] Mourning Apparel."[38] Similarly, important people in Marblehead rallied to the cause. The funeral of the wife of Captain William Curtis was "attended by principal Gentlemen of the Town and a great Number of others: This being the first Instance of that Kind in this Town, due Care was taken to conform to the *Boston Method,* which seems to be universally approved; and 'tis not to be doubted but that so laudable an Example will be followed here in all future Funerals."[39] By their participation, leaders showed that a funeral could be frugal without sacrificing solemnity, dignity, and respect for the dead.

*   *   *

Funerals were visible ceremonies that had to take place. Therefore they could be used to set up a test of membership in a political community. A death in a family required the head of the family or executor of the estate to make a choice that would have political implications. It was impossible to avoid making a public statement. Frugal funerals offered proof of political purity, and each frugal funeral increased the membership of the politically pure. Since people continued to die and be buried by their families, recruitment to the cause was cumulative. The more people chose frugal funerals, the easier it was for others to follow and the harder it was to deviate from what had become community practice. Because newspapers gave so much publicity to funeral regulations, people who conducted funerals in the old mode had to consciously make a decision. Either they cared more about funeral traditions than about politics, or they thought the British Parliament did have the power to tax and legislate for the colonists and wanted to make public their position. Meanwhile, public opinion in favor of the new mode undermined the very reason for elaborate funerals in the old mode: social prestige. The public aspects of the funeral took precedence over the private. Families no longer set themselves apart in visible mourning clothes; they joined a common cause. The overall effect of the new mode of funerals was to level social distinctions (distinctions between the family and the rest of society and distinctions between the

38. *Boston Post-Boy,* 25 February 1765.
39. Ibid.; *Massachusetts Gazette and Boston News-Letter,* 17 January 1765.

rich and important and the poor and insignificant) and to enhance political ones (the distinction between dedicated patriots on the one hand and neutrals or loyalists on the other).

Funeral reform operated as a political strategy in very particular ways. Some political demonstrations are more susceptible to governmental restraint than others; some are more prone to violence; some inhibit, others encourage the development of a class-based ideology. The funeral ceremony—that one small wedge of colonial resistance to parliamentary taxation and legislation—defined, modulated, and controlled political tension. To understand how New England funerals made a political statement we should look at the funeral ceremony itself, both at its structure and at its function within a particular society. The funeral ceremony, removed from the jangle of political grievances, contained beliefs, values, and assumptions. These beliefs, values, and assumptions, once distilled, can annotate the political crisis that elicited funeral reform and benefited from it.

ii

New England funerals had certain elements that funerals of other cultures often have. That is, they conformed to structural patterns that transcend time and place. But New England funerals also encased a particular theology. To a certain extent they were fashioned by the beliefs and values of the particular culture they were a part of. Both the transcendent and particular elements of the New England funeral enhanced the political effectiveness of the ceremony. The funeral not only gave patriots a means of expressing political resistance, but also conditioned that resistance—shaped it, colored it, and set it on a defined course.

Funerals in many different societies seem to have common features. Often people create noise at funerals, usually discontinuous, cacophonous noise: drumming, tapping, knocking, rattling, tolling.[40] The people of eighteenth-century New England tolled muffled bells. Tolling occurred at least twice (sometimes three or even four times), and each toll usually lasted about thirty minutes, sometimes

---

40. Claude Levi-Strauss, *From Honey to Ashes* (New York, 1973), 371, 373; Richard Huntington and Peter Metcalf, *Celebrations of Death: The Anthropology of Mortuary Ritual* (Cambridge, 1979), 47.

up to an hour.[41] The bells alerted the community. One series called people to gather at the house of the deceased. Another series tolled while the funeral procession wound its way through the town, arriving eventually at the burial ground, but not by the most direct route. At funerals for civic or religious leaders, guns would be fired along the way, probably when the procession passed the green, and then big guns would be fired over the grave itself. These military-style funerals harked back to the seventeenth century. A bystander describing the funeral of Deputy Governor Francis Willoughby in 1671 expressed pleasure at the noise.

> He was solemnly interred with the attendance of 11 foot companys (with the doleful noise of trumpets and drums) in their mourning posture all marching. 3 thundering volleyes of shot discharged, answered with the loud roaring of the great guns, rending the heavens with noise at the loose of so great a man.[42]

New Englanders in the eighteenth century, like people of many other cultures, ate and drank at funerals and received presents. Participants in a funeral gathered at the house of the deceased where they might receive from the family a pair of gloves to wear at the funeral. Here the mourners might read elegiac poems they had composed, and then, before the funeral march began, pin them on the pall that covered the coffin.[43] After the burial, participants again gathered at the deceased's house where everyone drank wine or rum with sugar and lemons, while the men smoked pipes. (The family provided pipes and tobacco for the occasion.) Close friends and important mourners might receive mourning rings—rings (usually of gold)

41. *Records of the Boston Selectmen, 1701–1715* (Boston, 1885), 52, 129. For an excellent description of New England funerals in the seventeenth century, see Gordon Geddes, *Welcome Joy: Death in Puritan New England*, in *Studies in American History and Culture*, no. 28 (Ann Arbor, Mich., 1981). Much of his descriptive material pertains also to New England funerals in the eighteenth century.

42. William Adams, "Diary," in Massachusetts Historical Society, *Collections*, 4th series, V. I (Boston, 1852): 12.

43. Samuel Sewall, *The Diary of Samuel Sewall, 1674–1729*, M. Halsey Thomas, ed. (New York, 1973), 9 June 1685, V. I:66; Samuel Danforth, "Elegy for Major Thomas Leonard" (1713), in Harrison T. Meserole, ed., *Seventeenth-Century American Poetry* (New York, 1968), 489; Jeremiah Lane, *A Memorial, and Tear of Lamentation* (Portsmouth, N.H., 1766), [2].

decorated with a coffin, a skeleton, or perhaps an hourglass, and engraved with the name of the deceased and the dates of her or his life.

Special funeral clothes to set the family apart from the rest of society or to mark social distinctions occur in funeral ceremonies of many cultures.[44] In England in the eighteenth century, when one of the royal family died, the whole country went into mourning. Elaborate protocol dictated what male and female members of the court should wear on both formal and informal occasions.[45] In New England, members of the deceased's family dressed in black, and sometimes pallbearers also wore full mourning. The widow might buy a new black dress made of crepe or bombazine, both flat materials with no sheen. She would wear a black bonnet, black gloves, and carry a black handkerchief and perhaps a black fan. (Merchants ran advertisements for renting funeral accoutrements: black bonnets, fans, and handkerchiefs.) Men also wore black and might buy special black buckles for their shoes. Sometimes families provided mourning apparel for the servants.[46]

Many funeral ceremonies deal with the opposition between life and death. Often ceremonies try to dissolve the opposition by bringing the dead back among the living in some sense (by translating death into another form of life), or by having the living approach the state of the dead (by entering into a trance, perhaps), or by having the living accompany the dead on their journey between the two states of being.[47] But another way to deal with the opposition between life and death is to re-create in the funeral ceremony other oppositions, to build up layers of oppositions holding each other in balance. Balanced oppositions are especially characteristic of funerals, like the New England funeral, that seek to control emotions.

44. Arthur P. Wolf, "Chinese Kinship and Mourning Dress," in Maurice Freedman, ed., *Family and Kinship in Chinese Society* (Stanford, Calif., 1970), 189–207.

45. *Massachusetts Gazette and Boston News-Letter,* 7 January 1768.

46. Probate records contain executors' accounts of the debts and credits of estates. Sometimes executors itemized funeral expenses, and mourning clothes sometimes show up in these itemized lists. I have derived most of my information on mourning clothes and funeral entertainment from them.

47. For further discussion, see Donald Tuzin, "The Breath of the Ghost: Dreams and the Fear of the Dead," in *Ethos* III (1975): 555–78.

New Englanders, being Christians, were tied to a theology that explained death in terms of life. "I am the resurrection and the life, saith the Lord: he that believeth in me, though he were dead, yet shall he live: and whosoever liveth and believeth in me shall never die." Ministers, particularly at funerals, spoke in the language of opposites: sin *versus* redemption; time *versus* eternity; the soul *versus* the body; the dissolution of the body *versus* its resurrection; sorrow over the loss *versus* joy at the dead person's deliverance. Ministers told their flocks that death "mortified" sin, because bereaved people, faced with their own mortality, would surely strive to lead a better life. "Every *Death* upon our *Friends,* let it add *Life* unto our Prayers," urged one minister.[48]

Theological oppositions had ceremonial counterparts. Funerals "enlivened" religion (because suffering people were more sensitive spiritually), and yet Puritan funerals were civil, not religious, affairs (because the living could do nothing for the dead). Mourners, dressed in black, were expected not to show grief.

> Ye then that mourn, suppress the pious Tear;
> You wish her out of Heaven to wish her here.[49]

Grieving displayed an inability to accept God's will and a tendency to love God's creatures more than God. Mourners were meant to express joy at the deceased's deliverance and her or his embarkation into eternal life. Appropriately, mourners engaged in festive activities, social gatherings where people ate and drank together as a kind of celebration. Puritan theology undermined the notion of a funeral as a time of sadness. Puritans were not meant to grieve over the death of a friend or relative because his death was really the beginning of everlasting life and because the living should not rebel against God's will. In the process of acting out paradoxes, people controlled emotions; they diluted human grief with theological joy.

The funeral ceremony in New England contained layers of paradoxes, oppositions, and reversals, some of which people would have been conscious of, others, possibly not. In funerals conducted in the military style, the weapons of soldiers were reversed. In all funerals

---

48. Cotton Mather, *A Christian Funeral* (Boston, 1713), 8.
49. Isaac Backus, *Gospel Comfort* (Providence, R.I., 1769), 17.

the drums and bells were muffled, which made the beating and tolling sound unnatural. The muffled drumbeats and bells and the firing of guns contrasted with the "silence of the grave." The motif of the "silent grave" was part of English culture.[50] Hamlet, as he is dying, identifies death with the end of speech: "The rest is silence." In the eighteenth century, English and American elegies and funeral sermons, whether romantic elegies bathed in moonlight and vibrating with lyres, or religious ones heavy with supplication and resignation, returned to the theme of the silent grave.

> Ah! how dark
> Thy long-extended Realms, and rueful Wastes!
> Where nought but silence reigns, and night,
> dark night,
> Dark as was Chaos.[51]

Silence was associated with darkness and chaos as a form of negation. In England, "mutes" were hired to attend funerals. These paid mourners were prohibited by their employment from the exercise of speech. New Englanders of the eighteenth century, like their English brethren, were preoccupied with the silence of death, a silence that had to be turned into communication. Cotton Mather told people how to get spiritual benefit from a funeral procession. "When you see the coffin of this Man of God, anon carried along the streets, imagine it a mournful pulpit, from whence, being dead, he yet speaks thus unto you; *Whatever you do, commit your perishing souls into the hands of the Lord Jesus Christ, as you have been advised.*"[52] Mather was so bothered by the silence of funerals that he took it upon himself to regale mourners in funeral processions with instructive chatter. "In walking to a Funeral, I would be forever careful, that the Gentleman

---

50. It occurs in Eastern cultures, too. In Bombay, the Parsees, Indian descendants of Persian refugees, build stone funeral towers on the hilltops where bodies are exposed to be picked clean by vultures. These towers are called *dakhmas*, "towers of silence." Jivanji Jamshedji Modi, *Religious Ceremonies and Customs of the Parsees* (Bombay, 1937), 65–70; R. C. Zaehner, *The Dawn and Twilight of Zoroastrianism* (New York, 1961), 23–24, 161–62.

51. Robert Blair, *The Grave* (New York, 1753), 4.

52. Cotton Mather, *Magnalia Christi Americana* (Boston, 1820), Vol. I, Book III, p. 560.

whom I walk withal shall be Entertained with some Communication, that shall be instructive to him, and assist our Preparation for the future State."[53]

New Englanders, drawing on Jewish theosophy, also confronted the silence of the grave with elegies that contained anagrams, acrostics, and puns on the names of the dead. These elegies, sometimes printed in the newspapers or as broadsides, conformed to a particular pattern. The sheet, edged with black, had emblazoned on it some of the symbols of death: a winged hourglass, a funeral procession, a pickax and shovel, a skull and crossbones, a skeleton, a scythe, a coffin. The elegy might well begin with an anagram on the deceased's name. Isaac Stetson, who was drowned off the fourth cliff of Scituate, Massachusetts, was scrambled up and reassembled as "'Tis Cast on Sea: — A! Son It's Ceast." The anagram, whose sense was often lost in mutilated grammar and procrustean syntax, was rescued from obscurity by the first few lines of the elegy.

> On Sea being Cast, his Life is Cast away,
> A! Son it's Ceast, Thou finish'd hast thy
> day.[54]

Anagrams, acrostics, and puns illustrated the malleability of language. The shuffling of letters and the double entendres, the slipping from one form to another and from one meaning to another, offered analogies of death for those who believed that death was another form of life. Anagrams, for example, which scrambled up the letters of the name and then reassembled them into a moral message, reconstructed on a verbal level the dissolution of the body and its rebirth into a new moral order.

While New Englanders were self-conscious about the mechanics of their elegies—the anagrams, acrostics, and puns—and knew they were drawing on Jewish mystical traditions, they may not have recognized other oppositions and analogues of death embedded in their funeral ceremony: the sweet and sour of the sugar and lemons, for

---

53. Cotton Mather, *Diary*, 21 June 1713, in *American Classics* 2 (New York, n.d.): 117.

54. *Words of Consolation to Mr. Robert Stetson & Mrs. Mary Stetson, his Wife, on the Death of their Son Isaac Stetson, November 7, 1718* (Boston, 1718).

example, or the dissolution of tobacco. In smoking a disposable clay pipe of tobacco, mourners engaged in an activity with biblical undertones. The tobacco turned to dust and ashes. People in relation to God were dust and ashes. "Thou art but dust and ashes." "For dust thou art and unto dust thou shalt return." The pipe, made of clay, was discarded. In the Bible God was often described as a potter who worked with clay, an image that ministers picked up on in their sermons. "The God that has Kill'd our Friends, is a *Sovereign* God. And, Shall the Clay *strive with the Potter,* for Casting the *Clay,* where it was before?"[55] The tobacco changed form; solid matter turned into insubstantial smoke. Christians often referred to death as the last great change. Death, that is, did not signify the end of one being and the creation of a new being out of nothing. Death was instead a reshuffling of the elements. The elements (fire, earth, air, and water) were all present in the social solemnities that rounded off the funeral: smoking clay pipes and drinking wine. Smoking, in replicating the change of death, offered a physical counterpart to the intellectual exercise of composing anagrams. The rules for composing anagrams that the Jews compiled in their cabalistic writings were called *Temurah* (change).[56] When God, taking Abraham to his bosom, made a covenant with him and bound the twenty-two letters of the *Thora* to his tongue, He let the letters "soak in water, burn in Fire, and sway in the Air."[57] God associated the letters with the elements. The creative power of the elements, like the creative power of the letters, lay in combinations: different combinations of letters and different combinations of elements formed different concepts and beings. Death was a recombination of elements and letters, of matter and spirit. The reversals, the word games, and the balanced oppositions, both in the ceremony and in the language, structured the funeral and kept emotions under control.

*   *   *

New Englanders could use funeral reform as a political strategy because of the structure of the New England funeral. It was noisy,

---

55. Mather, *Christian Funeral,* 11.

56. *Jewish Encyclopedia,* 551; Mather, *Magnalia* I:288–89.

57. Rabbi Akiba Ben Joseph, *The Book of Formation* (Sepher Yetzirah), trans. from the Hebrew by Knut Stenring (London, 1923), 32.

visible, social, and public. The ceremony was ideal for conveying the political message because, as a community event, it had been designed to attract public attention: the bells and the guns made funerals audible, and the processions winding all through the town made them visible. The unchanged aspects of the funeral ceremony therefore could draw attention to the modifications in dress of the mourners, which imparted a political message.

The success of funeral reform as a political statement depended both on the structure of the funeral and on the issues and goals of the political crisis. New England funerals contained layers of balanced oppositions that held the ceremony in control. Not all types of funerals could have served as an appropriate political tool in the context of colonial discontent from 1764 to 1776. The funeral of the Nyakyusa people, for example, in which emotions are whipped up into a frenzy, and the funeral dance duplicates the war dance with howling warriors hurling their spears into the ground, would not have encouraged nonviolent resistance. Open rebellion, yes. But colonists did not wish to rebel. New England funerals, designed to control emotions, could be used to make a political statement and at the same time to contain potential violence.

iii

Theories that lump together scattered funeral customs can prove difficult to formulate. The diversity of funeral customs and rituals and the diversity of meanings that can be ascribed to customs and rituals can distort transcendent categories and patterns and induce theoretical bloat. After all, bodies are buried, burned, conserved, exposed, even eaten. The details of the place leap out and demand their own specific explanation. They render their own satisfaction in the context of a particular society. New England funerals, while they had elements that related them to funerals of other cultures, also belonged very much to their own particular culture. Aspects of the New England funeral ceremony that rooted it in its own time and place, like the more transcendent aspects of the ceremony, fitted the ceremony for the role it would play in the political crisis. In 1765, New Englanders cut back on the cost of funerals as a political statement. They scored political points by ostentatious frugality. Before the political crisis, theological beliefs had dictated funeral expenses, while social and political beliefs had colored attitudes towards expenditures and determined whether expenditures constituted extravagance. The political crisis rearranged priorities. When American colonists associated virtue and frugality with resistance to parliamentary taxes, funeral expenses became extravagances, and extravagance became both a political and a moral issue.

New Englanders may not have been aware of the symbolic undertones of smoking a pipe of tobacco, but they did have definite ideas about the function of the funeral ceremony. These ideas were grounded in Puritan hostility toward the Anglican Book of Common Prayer. The hostility not only structured the New England ceremony and gave it its own particular meaning, but it diverted money away from certain funeral objects and channeled it into others.

The Puritans who settled New England objected to the burial service of the Anglican prayer book on three accounts. 1) The service did not distinguish between the saintly and the vile. Therefore it could not be a religious ceremony. Puritans recognized that everyone had to be buried, but because everyone had to be buried, and only a few were saved, and because only God knew who was saved, the burial service could not have religious significance. It was a civil ceremony that stressed decency. 2) Since it was a civil ceremony, it should not take place in church and ministers should not officiate. Puritans believed Anglican ministers officiating at the burial of the dead violated the separation of church and state. 3) In the Anglican burial service, prayers were said over the body. Technically the people who prayed were not attempting to mediate with God, but the scrupulous detected the taint of mediation.

The civil nature of New England funerals controlled funeral expenses. Towns set rates for tolling bells, carrying the coffin from the house to the grave, and digging the grave. In Boston in the beginning of the eighteenth century, the rate for digging the grave varied according to the age, sex, and race of the deceased, according to the season of the year, and according to the burying ground. Men cost more than women; whites more than blacks; adults more than children; and, perversely enough, black children more than white children. Digging a grave in winter when the ground was hard cost a shilling more than digging a grave in summer. In Boston in 1701, the gravediggers seem to have staged a revolt of sorts. They pointed out that digging graves in the summer had its own unpleasantness—

the noisomeness of the body.[58] By mid-century the distinction in pricing between the seasons and between male and female corpses was eliminated.[59] Town and provincial regulations that established fees kept the cost of funerals down and limited the outlets for personal aggrandizement and competition in funeral magnificence.

The Puritan fear of Catholic superstition also affected the funeral ceremony and its price structure. Because New Englanders wished to eliminate the slightest suspicion of mediation on behalf of the dead person, they took the focus away from the body. Little information exists on the procedures for preparing the body for burial. We do know that towns, which were responsible for burying people whose estates could not afford the burial, often appointed poor women from the town to lay out the corpse and perhaps to stay with it during the night.[60] Not much attention seems to have been given to decking out the body or making it presentable for public viewing. Shrouds rarely appear in the probate records as a funeral expense, and when they do they are often tarred shrouds.[61] Tarred shrouds were used as a sanitary precaution for people who died of an infectious disease and would have been a special expense.

It may be that the coffin was open when people met at the house of the deceased before the procession, but if so, the physical appearance of the corpse elicited little comment from mourners, whose attention was far more engaged by who was present, who received what gifts of what quality, and who stood where in the funeral

58. *Records of the Boston Selectmen, 1701–1715,* 8 May 1701, p. 3.

59. In 1745 in Boston it cost nine shillings (old tenor) to have a grave dug for a white adult at the south burying places, four shillings for a white child, seven shillings for a black adult, and five shillings for a black child under twelve years old. It cost twelve shillings to have a wall tomb opened, and fourteen shillings to have an old tomb opened. For the most part, digging graves at the north burying ground cost one or two shillings more. Underporters (town appointees, unlike the pallbearers, who were honorary figures chosen by the family of the deceased) received seven shillings each for carrying the body to the grave and attending at the funeral. The sexton received one shilling for each time he tolled the bell. Only men appointed by the selectmen could perform these funeral tasks. *Records of the Boston Selectmen,* 13 September 1745, p. 120.

60. *Watertown Records,* June 1756, 21 December 1758, 17 January 1766 (Newton, Mass., 1928), 183, 203, 206, 208, 304–6.

61. Executor's account, Estate of Nathan Ames, 2 June 1769, Probate Records, Suffolk County, Massachusetts, Vol. 68, p. 92.

procession. Coffins were not an expensive item, and their price did not vary much. They usually cost around a pound and a half. Three-quarters of the coffins that appear in the Suffolk County probate records from 1760 through 1764 cost less than three pounds; one quarter cost less than one pound four shillings. The rich did not draw attention to their social rank by providing deceased members of their family with fancy coffins. Nor would there have been much point in lavishing money on a showy coffin, because the coffin was wrapped in a pall when it was carried through the town on the bier, and New Englanders, except those who were Anglicans, did not hold church services with the coffin present. The town owned the bier and the pall. Jonathan Atwater, for example, gave the town of New Haven "a cloath to be Servisable at funeralls the said cloath to be Kept at the house of ensign Isaac Dickermans and when upon any ocation feched from said house to be carefully Return'd theither again."[62] The same pall was used for everyone. Palls, therefore, offered no outlet for pomp and family pride.

Were New England funerals extravagant? It is, of course, impossible to say, since extravagance is a subjective notion. The cost of funerals in Boston just before the imperial crisis ran from one pound to 194 pounds, with most costing between four and fifteen pounds (see Table 1). The wine, rum, sugar, lemons, pipes, and tobacco altogether usually cost well under a pound. Gloves for the whole funeral ranged from three shillings to fifty-seven pounds; mourning clothes, from eight shillings to sixty-nine pounds. Most people who recorded their expenditures on gloves and mourning clothes spent around two pounds on gloves and seven pounds on mourning clothes. The sexton's bill for tolling the bell and digging the grave usually ran a pound and a few shillings; gravestones, about a pound and a half.[63] But the question is not how expensive funerals were, but

---

62. *New Haven Town Records 1684–1769,* 19 December 1715, ed. by Zara Jones Powers (New Haven, Conn., 1962), 382. For other examples, see *The Old Records of the Town of Fitchburgh Massachusetts, 1764–1789* (Fitchburg, 1898), 182; *Town of Weston, Records of the first Precinct, 1746–1754, and of the Town, 1754–1803* (Boston, 1893), 202.

63. Gravestones were often bought in pairs (one for the head and one for the feet), but a pair seemed to cost about the same as a single stone. Evidence exists that the price of gravestones might have been higher in other colonies. John Blair of Virginia imported his tombstone, and James Reid, also of Virginia, cautioned his executor not

TABLE 1
Funeral Expenses, Suffolk County, Massachusetts, 1760–1764*
(Number of cases = 188)

	L	Q1	M	Q3	H	A
Total Funeral Cost	18	80(4)	142(7)	298(15)	3,878(194)	267(14)
Mourning	8	55(3)	137(7)	278(14)	1,385(69)	208(10)
Gloves	3	25(1)	41(2)	100(5)	1,154(58)	97(5)
Wine, etc.	1	6	13	30(2)	144(7)	25(1)
Gravestone(s)	3	24(1)	30(2)	40(2)	56(3)	32(2)
Coffin	5	24(1)	34(2)	60(3)	212(11)	44(2)
Sexton	3	14	26(1)	30(2)	72(4)	24(1)

*Prices rounded off to the nearest shilling. (The figures in the parentheses are prices rounded off to the nearest pound.)

L = low   Q3 = third quartile
Q1 = first quartile   H = high
M = median   A = average

whether New Englanders considered them too expensive (i.e., extravagant). The answer is yes and no: In theory, yes; in practice, no.

In 1721, Massachusetts legislators, in an attempt to curtail what they perceived as funeral extravagance, passed a law that prohibited people from giving away scarves at funerals.[64] It was the custom in Massachusetts, as in other colonies, for the family to give scarves—sometimes expensive silk scarves painted with the family escutcheon—to friends and important members of the community who attended the funeral. The letter of the new law was obeyed, and scarves disappeared from the Massachusetts funeral scene. (The people of Rhode Island and Connecticut were still giving away scarves at funerals when the imperial crisis broke in 1764.) But the Massachu-

---

to pay more than twenty pounds sterling for his tombstone. ("Diary of John Blair," 20 February 1751, *William and Mary Quarterly*, 1st series, Vol. 7 (1898–1899): 136; James Reid, Will, Book E, Middlesex County, p. 186.) Even in New England, taste occasionally ran to the elaborate. Josiah Quincy, austere Puritan and republican though he was, when dying at sea let his fancy alight on funeral monuments of perpetuity. "My inclination would be that my body should rest in the tomb of my ancestors at Braintree, until my executor . . . should be able to erect a large durable stone tomb, on which I would have placed a small durable stone monument and on the top of all be placed a slab of the most durable marble." (Quincy, "London Journal," MHS, *Proceedings*, 49 (1915–1916), 466.)

64. "An Act to Retrench the Extraordinary Expence at Funerals," *Acts and Resolves of the Province of Massachusetts Bay* (hereafter, *A&R*) 2 (Boston, 1878), 229–30.

setts legislators, worried that people had merely transferred their outlay from scarves to gloves and other items and that funeral costs were still too high, passed another law in 1742 that reiterated the ban on scarves, prohibited people from giving away mourning rings, and limited the gift of gloves to the pallbearers and to the minister or ministers of the church whose congregation the deceased belonged to. Furthermore, no wine or rum was to be served at funerals.[65] This law was not obeyed. People did not openly object to the law—they did not write to the newspapers or draw up petitions to the legislature—but they did disobey it with impunity. The legislature re-enacted the law in 1750 to be in effect for ten years, and again in 1760 to be in effect for another ten years. Many people continued to give away mourning rings and more than seven or eight pairs of gloves and to serve wine and rum after the burial. Executors of estates continued to charge these illegal expenses to the estate, and the probate judge continued to allow the charges.

Why was the law disobeyed? First of all, the purpose of the law was to curtail extravagance, and neither wine nor gloves usually were a great expense. Furthermore, it may be that the law tried for too drastic a reform. The law virtually eliminated gifts and stripped the funeral of its social aspects. By weakening the bond that tied people together at the time of death, the law, if strictly obeyed, would have changed the function of the funeral. Therefore, while people might agree with the principle in whose name the law was enacted—frugality—they did not always modify their behavior to conform to the principle. The method of enforcement set forth in the law also presented problems. An informer had to file an action in a court. If he won, he received one half of the fine of fifty pounds, while the poor of the town where the offense took place received the other half. The social cost of criticizing someone for the way he buried his dead probably exceeded the twenty-five-pound reward. Because funerals had no victims, there was no incentive to initiate a feud. Indeed, the enforcement procedures of the law undermined the very function of the funeral. The funeral nourished social solidarity and harmony in a time of stress, and yet the method of law enforcement offered a reward to people who would instigate proceedings bound to bring about discord.

65. Ibid., 1,086.

Not only social pressures but legal pressures worked against strict compliance with the funeral law. The laws concerning the distribution of estates in Massachusetts contained hidden directives that undermined both official policy and stated values and actually encouraged people to spend money on funerals. The first expenses to be paid out of an estate were debts due to the Crown and medical and funeral expenses.[66] The procedure of taking funeral charges out of an estate before it was distributed benefited certain types of people. If, for example, the estate had several legatees (perhaps some outside the family) or if the estate were insolvent—if, that is, it did not have enough assets to meet the claims of its creditors—then the family would benefit by spending money on the funeral. Durable funeral paraphernalia (such as mourning clothes) were particularly valuable. These expenses having been paid before the estate was distributed, less would remain for the heirs or the creditors. Take the case of a widow whose husband died intestate. Widows received a dower, a one-third share in the houses and lands of the estate for their use during their life. When their husbands died intestate, widows also received, besides their dower, one-third of the personal estate. It was therefore to the advantage of the widow to spend money on valuable funeral items that would be paid for out of the estate before it was distributed. If the estate was insolvent, the widow lost her share of the personal estate, which had to go to the creditors.[67] The widow might be left without any funds. But before the creditors' claims could be settled and before the estate could be distributed among the legatees, the estate paid funeral charges. When the estate was intestate or insolvent, indirect pressure was therefore exerted on the

66. "An Act for the Settling and Distribution of the Estates of Intestates," *A&R* I:43–45; "An Act for the Equal Distribution of Insolvent Estates," *A&R* I:251–52.

67. The dower was exempt from creditors, but the dower was real estate, not personal property. "An Act for the Settlement and Distribution of the Estates of Intestates," 22 August 1695, in *Acts and laws, passed by the Great and General Court or Assembly of the Province of Massachusetts-Bay in New-England, from 1692, to 1719* (London, 1724), 3. See also "An Act for the Equal Distribution of Insolvent Estates to be distributed to Creditors in Proportion to the sums to them respectively owing," 24 November 1698, ibid., 99–100; and "An Act for preventing Fraud in Debtors, and for securing the Effects of Insolvent Debtors for the benefit of their Creditors," 1765, *Temporary Acts and Laws of his Majesty's Province of the Massachusetts-Bay in New-England* (Boston, 1736–1774), 223.

widow to spend money on the funeral. Widows of insolvents could stash away money in valuable mourning clothes, and widows of intestates could add to their one-third share in the personal estate.

The frequently high cost of funerals of insolvents bears witness to the legal loophole. From 1760 to 1764, the years that immediately preceded the political crisis, executors of insolvent estates in Suffolk County spent, on the average, 209 shillings on the funeral, while for the same period executors of estates valued at from one to fifty pounds in personal property (small but solvent estates) spent on the average ninety-nine shillings for the funeral. Small-scale insolvents were buried with parsimony. But if the estate had many debts, it probably also had assets. Such an estate could afford an expensive funeral, even it if could not cover the debts of the deceased. Merchants who dealt in funeral wear might know the estate was insolvent, but they would have nothing to lose by extending credit to the widow, since a large insolvent estate with assets as well as debts would be able to cover funeral charges. Widows of insolvents might have spent money on their husbands' funerals partly for psychological reasons, to vindicate socially a husband who had failed economically and perhaps to punish creditors who in the recesses of the conjugal psyche might be perceived as persecutors. But the pragmatic widow also had purely economic incentives. By spending money on mourning clothes for herself and her children, she could salvage some of the personal estate for the family.

Executors of estates filed an account of the expenses, debts, and credits of the state in the probate court. When the probate judge caught an unreasonable funeral charge, he responded in one of three ways. He might simply disallow it.[68] But if a widow was obviously trying to put something aside for the maintenance of her family, the judge might disallow the funeral charge, add another charge for the same amount, and call it an allowance for the widow, merely renaming the claim on the estate.[69] Sometimes an executor charged the

68. Executor's account, estate of Captain Edward Foster, 13 August 1762, Probate Records, Suffolk County, Massachusetts, Vol. 60, p. 544; Estate of William Brown, 26 February 1762, Vol. 60, p. 154; James Tilestone's account of his father's estate, 8 March 1762, Vol. 60, pp. 186–88; Estate of Samuel Allen, 27 December 1765, Vol. 64, pp. 638.

69. Estate of Joshua Thorton, 19 July 1765, Vol. 64, p. 392.

estate for his own mourning clothes and the mourning clothes of his immediate family, but failed to charge the estate for the mourning clothes of other members of the family. Then the judge might charge the estate for the value of the mourning clothes and distribute this money to members of the family who had been defrauded.[70] Such additional charges show that people did recognize clothes as a form of wealth. Probate judges did not in general disallow funeral charges merely for being high. If the estate could afford a lavish funeral and if the executor was the primary legatee, probate judges did not interfere with funeral costs. In making decisions, they were concerned with the social welfare of the survivors and with equity. They did not, however, enforce the law against extravagant funerals.

In Massachusetts, right before the imperial crisis, town regulations and provincial laws stood out against funeral customs and practices as public statements of an ideal attitude. These regulations and laws, while they failed to be translated into reality, appeased the public conscience. Public statements in conflict with public practice accommodated divergent social needs and values. The contradictions, as long as they remained unresolved and in abeyance, broadened the social usefulness of the funeral ceremony. From 1742 to 1764, the people of Massachusetts ignored the law against funeral extravagance without denying its validity. The noncompliance, which received little publicity, allowed people to gratify social needs without sullying principles. People could spend money on funerals to demarcate status and rank and to honor the dead at the same time that they, as a people, publicly acknowledged the value of frugality. The political crisis dissolved the bonds holding the paradox together.

In 1764, funeral regulations became politicized in New England. Funeral data should therefore yield some rough estimate of the degree of participation in the political cause and the composition of the participating population. Even though funeral data do not provide an exact assessment of public opinion and political activity, perhaps the figures from one county—Suffolk County, Massachusetts, where it all began—can offer some clues to the general climate.

---

70. Executor's account, estate of Jonathan Bill, 26 November 1762, Probate Records, Suffolk County, Massachusetts, Vol. 61, pp. 207–10; estate of Nathaniel Davis, 28 August 1767, Vol. 66, pp. 144–45.

iv

The call for funeral frugality initiated by the Boston merchants in the summer of 1764 succeeded. From 1760 through 1764 in Suffolk County (the county that included Boston), funerals on the average cost 13 pounds 7 shillings; after 1764, 8 pounds 13 shillings. People of all income brackets (except for insolvents) cut down on funeral expenses. For people with estates worth 50 pounds or less in personal property, the average cost dropped from 6 pounds 14 shillings to 4 pounds 5 shillings; for people with estates of 51 to 682 pounds in personal property, the average cost dropped from 12 pounds and 14 shillings to 9 pounds and 3 shillings; and for people with estates of over 682 pounds, from 37 pounds and 14 shillings to 18 pounds and 8 shillings (see Table 2).

The cost of funerals declined so dramatically because people spent less money on mourning clothes. Fewer people bought mourning clothes, and those who did, spent less money on them. From 1760 to 1765, 40 percent of the executors who included funeral charges in the account they filed at the Suffolk County probate court charged the estate for mourning clothes. In the decade from 1765 through 1775, the figure dropped to 18 percent (see Table 3). Even those who continued to spend money on mourning cut down on their expenses. Rich and poor alike showed a sensitivity towards the funeral regulations (see Table 4). Only insolvents as a group failed to modify their behavior. Political consciousness in their case was sacrificed to economic needs.

Other aspects of funeral behavior did not change so dramatically, although people did spend less money on gloves. The funeral regula-

TABLE 2
Average Funeral Cost, Suffolk County, Massachusetts, 1760–1764*
(Number of cases = 512)

Size of Personal Estate in Pounds	Before 1765	1765–1775	Change
1–50	134(41)	81(75)	−53
51–682	256(110)	183(185)	−73
682+	754(19)	368(26)	−386
Insolvents	160(18)	186(38)	+26

*Cost in shillings, compiled from probate records. (The figures in the parentheses are the number of cases in each category.)

TABLE 3
*Suffolk County Estates Charged with Mourning**

	1760–1764	1765–1775
No Mourning		
No. of Estates	116	271
percent. of total no. filing funeral charges	60.1	82.37
Mourning		
No. of Estates	77	58
percent. of total no. filing funeral charges	39.9	17.63

*Compiled from the probate records.

TABLE 4
*Average Mourning Cost for Estates Charged with Mourning**
(Number of cases = 132)

Income Group	1760–1764	1765–1775	Change
Poor (1–50)**	143(13)	68(6)	−73
Middling (51–682)	203(45)	188(37)	−15
Rich (682+)	344(9)	227(7)	−117
Insolvents	173(7)	277(8)	+104

*Cost in shillings, compiled from Suffolk County Probate Records. (The figures in the parentheses are the number of cases in each category.)
**Value of personal property in pounds.

tions of 1764, 1765, and 1767 still allowed gloves for the bearers and the minister, and no limits were placed on gloves made in the colonies. Consequently, it is somewhat difficult to pinpoint in the probate records violations of the glove regulation. Executors, when they mentioned gloves in their account, never said where they were made. Assuming that all funeral gloves in the probate records were made in England, some rough indication of sensitivity to the glove regulation can be made by determining whether there were fewer funerals after 1764 in which large numbers of gloves were given away. Since gloves cost around two shillings per pair, any executor who paid more than twenty-five shillings for gloves was almost certainly violating the regulation. In Suffolk County, 19 percent of all executors' accounts filed in the probate court from 1760 through 1764 that mentioned funeral expenses charged the estate twenty-five shillings or more for gloves. After 1764 this figure dropped to 13 percent.

The political crisis did not have a measurable effect on the number of people who served wine at funerals. Both before and after 1765, about 10 percent of executors who mentioned funeral expenses charged the estate for one or more items of entertainment: wine, rum, loaf sugar, lemons, pipes, and tobacco. (The number offering entertainment would have been greater, of course, because many executors did not itemize funeral expenses, and except at very large funerals, drinks, food and tobacco did not amount to much and could easily have been subsumed under "funeral expenses.")

The funeral regulations found broad-based public support, and yet not all people passed the funeral test. The regulations did result in heightened awareness and modified behavior, but some people still clung to the old methods. In the decade from 1765 to 1775, fifty-eight executors charged Suffolk County estates for mourning clothes, and forty-three charged estates more than twenty-five shillings for funeral gloves. On these cases of impropriety the newspapers maintained a silence. No towns took action; no mobs assembled. People were encouraged to comply with funeral regulations, and they were praised for doing so; but failure to comply did not elicit public condemnation. In some cases violators were Englishmen who were residing in the colonies on business. These men would obviously not have modified their behavior for the sake of the political cause. But what is curious is the attitude of Bostonians towards these funerals. When Captain Hay of a British man-of-war died in March 1773, he received a standard military funeral in the Anglican style. Most of the participants were Navy men and top public officials. A band playing solemn music preceded the coffin to King's Chapel along with Navy officers and mariners. Following the coffin came the admiral, the governor, the secretary, the commissioners, and two by two, the lieutenants of the Navy, the officers of the Army, the midshipmen, and the warrant officers. But the people of Boston also participated. The clergymen walked before the coffin, and at the end of the procession came the gentlemen of Boston in coaches, chariots, and other carriages. Two ministers attended in full mourning.[71] This funeral violated the regulations. Yet Bostonians did not criticize the funeral, and many participated in it: perhaps because the deceased was English, perhaps because March of 1773 was a time of relative ease in the relations between Great Britain and the colonies, perhaps because the funeral was official. In general, however, colonists chose to praise frugal funerals instead of calumniating elaborate ones—a wise decision psychologically. After all, how people respond to the death of a relative—the style of the funeral they choose to give—is a personal and highly emotional issue. To attack people for honoring the dead in a particular style could have engendered needless hostilities. To praise them for exercising restraint, on the other hand, strengthened community feeling. It was one thing to praise funeral frugality and associate it with political resistance. It was another thing to stigmatize a munificent funeral as complaisance towards, or approval of, British taxation. Bostonians did occasionally express political indignation at funerals. They intimidated Peter Oliver, keeping him from attending the funeral of his brother Andrew, the hated lieutenant governor. And at Oliver's funeral the crowd behaved rudely towards the mourners.[72] But even in this notorious case when Bostonians used the funeral to express their feelings, they did not criticize the funeral itself. The funeral had always been an event to bring the community together. When funeral reforms were adopted for political purposes, the reforms were undertaken in the spirit of cohesion. Funeral regulations were a test that people could only pass.

*   *   *

The terms of the political crisis made the people of Massachusetts take seriously the law against funeral extravagance, which had stood listless for twenty-four years. The crisis brought out into the open a paradox that had long existed in New England unresolved. The modified funeral did not change public values; it merely made people act in accor-

71. John Rowe, *Letters and Diary of John Rowe, 1759–1762, 1764, 1779,* Ann Rowe Cunningham, ed. (Boston, 1903), 240–41.

72. *Peter Oliver's Origin & Progress of the American Rebellion, a Tory View,* Douglass Adair and John A. Shutz, eds. (Stanford, Calif., 1961), 111–12; *Diaries and Letters of Thomas Hutchinson* 1 Peter Orlando Hutchinson, ed. (Boston, 1884), 130–33; *The Literary Diary of Ezra Stiles,* Franklin Bowditch Dexter, ed. (New York, 1901), entry for 12 March 1774, V. 1, p. 437.

dance with the values they professed. In 1764, frugality became politically expedient. Modifications in funeral attire reflected social and political awareness and did not undermine religious beliefs.

Funerals, with their intimate connection with biological inevitability, offered frequent opportunities for a public display of frugality. Nor could the authorities interfere. They may have abhorred the message of economic independence expressed in the public display of frugality, but they could not reasonably object to funerals or the way they were conducted as long as they were orderly. Funerals had a reason for taking place quite apart from the political crisis. The dead had to be buried. If colonists expressed a political attitude in the way they disposed of bodies, still, authorities could not reasonably label funerals as riots or unlawful assemblies. Indirection of protest avoided confrontation.

Modified funerals, like other sartorial restrictions, abstinence from tea, and projects for home manufactures, traced a design on the colonial mind. The modifications in daily routines cut channels in complacency through which emotions could surge, and these emotions succeeded in bringing people together. In the case of funerals, the emotional commitment would have been particularly strong. Even if people decided to modify funerals solely in response to social pressure, the decision could still have had political effects. Death generates an emotional crisis for survivors, and personal grief does not easily dissolve in theological reconciliation. Bereaved families, by modifying funeral procedures in the name of a political cause, must have transferred some of their pent-up emotions to the cause for which they were making modifications. Because funerals take place in a time of emotional crisis, modified funerals offered a psychological source of political commitment.

New Englanders transposed the values that justified funeral reform to the political cause. In the process of adhering to the regulations, they defined a character for themselves, drew attention to the fact that many elements of this character applied to all colonists, and underscored the difference between the colonial character and the English character. The New England reforms and their political resonances proved appropriate for other colonies. Other colonies also had critics of funeral extravagance, and these critics had appealed to the same values and had couched their criticism in the same terms as New England critics. Consequently, the funeral reforms New En-

glanders had linked to political resistance could serve to attract people from other colonies to a common cause. What started off as a
measure initiated by a few Bostonians to put economic pressure on
British merchants and to keep money from draining out of Massachusetts became a statement of values that all colonists could endorse
and live in accordance with.

v

The initiative of a few Boston merchants who advocated funeral reform in the Sugar and Stamp Act crises developed into an intercolonial
policy ten years later when the First Continental Congress met in
Philadelphia. At first glance the policy of applying funeral regulations
to all colonies does not seem like a very promising way to cement
political solidarity. Religious dissension had at times shattered the
peace of various colonies, and funeral customs varied among denominations. Nonetheless, American colonists, of whatever denomination,
did share common values, define funeral corruption in the same way,
and recognize civil aspects of the funeral ceremony.

People of different denominations had slightly different funeral
customs. Members of the Dutch Reformed Church, like other colonists, gave away gloves and scarves, but they also gave bottles of
wine, monkey spoons, and *doed-koecks* (dead cakes), and they were
less likely to give away mourning rings.[73] And, of course, Anglicans
and Dissenters had their differences. Anglican ministers preached a
funeral sermon over the body before burial; Dissenting ministers, if
they preached a funeral sermon, did so the Sunday after burial. In
Virginia, which was mainly Anglican, a person who did not want a
funeral service might specify his disinclination in his will.[74] In New
England, on the other hand, where Dissenting denominations held
sway, an Anglican who was afraid that he might be deprived of a
funeral sermon or the prayer book service might tell his executor
exactly how he wanted to be buried.[75] The Anglican procession

73. Alice Morse Earle, *Colonial Days in old New York* (New York, 1896; reprint New
York, 1938), 293–312.

74. Edwin Conway, Will, 27 July 1768, Deeds and Wills, no. 17, Lancaster County,
Virginia.

75. Samuel Spare, Will, 22 April 1767, Suffolk County Probate Records, Massachusetts, Vol. 67, p. 119.

might take place after dark with candles; the Dissenting procession took place in the afternoon. The Anglican burying ground was consecrated and owned by the church. Occasionally an Anglican, on spotting a cow grazing or hog rooting in a burying ground, might grumble about the lack of decency.[76] In New England, towns owned the burying grounds. The town bought the land, laid it out, and maintained it.[77] Sometimes the man who rented the land for grazing was responsible for its upkeep; sometimes the town required all men over a certain age to do the work.[78] But in the political turmoil these divergences in practice proved trivial, because Americans shared fundamental beliefs about the function of the funeral and defined funeral corruption in the same way.

Although Anglicans might endow funerals with more religious significance than Congregationalists did, American colonists in general thought of their funerals as civil affairs. They called the gifts "civilities," and these civilities were bestowed according to social rank. Robert Newman of Northumberland, Virginia, directed his executor to bury him "in a decent manner according to my rank and quality."[79] Important people received more gifts of better quality, and important corpses had larger funerals in which more presents were bestowed. Philip Livingston even had two funerals, one at his New York City house and one at his manor in the country.[80] Colonists measured the success of a funeral by the number of participants and their social prominence. People in funeral processions marched according to social rank, and often members of a society or profession clumped together: judges, lawyers, militiamen, members of the assembly, Masons.[81] Because colonists thought of funerals as civil

76. Philip Vickers Fithian, *Journals and Letters* (Williamsburg, Va., 1957), 41, 61.

77. *Records of the Boston Selectmen, 1701–1715*, 32, 63, 74, 82, 89, 91, 111, 157, 184; *Records of the Town of Fitchburg, Massachusetts, 1764–1789*, (Fitchburg, 1898), 7.

78. *Records of Boston Selectmen, 1701–1715*, 182–83; Gloucester Town Records, microfilm, Early Massachusetts Records Inventory (Graphic Microfilm, Waltham, Mass.) Vol. 2, pp. 53, 111.

79. Mary Newton Stanard, *Colonial Virginia: Its People and Customs* (Philadelphia, 1917), 342–43.

80. Earle, *Old New York*, 298.

81. *Massachusetts Gazette and Boston News-Letter*, 30 August 1764; Sewall, *Diary*, II:1,016–1,017; Rowe, *Letters*, 141–42.

affairs that reinforced community order, status, and values, the ceremonial aspect of funerals for civil, military, and religious leaders did
not vary much from colony to colony. John Gardner, who had served
in various government offices and had been deputy governor of
Rhode Island for eight years, received the same sort of military
funeral in Newport, Rhode Island, that Arthur Dobb, the governor
of North Carolina, received in Brunswick, North Carolina, and that
the Virginian, Peyton Randolph, who had been the president of the
First Continental Congress, received in Philadelphia.[82]

Colonists throughout the colonies thought of funerals as civil affairs; they also shared the same values. Although before the imperial
crisis began in 1764 only one colony, Massachusetts, had taken public measures to curtail funeral extravagance, Americans from other
colonies also expressed concern over funeral extravagance. Protests
appeared in newspaper editorials or synod minutes, or tucked away
in the privacy of wills. A protest from New Jersey rings from the will
of a political leader.

> I forbid any *rings,* or *scarfs* to be given at my funeral, or any man to be
> *paid* for preaching *a funeral sermon* over me. Those who survive will
> commend or blame my conduct in life, as they think fit, and I am not
> paying any man for doing either. . . . I would not have *mourning* worn
> for me by any of my descendants, for I shall die in a good old age; and
> when Divine Providence calls me hence, I die when I should die, and
> no relative of mine ought to mourn because I do so.[83]

An echo of the same sentiment sounds in Tidewater Virginia.

> My body I desire may be buried in the Church Yard near my dear
> Relations with Christian Decency, but as little Ceremony and Expence
> as possible, I desire that Prayers only may be read, having observed,
> that Funeral Sermons are generally prostituted by fulsome Flattery and
> too often by Untruths, not the least Regard being had to the sacred
> Place and divine Presence in which they are delivered. I direct that there

---

82. *Massachusetts Gazette and Boston News-Letter,* 16 February 1774; *The Boston Post-Boy,* 1 April 1765; "Dr. Solomon Drowne to Miss Sally Drowne," *Pennsylvania Magazine of History and Biography* 5 (1881, No. 1):112.

83. Will of Governor Morris of New Jersey, quoted in Gabriel Forman, unnumbered MS history in the New-York Historical Society.

be no outward shew of Mourning made Use of among my Family, my Wife only excepted, who may conform to the common Custom if she pleases, nor will I have any Tomb erected over me.[84]

A Presbyterian New Light preacher wants a dry funeral. "It is my desire that there be no liquor at my funeral."[85] Three years later, his brethren, meeting in a synod, pass a resolution that goes out to all the presbyteries of New York and Philadelphia.

> That as the too great Use of spiritous Liquors at Funerals in some Parts of the Country is risen to such an Height as greatly to endanger the Morals of many, and is a Cause of much scandal, the Synod earnestly enjoin that the several Sessions & Committees shall take the most effectual Methods to correct these mischiefs, and discountenance by their Example and Influence all Approaches to such Practices, and all Ostentations and expensive Parades, so inconsistent with such mortifying and distressing Occasions.[86]

These expressions of concern did not sound a message in a public voice promulgated in official acts. (Even the regulation of the synod was couched as a recommendation, to be encouraged by example.) But they show that concern over funeral extravagance and impropriety was not limited to New England.

In general, cities bred funeral pomp and circumstance—an understandable phenomenon, since, to be effective, ceremony needs an audience. New York, Albany, Philadelphia, and Charleston all hosted expensive funerals. In Albany, at the funeral of the first wife of Stephen Van Rensselaer, 2,000 linen scarves were given away. At another lavish funeral in Albany, the mourners, having consumed a pipe of wine (a large cask) and smoked pounds of tobacco, smashed all the decanters and glasses in the house and hundreds of clay pipes and burned all the funeral scarves.[87] When a New York landlord died,

---

84. Philip Grymes, Will, 18 December 1756 (probated 1 February 1762), in Wills, Book E (Middlesex, Va.).

85. Gilbert Tennant, Will, in the Presbyterian Historical Society, Philadelphia. This and the following reference I owe to Annette Becker.

86. *Minutes of the Synod of New York and Philadelphia,* ed. by Guy Klett, Presbyterian Historical Society (Philadelphia, 1975), 421.

87. Earle, *Old New York,* 299–300.

his heir might feast the tenants at the manor house for several days. In the rural colony of Virginia, on the other hand, the rich who could afford to turn funerals into a show to reinforce social prestige were planters who lived in isolation and had slaves rather than tenants. With no effective means of preserving the body and with communication and transportation slow, Virginia planters often buried their dead in their own burying grounds on the plantation witnessed by the slaves and perhaps a few neighboring planters. According to one outside observer, only the "lower sort" were buried in church-yards, "for the Gentlemen have private burying-Yards."[88] Anglican ministers tried to browbeat their parishioners into using the conse-crated burying grounds of the church, only to be rebuffed. If a minister persisted too vigorously in his exhortations, he stood to be excluded from the funeral altogether and to lose his stipend of forty shillings for the sermon.[89] Sometimes a parishioner outfoxed the minister by specifying burial instructions in her or his will. "I bequeath my . . . body to the ground to be decently and privately buried in the Burial place in the Orchard by my deceased Husband," said a widow, with optimistic syntax.[90] While the burial could not always await the arrival of distant guests, the guests, when they did arrive, were lavishly entertained. Rural funerals did not have elaborate ceremonies, but deaths were the occasions for social visits. A steer, three sheep, five gallons of wine, two gallons of brandy, ten pounds of butter, and eight pounds of sugar helped soothe the grief of those who came to mourn Frances Eppes of Virginia.[91]

Colonists did not object to the public aspect of funerals—to cere-mony that honored the dead and in honoring the dead drew the community together to express approval of certain ideals or a certain way of life. Even sartorial trappings, as such, did not raise objections: military uniforms, lawyers' robes, Masonic dress—all had a use apart from the funeral. Formal dress of this nature served merely to high-

88. Fithian, *Journals and Letters,* 41.

89. Hugh Jones, *The Present State of Virginia* (London, 1724), 67–68.

90. Elizabeth Elliott, Will, 8 August 1776 (probated 29 July 1779), Wills, Book F, 1771–1787, Middlesex County, Virginia, p. 139.

91. Stanard, *Colonial Virginia,* 341.

light the activities of the dead man's life. But while colonists did not begrudge important people recognition at their funerals, they did separate the public from the private aspect of the ceremony. Money spent on scarves, gloves, rings, funeral invitations, apostle and monkey spoons, and silk escutcheons might glorify the family of the deceased, but such expenses did not benefit the community and in fact endangered its social health. Reformers in all colonies believed that extravagant funerals wasted money (that is, drained it away from more worthy causes) and set a bad example. A New York reformer argued that people spent money on extravagant funerals to protect their reputation. If they did not spend lavishly, "they would be obnoxious to the ill-natur'd Censures of a malicious World, who would interpret their commendable Parsimony into Avarice, or something more unnatural."[92] Reformers feared that expensive funerals might impoverish families who, feeling the social pressure, would spend beyond their means.[93]

Colonists up and down the seaboard from Massachusetts to South Carolina, if they expressed concern about funerals, concentrated on the social evils of extravagance. They attacked the waste of money on gifts, special clothes, and lavish entertainment, but they did not attack the ceremony itself. They held to the belief that the funeral was a civil as well as religious affair, which strengthened communities by honoring the dead. To attack the funeral ceremony itself would have been to attack the community. The English in the eighteenth century were also concerned about funeral corruption, but they defined corruption differently, and they pressed for reform in an acerbic voice. The contrast between American funeral reform and British funeral reform shows that Americans were more concerned about protecting the community and appealing to positive values; the British, about exposing corruption.

92. William Livingston, *The Independent Reflector* (New York, 1753), 115–17.

93. Probate records verify the general impression that funeral expenses put a greater financial strain on families of modest means. In Suffolk County, Massachusetts, from 1760 to 1764, a funeral cost on the average 35 percent of the personal estate for those with a personal estate of 1 to 50 pounds; 9 percent for those with a personal estate of 51 to 682 pounds; and 2 percent for those with a personal estate of over 682 pounds.

vi

Americans thought of funerals as civil affairs that reinforced community values and celebrated a person's contribution to the community, and when they talked of reforming the funeral ceremony they directed their energies to reducing expenses that they thought jeopardized the health of the community by draining money from more socially beneficial projects and inculcating the wrong values. The English, on the other hand, dealt with funeral corruption ironically and in so doing reduced everyone who participated in the ceremony to a stereotype of evil: the mourners, the undertakers, and even the corpse. Irony might expose corruption, but it also could exacerbate divisions. Americans avoided irony when they sought funeral reform and instead stressed positive values that bound people together in communities. These values could also bind communities together as a people. The British saw funeral corruption as part of a larger national corruption that permeated society and government. In exposing and ridiculing funeral corruption and in relating it to corruption that pervaded all aspects of life, the English presented themselves as a corrupt people.

American reformers offered charity as an antidote to waste. They pointed out that funerals could be used to advertise the virtue of charity. Rich people could draw attention to the simplicity of their family funerals and make a public statement that they were directing the money they saved to charity. Cotton Mather suggested that public benefactors who diverted money from funerals to charity should be given credit for their sacrifice. Publicized charity could replace dramatic funerals as a way of enhancing a person's honor in the community.

> There are some Gentlemen, who are willing upon Funerals in their families, to devote some of the Money, they save out of needless Expences on such Occasions, unto the Service of our three Charity-Scholes and the Education of poor Children. I would move, that the three Gentlemen who are the Stewards for the Supporters of the said Scholes, may unite in calling on the Gentlemen proper to be address'd for their Bounty on such Occasions.[94]

94. Mather, *Diary,* 4 February 1711, V. 2:45–46.

Not only could the funeral be used as an occasion for charitable donations that would receive public attention, but towns and cities could stage large civil funerals for well-known benefactors and thus publicize the virtue of charity.[95] Promoting charity presented a sticky problem. People, after all, should not give in order to aggrandize themselves and get attention. Funerals offered a convenient way of drawing public attention to charity without making the charitable seem vain and self-serving. A dead man could derive no personal pride from the show of public esteem generated at his funeral, and, while it might be in bad taste to praise a living man for his beneficence, his death could safely be used as an occasion to honor him and encourage others to follow his example.

Colonial funerals, while they stressed community cohesion, did harbor ironic inconsistencies. Cotton Mather, who chafed at the waste of money that funerals entailed, would say to himself, as he put on the mourning gloves or ring or scarf that he had received from the family of the deceased, that these gifts spurred him to be worthy of the attention. The gifts, of course, did nothing for the dead person, but theoretically they reminded the recipient of his own impending death and enhanced the urgency of living a moral and useful life.

> And inasmuch as I have a distinguishing Share, above the most of them who ordinarily attend a Funeral, in such Civilities, I would look at it, as an Obligation on me to press after the Instances of Godliness and Usefulness, that may render me more excellent than my Neighbour; and particularly, in an holy Behaviour at a Funeral.[96]

Mather received "a distinguishing share" of the goods because of his social and religious prominence. Death took its course unmindful of social rank, yet funeral ceremonies, by especially honoring important mourners, gave them a certain advantage in what could be viewed as a spiritual competition. Cotton Mather did not strive to be good, he strove to be better than his neighbors. Because of the hierarchical structure of society, gifts, bestowed according to rank, could easily

---

95. See, for example, the funeral of Peter Faneuil, a prosperous and generous Boston merchant. *A Report of the Record Commissioners of the City of Boston Containing the Boston Records from 1729–1742* (Boston, 1889), 8–9, 16, 307.

96. Mather, *Diary,* 17 August 1711, Vol. II, p. 96.

become a cause of competition and undermine the social harmony that the funeral was meant to reinforce. The rich and important, laden with rings, gloves, and scarves that stimulated thoughts of mortality, would be better prepared than the poor and insignificant. Gifts, criticized for their uselessness, were meant to encourage people to lead useful lives.

But colonists did not press on to unmask the ambivalences of the funeral ceremony: the conflict between social values and religious ones. They did not attack the funeral ceremony as a false language. Instead, they maintained that the ceremony served a social function, and they criticized, not the ceremony itself, but the excesses in conducting the ceremony that threatened the stability of the community. The political crisis ended the unexpressed conflict between social and religious values in the funeral ceremony by transforming the funeral from a ceremony of social demarcation to a ceremony of political solidarity. All colonists were to scour waste from funerals, and waste meant money spent on mourning clothes, gloves, and scarves—the very elements that distinguished the rich from the poor. A movement designed to include everyone and to encourage everyone to take measures that eliminated the telltale signs of social distinction had a leveling effect, even if that was not the intention of the reformers. The moral movement blurred class distinctions and helped keep the political movement from fragmenting along class lines.

Colonists, who saw the funeral as a social ceremony with a social purpose, organized their calls for reform on the theme of waste. English reformers, on the other hand, while they also criticized funeral extravagance, organized their calls for reform on the theme of hypocrisy. English satirists, critics, and reformers concentrated on aspects of mortuary corruption that did not capture the imagination of colonial reformers, partly because English funerals differed from colonial funerals both in ceremony and in function, and partly because the constellation of English values differed from the colonial constellation. In the imperial crisis that preceded the Declaration of Independence, moral values carried a political freight, and the response to corruption influenced political behavior. English funerals were more corrupt than colonial funerals, and English reformers saw funeral corruption as symptomatic of the more general corruption that pervaded their society and government. They responded to corruption with satire, and one of their favorite satirical conceits was the mock funeral. Since real funerals exuded hypocrisy, it took only a small leap of imagination to use a hypocritical ceremony to expose hypocrisy in government.

In the colonies, funerals were part of community life. In London the hugeness of the city sapped the funeral's communal significance and encouraged families to stage magnificent funerals for a gaping but anonymous public. "Great Gluts of People / Retard th' unwieldly Show; whilst from the Casements / And houses tops, Ranks behind Ranks close-wedg'd / Hang bellying o'er."[97] The funeral became a performance and the participants, actors in a show, who projected an image of themselves for the public to consume. "There are few, very few in the whole world that Live to themselves, but sacrifice their Bosom-Bliss to enjoy a vain Show, and Appearance of Prosperity in the Eyes of others."[98] The "vain show" could have a mix of various elements of pomp: horses decked out with special plumed harnesses, feathers on the coffin, paid attendants, canopies, candles, costly palls, escutcheons, carriages. Perhaps several men on horseback dressed in long black cloaks and bearing painted banners headed the procession. Coaches carrying the pallbearers might follow. Then the hearse itself, drawn by plumed horses: on it the coffin laden with escutcheons, smothered with plumes, and covered with a canopy. Then the carriage with the chief and perhaps sole mourner. Then empty carriage after empty carriage rattling behind.[99]

97. Blair, "The Grave," 10.

98. Richard Steele, *The Funeral: or Grief à la mode* (London, 1712), Act I, scene ii, pp. 2–3.

99. *Universal Spectator* II (1736): 48–49; Blair, "The Grave," 10; William Dodd, *Reflections on Death*, 5th ed., (Boston, 1773), 11; *The Ceremonies and Religious Customs of the Various Nations of the Known World*, illustrated by Bernard Picart, trans. from the French (London, 1737), VI:88–91. Contemporary information on eighteenth-century English funerals can be found in: Frances Arblay, *The Early Diary of Frances Burney, 1768–1778*, ed. by Anne R. Ellis (London, 1913); Mary Granville Pendarves, *Autobiography and Correspondence of Mary Granville, Mrs. Delany*, ed. by Lady Llanover (London, 1861–1862); *The Yale Edition of Horace Walpole's Correspondence*, W. S. Lewis, ed.; James Woodforde, *The Diary of a Country Parson*, ed. by John Beresford, 5 vols. (London, 1924–1931); Sir Walter Calverley, *Memorandum of Sir Walter Calverley*, ed. by S. Margerison, in *Yorkshire Diaries and Autobiographies of the Seventeenth and Eighteenth Centuries*, Surtees Society Publications, vols. 75 and 77 (Durham, England, 1886).

The physical reality of London—its enormousness and sharp contrasts in wealth—had much to do with the evolution of English funerals. In the middle of the eighteenth century, London, the largest city in Europe, had 675,000 inhabitants. In contrast, Philadelphia had around 23,700; New York, 18,000; Boston, 15,600; Charleston, 8,000; Newport, 7,500. These cities, unlike London, still had a recognizable community. The rich did not have to strive for recognition; everyone knew who they were. In London, empty carriages rolled along behind the hearse as a testament to the wealth of the deceased, even though no mourners bore witness to his popularity— a show of family pride before an uncaring and indifferent world rushing on in pursuit of its daily tasks. A paid herald preceded the funeral and brushed aside the hurrying crowd. Paid mourners filled the emptiness left by the indifference of a vast and busy metropolis. In England, where the funeral was a religious ceremony, not a civil one, towns, cities, and counties did not control funeral expenses. Parliament did pass a law requiring corpses to be buried in wool in order to protect the wool industry. But many people preferred to pay the fine and dress the body up in fine clothes. "Harkee, Hussey," says a character in a play, "if you shou'd, as I hope you won't, out-live me, take care I an't buried in Flannel, 'twould never become me, I'm sure."[100] In general, the lack of civil regulations left the field wide open for professional undertakers to exploit.

Certain themes surfaced in English attacks on funeral corruption. English reformers concentrated on hypocrisy that had various manifestations: the inappropriate response of survivors to death, the exploitation of the bereaved by professional undertakers, the unworthiness of the deceased and the consequent emptiness of the ceremony commemorating him.

English critics condemned the behavior and attitude of heirs: sons rejoicing in their fathers' death, legatees dissatisfied with the will, hypocrites pretending to mourn. Heirs, the critics charged, often spent vast amounts on the funeral of their legator in order to cover up their own joy at the death. Widows dressed up in elegant weeds rejoiced at their husbands' death and fell in love with the role of sufferer.

---

100. Richard Steele, *The Funeral, or Grief à la mode,* Act V, scene i, p. 68.

Now you talk of Equipage, I envy this Lady the Beauty she'll appear in a mourning Coach, 'twill so become her Complexion; I confess I my self mourn'd two Years for no other Reason. Take up that Hood there; Oh! that fair Face with a Vail.[101]

Both American and British critics voiced concern over funeral extravagance, but Americans seeking reforms championed the poor, while the British exposed hypocrisy and corruption. In eighteenth-century England, the people who ran funerals and even those who participated in them were paid professionals. Undertakers who had a financial stake in elaborate ceremony hawked their wares to the bereaved who, in their emotional state, were easy victims. The divorce of the funeral from the community spawned funerals "adorned with all that senseless Pageantry which the Undertakers have invented to inrich themselves at the cost of other People."[102] The senselessness of the pageantry underscored the selfishness and greed of the entrepreneurs who raised "an Estate by providing Horses, Equipage, and Furniture, for those that no longer need 'em."[103] Professional undertakers not only exploited the bereaved, but by encouraging ceremonial extravaganzas enhanced the hypocrisy of the funeral. Virginity was treated as a commodity. Virgin corpses were attended by professional virgin mourners, dressed in white. In a satire on funeral hypocrisy, an undertaker rebukes his hirelings. "I wonder, Goody *Trash,* you could not be more punctual; when I told you I wanted you, and your two Daughters, to be three Virgins to Night to stand in White about my Lady *Katherine Grissel's* Body, and you know you were privately to bring her home from the Man-Midwife's, where she dy'd in Childbirth, to be buried like a Maid."[104] This same undertaker, lining up his professional mourners, gives them a lesson in hypocrisy and laments the logistical difficulty of paying people to be unhappy.

Well, come you that are to be Mourners in this House, put on your sad Looks, and walk by me that I may sort you: Ha you! a little more upon the Dismal; [*forming their Countenances—*] this Fellow has a good

101. Steele, *Funeral,* Act III, scene i, p. 45.
102. *Universal Spectator* II (1736): 48–49.
103. Steele, *Funeral,* Act I, scene i, p. 2.
104. Ibid., p. 6.

Mortal Look—place him near the Corps: That Wainscoat Face must be o'top of the Stairs; that Fellow's almost in a Fright (that looks as if he were full of some strange Misery) at the Entrance of the Hall—So— but I'll fix you all my self—Let's have no Laughing now on any Provo- cation: [*makes Faces*] Look yonder that hale well-looking Puppy! You ungrateful Scoundrel, did not I pity you, take you out of a Great Man's Service, and show you the Pleasure of receiving Wages? Did not I give you Ten, then Fifteen, now Twenty Shillings a Week, to be Sorrowful? and the more I give you, I think, the Gladder you are.[105]

The emptiness of the cavalcade of coaches that rattled behind the hearse reflected the emptiness of the whole ceremony. The partici- pants in the funerals—the coachmen, the paid mourners, the heralds, the mutes—did not know the deceased, felt no emotion at their death, and often did not even know their names ". . . for they being continually employed in Works of this Nature, consider nothing but their Pay, and seldom give themselves the Trouble of asking whom they are carrying to the Grave."[106] Undertakers were criticized for the unnaturalness of their profession. Not only did they feel no sorrow over death, they rejoiced in it. "A flock of Ravens that attend this numerous city for their Carkasses," they waited eagerly for peo- ple to die, and in their eagerness they sent out spies to spot the dying and claim the bodies.

Making money out of burials bred hypocrisy that deadened natu- ral feelings; it could also breed corruption. When people stood to gain by the death of others, they were tempted to push things along. Undertakers might collude with doctors who could hasten the de- sired end with well-timed administrations of this or that powder. Undertakers might employ gravediggers and sextons to get a little of the funeral booty back from the body, or to make money on the body itself.

Gravedigger: I carry'd home to your House the Shrowd the Gentleman was buried in last Night; I could not get his Ring off very easily, therefore I brought the Finger and all; and, Sir, the Sexton gives his Service to you, and desires to know whether you'd have any Bodies remov'd or not: If not, he'll let 'em lye in the Graves a Week longer.

105. Ibid., p. 5.
106. *Universal Spectator* II (1736): 49.

Sable [the undertaker]: Give him my Service, I can't tell readily; but our Friend, tell him, Dr. *Passeport,* with the Powder, has promised me Six or Seven Funerals this Week.[107]

The play, of course, is a satire and cannot be used as courtroom evidence to convict any particular undertaker; but whatever undertakers may or may not actually have done, they exuded an aura of corruption by virtue of their profession.

The hypocrisy of heirs, the unnaturalness of undertakers, the senselessness of the funeral ceremony: all were exposed. But even the corpse drew the fire of critics, who treated the precept "speak no ill of the dead" with total unconcern. Funeral critics cast the corpse as a miser. They might cite with approval the punishment that Minos, in the Greek myth, meted out to the miser who swam the Styx in order to avoid paying Charon the penny toll. "Open the Passage for him immediately," decreed Minos, "and turn him back into the World.— I condemn him to behold what Use his Heirs are making of his Estate."[108] Misers raked together vast hoards of wealth by exploiting society and denying themselves and their family the comforts that wealth could buy and even the necessities of life. They increased their wealth by usury, and they protected it by depriving their children of education and clothes, their wives of food and medical care. "Full threescore years and ten had BUBULO encumbered, with his heavy load, this sublunary world. And it would be difficult to point out any works of benevolence or religion, any works of real worth or humanity, which distinguished these seventy years!"[109]

Misers came in two varieties: the lean and the obese. The lean, "lank-sided" misers—"muckworms" who starved in the midst of plenty while living, only to become food for worms when dead—abused their bodies and damned their souls.

> Oh! Cursed Lust for Gold; when for thy Sake
> The Fool throws up his Int'rest in both Worlds
> First starv'd in this, then damn'd in that to come.[110]

---

107. *Funeral,* Act I, scene i, p. 5.
108. *Universal Spectator* II (1736): 52–53.
109. Dodd, *Reflections on Death,* 67.
110. Blair, "The Grave," 17.

Self-inflicted torment in this life assured the miser perpetual torment in the life to come. In the end, the lean miser might die because of his unwillingness to spend money on a doctor. The fat miser, "fond of vile pelf," starved his relations in order to indulge himself. He, too, abused his body and in so doing denied his humanity. "The hours which were not devoted to gain, were consecrated to the service of his nice and enormous appetite, to devouring of *flesh,* and drinking of *wine:* He was, in this respect, a perfect animal."[111]

Satirists underscored the extravagance of the funeral and also its hypocrisy by casting the corpse as a miser. The occupation of the miser, the hoarding, day after day, the skimping on the necessities of life: food, clothes, medicine, contrasted with the extravagance of the funeral—the dissipation of money in a single evening on vanities. Alexander Pope laughed at the money spent on candles for the funeral of a miser.

> When Hopkins dies, a thousand lights attend
> The wretch, who living sav'd a candle's end.[112]

And all the money spent on the funeral of a miser commemorated and honored a person whose life had nothing worth commemorating or honoring. "The Obsequies which are due only to the Best and Highest of human Race (to admonish their short Survivors that neither Wit, nor Valour, nor Wisdom, nor Glory can suspend our Fate) are prostituted, and bestow'd upon such as have nothing in Common with Men, but their Mortality."[113]

English critics ridiculed and deplored the funeral ceremony as a tangle of hypocrisy, greed, and manipulation. They heaped sordid connotation upon sordid connotation and presented the funeral as a public display of human corruption. Funerals, laden with hypocrisy, became an analogue for the corruption that permeated society. English funerals bred hypocrisy, greed, exploitation, and backbiting—and so did English politics. Given this congruence, satiric artists swooped on the funeral ceremony to portray the nastiness of politics.

111. Dodd, 67.

112. Alexander Pope, "Epistle 3: to Bathurst," in *The Poems of Alexander Pope,* F. W. Bateson, ed., second edition (London, 1961), vol. III-ii, pp. 116–17, ll. 291–92.

113. Steele, Preface, *Funeral,* p. A5.

Political prints used the funeral to highlight political squabbles, corrupt elections, unpopular laws. Robert Walpole, safe after an attempt to oust him from office, laughs merrily, his hands on his hips, as the bier of "Faction" rolls by. When the House of Commons rejects the election of John Wilkes as the representative of Middlesex, mourners cluster around the coffin of "Freedom." After a corrupt election in which victory is bought, four bearers struggle with the coffin of "Independence": "Folly," decked out in a fool's cap and bells with a bauble in his hand; "Contradiction," with two faces; "Ignorance," with ass's ears; and "Deceit," whose face is hidden by the coffin. When Parliament passed an act for the suppression of gin (called Geneva), the beggars of London—starving, naked, and drunk—lurched in the funeral procession of Madama Geneva and cried over the death of their queen.

> No, 'tis resolv'd DIVINE GENEVA!
> We'll bravely perish e'er we'll leave ye:
> With that the brimming Glass they ply,
> And Poverty and Rags defy,
> Their Brains with fumy Vapours, turn,
> They fall to grace their Monarch's urn.[114]

English prints made funerals popular as an ironic device to expose corruption. The funeral, with its entourage of paid professionals milling about, its detailed and elaborate ceremony, its accumulation of display items and trinkets, attracted political satirists who stepped up and packaged political corruption and venality in funeral trappings for public consumption.

In contrast to the English funeral, the colonial funeral, criticized more for waste than for hypocrisy, had not been used much to score political points before the imperial crisis. Occasionally a political critic ventured onto satiric waters and a mock elegy appeared. Old tenor (a paper currency that was replaced) had its elegists. But the authorities, sensitive to the danger of mockery, were quick to take offense. In this case they attempted to punish the author and publisher of verse that contained "sundry expressions tending to bring

114. *Catalogue of Political and Personal Satires Preserved in the Department of Prints and Drawings in the British Museum* 3 (London, 1978): 191.

into Contempt and Subvert the Constitution of the Government."[115] In general, though, colonists did not undercut their leaders with irony and did not use the funeral to expose political corruption. For them, the funeral ceremony still served the social function of drawing the people of a community together. When colonial reformers leveled criticism against funeral abuses, they targeted exaggerations of the funeral ceremony that threatened to weaken the community. Their criticism, unlike the criticism of English reformers, was general, not personal. They constructed a positive ideal, a community held together by industry and charity; and showed how extravagance, expenditure on useless items, undermined the ideal. But in 1765, colonists felt the corruption of British politics impinge on their own life. Suddenly ridicule and mockery as a means of overcoming impotence attracted their attention.

*   *   *

Ten years after New Englanders initiated the association of funeral reform with political resistance, the First Continental Congress adopted the reforms for all colonists. The funeral reforms of New England could be used as a vehicle of colonial cohesion because funerals in other colonies, while they might vary slightly in ceremonial detail and religious import, were conducted in the same spirit, and because reformers from other colonies had criticized funeral extravagance with the same voice. Long before the political crisis, colonial reformers had appealed to people to cut back on funeral expense for the good of society. They did not use irony or satire in their appeal. They called for reform in the name of the poor, and they saw nothing to mock in poverty, which was an ever-present threat to social stability. Funeral reform could be undertaken in a political crisis that called for cohesion, because the language of reform had been the language of cohesion. Had colonial critics, like English critics, used mockery and ridicule and made victims out of their subjects, instead of approaching the subject of funeral extravagance obliquely by introducing the concept of helping the poor, funeral

---

115. Worthington Ford, "Check List of Massachusetts Broadsides, etc. 1639–1800," in Massachusetts Historical Society, *Collections*, 75:127, 131; Ola Winslow, *American Broadside Verses from Imprints of the 17th and 18th Centuries* (New Haven, Conn., 1930), 166.

reform could have been a divisive issue, hardly suitable for rallying people to a common cause.

Englishmen, on the other hand, criticized their funerals for hypocrisy, exploitation, and fraud, and in England mock funerals featuring political leaders and political events capitalized on the sordid connotations implanted in the public consciousness by funeral critics. The point of the satire could reside in the incongruity of the funeral (a funeral for gin, for example) or in the relationship between the mourners and the corpse. The mourners might actually be rejoicing or they might be mourning for a victim whom they had in fact killed. The corpse in the mock funerals was usually an object (gin) or an abstraction (faction, independency, freedom). But in developing the theme of hypocrisy, English funeral critics had also scored points by making the dead man a miser—someone who should be reviled and not commemorated. The vilification of the corpse banished sorrow from the funeral. Spectators were asked to be indignant, not sympathetic; to ridicule the corpse and scoff at the idea of lamenting the despicable.

In 1765, American colonists not only displayed frugal funerals as a statement of moral value with political connotations, but also adopted the English style of political protest and used irony to expose British officials and colonial collaborators and strip them of authority. The colonists buried abstractions, but they went further and buried people—stuffed people, to be sure, but identifiable people, who stood for evil. Taking their cue from English funeral critics, colonists made the corpse an outsider whose deviance defined the norms and values of society. This mode of irony set the corpse against society and turned the funeral into a social celebration. It remained to be seen whether colonists could uphold the moral mode of resistance embodied in their funeral reforms simultaneously with the ironic mode.

★ 6 ★

Mock Funerals
and Mock Executions

WHEN THE Sugar Act and the Stamp Act stunned the American colonists, they plunged elbow-deep into community activities that spelled resistance.[1] Funerals in the new mode made a dignified show of protest, but funerals had to wait for corpses—or at least they did until colonists hit on the happy idea of supplying corpses to get things moving. They made effigies of Liberty, who was slated to die on November 1, 1765, when the Stamp Act went into effect, and of stamp distributors and British ministers, who could be executed and then carted all over town in a come-one, come-all funeral procession that ended with their immolation on a sacrificial funeral pyre.

In 1764 and 1765, colonists launched a program for the cultural management of a political crisis: they changed their eating and drinking habits, donned homespun clothes, and made a display of frugality on public occasions. As part of a program to incorporate the

1. Many historians have dealt with crowd behavior, both in eighteenth-century America and in the American Revolution: Edward Countryman, Paul Gilje, Dirk Hoerder, Jesse Lemisch, Pauline Maier, Gary Nash, Peter Shaw, Alfred Young. Some have used crowd behavior as a way of studying class distinctions (Countryman, Hoerder, Lemisch, Nash, Young); others have focused on crowd behavior as a cultural and psychological phenomenon (Gilje, Shaw). This chapter, much narrower in conception, focuses not on the broad subject of crowd behavior but on mock ceremonies (by nature ironic) as a political strategy and addresses the strengths and weaknesses of irony as a community response to a constitutional and economic threat.

political issue into daily life, they modified their manner of conducting their funerals. They also used funeral and execution ceremonies in an ironic way to transform a political conflict into the ritual defeat of evil. Both the "new method" of conducting real funerals and the mock funerals had a political message, but in the one case the funeral ceremony was the object of reform; in the other, it was the medium for a message that had nothing to do with funerals. Consequently, the styles of the two types of funerals differed dramatically.

Scaffolds dotted the colonial landscape in the autumn of 1765, and processions wove their way to gravesites all over the colonies in small towns and large cities alike. This landscape of staged gloom punctuated by screams of joy had its own doctrine, a formula of principles assembled around the purpose, meaning, and effect of the mock ceremonies. The people watching or participating in the ceremonies or reading about them in the newspapers responded to the message wrapped in themes and packaged in metaphors that organized colonial political thought and channeled resistance along certain courses. Although the ceremonies did fulfill the intentions of the organizers (they succeeded in intimidating the stamp distributors and in rallying the community to the cause), the methods employed to achieve these ends had unforeseen effects that threatened to undermine social cohesion and in the long run led to the abandonment of irony as a principal mode of resistance.

i

Even before the Stamp Act went into effect, colonists prepared for the funeral of Liberty. In August 1765, Boston announced that Liberty had died on the seventh of February when the Stamp Act was passed in Parliament, and would be buried on the first of November when the Act went into effect. Meanwhile, the body had been embalmed. Charleston, South Carolina, buried Liberty a little early, on October nineteenth. Portsmouth, New Hampshire, waited until November first, and Wilmington, North Carolina, put Liberty into a coffin on December thirty-first and marched to the graveyard in a solemn procession.[2]

Although the funerals varied in detail, they followed the same

2. *Pennsylvania Journal:* 12 September 1765, 2 January 1766, 21 November 1765.

general pattern. The coffin bore a notice proclaiming the name of the deceased, "Liberty." In Portsmouth the townspeople prepared a coffin "neatly ornamented, on the lid of which was wrote LIBERTY, aged 145, STAMPED, computing from the aera of our forefathers landing at Plymouth from England."[3] Muffled bells would ring as a procession of people of all ranks, having assembled at the courthouse or statehouse, marched through the principal streets, past the parade ground where guns were fired and on to the gravesite. Some people in the procession might beat muffled drums; some might precede the coffin carrying banners with inscriptions or perhaps a copy of the Stamp Act or a liberty cap on a pole; and at the gravesite someone might deliver a funeral oration in praise of liberty.

The funerals for Liberty gave people a chance to respond emotionally to the Stamp Act, to make public their response, and, in doing so with many other people, to bring into being a visible community of belief. Organized demonstrations made it easy for people to participate, and once they had participated they felt they were part of the cause. Demonstrations in which people re-enacted a ceremony such as a funeral also served to control the crowd and protect the community from violence. Funerals followed a set pattern. In participating in mock funerals, people were bound by the pattern. The crowd did not act emotionally so much as they acted out emotions according to the rules of the ceremony itself. The muffled drums, the procession of mourners, the firing of guns, the funeral orations: all induced an aura of solemnity, but all also reminded the people who were participating of the limits of their action.

Colonists staged funerals for Liberty to dramatize the political significance of the Stamp Act, yet, were they actually to bury Liberty, they would be admitting the futility of resistance. Consequently, just as Liberty was being lowered into the grave, she often revived. Someone in the crowd would notice signs of life; she would be taken up and resuscitated; the Stamp Act would be pushed into the grave as a suitable substitute; the bells would ring out unmuffled; and everybody would go off to the tavern to drink a toast to Liberty and the king, and death to the Stamp Act. On October 31, 1765, the people of Wilmington, North Carolina, were about to lower a coffin containing Liberty into the grave. "But before they committed the body to

3. *Pennsylvania Journal,* 21 November 1765.

the ground, they thought it advisable to feel its pulse; and when finding some remains of life, they returned back to a bonfire ready prepared, placed the effigy before it in a large two-arm'd chair, and concluded the evening with great rejoicings, on finding that LIBERTY had still an existence in the COLONIES."[4] In Portsmouth, right after the funeral oration over the body of Liberty, someone noticed signs of life, at which "Liberty revived, —and the stamp act was thrown into the grave and buried."[5] The funeral of Liberty called off or transformed into the funeral of the Stamp Act fulfilled the wishes of the colonists. The crowd attending Liberty's funeral took an emotional pilgrimage. Each stage of the ceremony had its corresponding emotional response: at the death of Liberty, grief; at the resuscitation of Liberty, joy and relief at the escape from calamity; at the substitution of the death of evil for the death of good, satisfaction. The crowd emerged from the ceremony with the renewed sense of appreciation that comes from a threatened loss being averted. In their mock funerals, the colonists constructed the world of a fairy tale in which good and evil, clearly identified, vie with each other. Good triumphed, not because the gods (or God) willed it, not because the good character willed it or performed mighty deeds, but because it is the nature of a fairy tale to fulfill wishes and in fulfilling wishes to solve all moral problems.[6] The funerals for Liberty defied reality in two respects: the corpse was not a body but an incorporeal abstraction, and the corpse turned out not to be dead at all. Funerals climaxed in a resurrection, and the resurrection demonstrated that the community remained intact by very virtue of the fact that no death had occurred.

The colonists also staged funerals for the Stamp Act. Here the irony did not lie in a surprise ending, but in the response of the onlookers. During funerals for the Stamp Act, the streets rang with joy, hardly the normal response to death. In a county seat in Maryland, the Stamp Act, "having received a mortal Wound by the Hands of Justice . . . gave up the Ghost, to the great Joy of the Inhabitants of Frederick

---

4. *Pennsylvania Journal,* 2 January 1766, Supplement.

5. *Pennsylvania Journal,* 21 November 1765.

6. W. H. Auden discusses the fairy tale in "Interlude: The Wish Game," *The Dyer's Hand and Other Essays* (1956; New York, 1968), 209–17.

County."[7] The townspeople left the body exposed to public ignominy for a few days until the "stench" encouraged them to bury it. The funeral procession formed. Someone bearing the colors of the town company led the way; then followed drummers. Someone carried a banner inscribed "CONSTITUTIONAL LIBERTY ASSERTED BY THE MAGISTRATES OF FREDERICK COUNTY, 23rd November, 1765." Someone else carried a liberty cap mounted on a staff, with various inscriptions attached: "MAGNA CHARTA, CHARTER OF MARYLAND, TRIALS BY JURIES RESTORED, OPPRESSION REMOVED, LIBERTY AND LOYALTY." Porters carried the coffin, whose lid bore the inscription "THE STAMP ACT, EXPIRED OF A MORTAL STAB RECEIVED FROM THE GENIUS OF LIBERTY IN FREDERICK COUNTY COURT, 23rd November, 1765. AGED 22 DAYS." The coffin was decorated with labels and representations designating the various evils that accompanied the Stamp Act and arbitrary legislation—"Tyranny, Villenage, Military Execution, Soldiers quartered on private Houses, Court of Vice-Admiralty, Guarda de Costas to prevent Corruption in *North-Americans* from a Redundancy of *Spanish* Dollars, *Britons* employed in fastening Chains on the Necks of *British* Subjects, Fines, Imprisonment, Ruin, Desolation, Slavery taking Possession of *America,* in Order to extend her Dominion over *Great-Britain*"—all of which were to be buried with the Act. It was the custom for mourners to follow the coffin, but this funeral had only one mourner, Zachariah Hood, the man designated stamp distributor for Maryland. His effigy was carried in an open chariot right behind the coffin, "His Countenance pale and dejected—His Dress disorderly, unsuitable to his Rank, and betraying great inward Distraction of Mind. . . ." The Sons of Liberty, who (according to the account) participated as witnesses, not as mourners, followed the effigy of the stamp distributor in orderly ranks, two by two. While the bells rang and the crowds cheered, the procession marched through the principal street and stopped in front of the courthouse, where a gallows had been erected and, under the gallows, a grave dug. The drums ceased and a proclamation for silence was read. Zachariah Hood tried to speak but, struck with astonish-

---

7. *Maryland Gazette,* n.d. In early December 1765, a special edition entitled "An Apparition of the late *Maryland Gazette,* which is not Dead, but only Sleepeth" appeared.

ment, his features fixed as death, he was overcome with faintness and no words issued from his stuffing. A helpful bystander unpinned a paper from the effigy's breast, which turned out to be a funeral oration composed earlier by Zachariah, the Stamp Act's one friend—"a lamentation over the body of that beloved Act which had engrossed his whole Mind and Affections." As his speech was read, Zachariah grew weaker and weaker. Suddenly he toppled forward out of his chair and fell on the ground, cold, still, and dead—"a lifeless Figure scarce resembling Humanity." One of the Sons of Liberty called out, "Let him die like a dog!" and the crowd cheered its approval. To a loud "Huzza" and roll of the drums, his corpse was thrown into the grave with the Stamp Act and the grave filled. The company then marched in the same order back to the house of one of the organizers, "where an elegant Supper was prepared, and a Ball given to the Ladies, who made a brilliant Appearance on the Occasion; —many loyal and patriotic Toasts were drank, and the whole concluded with the utmost Decorum."

The funeral of the Stamp Act shared with the funeral of Liberty the harmonious ending and the emphasis on decorum, and in both funerals the cause of the main event—in the one case the revival of Liberty, in the other case the death of the sole mourner—was the wish that it might happen. But the funeral of the Stamp Act, unlike the funeral of Liberty, was a parody. People watching the funeral of the Stamp Act would see how different it was from a real funeral, not in form, but in substance. The ceremony of the funeral was used to demonstrate the lack of mourning, the absence of grief, the beneficial effects of death—death not as a loss, but as a gain. The irony lay in the vast gap between the trappings of woe and the feelings of joy. Far from sympathizing with the one mourner, the crowd condemned him for his grief and rejoiced in his suffering. When he passed, they cheered, and "on every Huzza by the Crowd, or loud Laugh of Female Spectators, Z_____ H_____, Esq. was observed to nod, or drop his Head into his Bosom, in Token of the utmost Sorrow and Confusion." Even the people who participated in the funeral as officials—those who marched with banners, or beat drums, or carried the coffin, or followed the one mourner—maintained an emotional distance from the event. They participated as witnesses and judges.

Funerals, whether mock funerals or real funerals, are a means of reaffirming community solidarity in the face of the threat of dissolution and of publicizing community values. But fundamentally funerals are passive, a response to an event over which the community has no control. When a community executes someone, on the other hand, it commits an act of will. The community controls the form of this act, and it tries to control the community's response to the event. Putting someone to death is an act of violence, but since violence can be contagious and might easily get out of control, colonial magistrates took pains to present the execution as an act of retribution.

In 1765 and 1766, colonists from Maine to Georgia staged mock executions that were also funerals. The crowd would hang effigies of stamp distributors, British ministers, and British sympathizers and later cut them down and carry their bodies through town in a funeral procession of joy and exultation. In funerals for Liberty, the crowd participated as mourners. In funerals for the Stamp Act, the crowd did not mourn. But although they condemned the deceased in their hearts, they still did not initiate the death. Liberty stabbed the Stamp Act and the crowd approved. The stamp distributor, the sole mourner at the funeral of the Stamp Act, died, and the crowd approved. But the crowd did not take responsibility for the "deaths"; they merely responded to them. In the mock executions, however, the crowd made a decision to put offenders to death and carried out that decision. Because the effigies represented particular men, some of whom were also available in the flesh, the potential for real violence lurked behind mock executions.

For whose benefit were the mock executions performed? In part for the benefit of the English, but only in small part. Violence, even mock violence, if it took place throughout the colonies, may have been meant to demonstrate England's inability to enforce her authority. But the latent violence of mock executions, while serving as a threat, could not have been translated into reality without undermining the colonial cause. Had the colonists been seeking better living conditions, redistribution of wealth, or religious freedom, they would not have been bound logically by law (although morally they might have been). Violence would not have been outside their compass. But since colonists were demanding rights guaranteed by the British constitution, they could not logically violate that constitution. The nature of their aims restricted the possible means of achieving those aims.

Still, there were those who could ill afford to rely on the colonists' sense of logic. On the stamp distributors who lived in the colonies, if not on the British ministers and members of Parliament, the mock executions had a powerful effect. Seeing an effigy of yourself dangling from the gallows might predispose you to acquiesce in the demands of the crowd that had engaged in this imaginative exercise. Even if the colonists intended mock executions as substitutes for, rather than harbingers of, real executions, someone so intimately involved in the outcome of events as a stamp distributor would not have wished to play the odds. Stamp distributors, no doubt, did not participate in the general hilarity and ebullience of the mock ceremonies. Looking on the somber side of things, they might well have been encouraged by these public demonstrations of emotion to resign their offices.

Even if the colonists did not intend to execute real people, the mock executions could have been the excuse for a spree of destruction, a chance for people to even old scores, for the poor to make the rich squirm, for frustrated colonials to victimize or harass all government officials. Yet for the most part, mock executions, like mock funerals, contained violence rather than inflaming it. Participants in mock executions were so occupied with the task at hand and so busy maintaining the form of a real execution and funeral that they did not go on rampages. Once or twice the attention of the crowd was diverted. On August 14, 1765, a Boston crowd hanged an effigy of Andrew Oliver, the man appointed stamp distributor for Massachusetts. As they were carting the "body" through town, they paused to tear down Oliver's newly constructed office building, which they reasoned would house the stamped papers, and then proceeded with the funeral procession, carrying the shreds of the demolished building to use for the funeral pyre. After the cremation of the hanged effigy, some of the crowd amused themselves by defacing Oliver's house.[8] In October of the same year, in Charleston, South Carolina, a crowd of 2,000 people attending the funeral of an executed effigy stopped at the house of George Saxby, the appointed stamp distributor, to inquire whether there were any stamp papers on the premises. The occupants of the house, understandably nervous, hesitated to open the door, and the impatient crowd started breaking windows.

8. *Connecticut Courant,* 26 August 1765.

When they gained entrance, however, and a search uncovered no stamp papers, they left the house standing (although they probably had some fun with the furniture) and continued the funeral procession in an orderly manner. An account of the affair concluded with the somewhat pious statement that "[n]o outrages whatever were committed during the whole procession, except the trifling damage done to Mr. Saxby's house, whose furniture, 'tis said, had been mostly removed into the country ten days before."[9]

For the most part the mock executions and the subsequent funerals that took place throughout the colonies did proceed without violent interruption. What destruction occurred was targeted property damage. The lieutenant governor of New York, an adherent of the Stamp Act, lost his coach, which the crowd commandeered as a vehicle for the effigies and committed to the flames when the ceremony was over. Unruly mobs had been known to destroy houses, and with the atmosphere so tense, stamp distributors occasionally found themselves unable to rent houses.[10] But the two most violent riots of the period did not take place in the context of an execution or funeral ceremony: the Boston riot of August 26, 1765, when Lieutenant Governor Hutchinson's house was gutted; and the Newport riot two days later, when the houses of Martin Howard and Thomas Moffat (two conservatives who sought the revocation of Rhode Island's charter and the establishment of a royal government) fell victim to the same fate. On August 27, when the Newport mob hanged the effigies of Howard, Moffat, and Augustus Johnston (the appointed stamp distributor), the violence had been contained. It was only the next day, after Newport had received news of Boston's spree of destruction, that the mob raged out of control. Many colonists were revolted by these two outbreaks of violence and complimented themselves on their own orderly demonstrations. In September, the people of New Haven put to death the West Haven Giant, a monster "twelve Feet high, whose terrible Head was internally illuminated." "It should be mentioned," said one conscientious (if somewhat smug) citizen, "that, through the whole of this Raree-show, no unlawfull Disorder happened, as was the Case in the last truly deplor-

9. *Pennsylvania Journal*, 2 January 1766: *South-Carolina and American General Gazette*, 23 October 1765 to 31 October 1765.
10. *Connecticut Gazette*, 8 November 1765.

able and truly detestable Riot in Boston."[11] In November, a citizen of Newport, recalling the violence of the August riot, praised the people of his city for conducting the funeral of Liberty with such decency, which "affords every rational Lover of Liberty the highest Satisfaction . . . and gives the strongest Assurance, of your manly, sensible Behavior on any future, public Exhibition."[12] On the first of November, Boston paraded effigies through the streets and burned them. The tone of the ceremony differed markedly from the "lawless ravages" of August 26, "for the horrid Violences of which Night we hope the good Order of this will in some Measure atone."[13] All three of these demonstrations that reporters contrasted with the violence of the Boston and Newport riots of August took place in the context of a ceremony. Mock ceremonies did seem to contain violence. Caught up in the fun of the performance, the crowd was controlled by the formal aspects of the ceremonies they were putting to ironic use. Although mock funerals and executions cropped up all over the colonies, only a few people suffered property damage, and no one was killed. Stamp distributors and British sympathizers feared for their lives, but the crowds seemed content to vent their hatred on effigies.

ii

The crowds behaved well partly because of the nature of funerals and executions and partly because of a thorough newspaper campaign that implicitly established rules for the mock ceremonies and instilled certain expectations in the participants. Mock executions, whether in big cities or in isolated villages, were caught and fixed in the glare of intercolonial publicity. As effigies went to their death from New Hampshire to South Carolina, the press fed its readers a rich mortuary diet of far-flung executions. Bostonians and Philadelphians, Virginians, Rhode Islanders, and Carolinians—all could relish each other's executions and appreciate the fine workmanship of a distant performance. A funeral in Portsmouth, New Hampshire; an execution in Lebanon, Connecticut—both would have their day in the sun

---

11. *Connecticut Gazette,* 13 September 1765.

12. *The Newport Mercury,* 4 November 1765.

13. *Connecticut Gazette,* 15 November 1765.

and contribute to the standardization of the performance. Newspaper accounts, like etiquette manuals, notified the public of accepted procedure and proper behavior. The more the executions proliferated and were dutifully publicized, the more pressure people performing the last rites of their own local effigies felt to comply with the rules outlined by the papers. A pattern of procedure and an aura of propriety settled over the colonies, and the mock ceremonies developed their own visual language, which worked in conjunction with the written tracts to politicize people.

Reporters took pains to portray mock executions as legitimate expressions of resistance and not as instances of mob violence. If the accounts are to be believed, the crowd almost always consisted of "reputable" people who behaved in an "orderly" and "decorous" way. After the ceremony the "gentlemen" would often adjourn to a tavern and drink loyal healths to the king, royal family, and liberty, and by this bibulous expression of allegiance put the seal of utmost "decency" and "good order" on the whole affair. If the leaders of the community conspicuously absented themselves from the ceremony, the crowd might enjoin their approval. In Wilmington, North Carolina, a crowd of 500, after hanging and burning an effigy of an unnamed "HONOURABLE GENTLEMAN" who supported the Stamp Act, went around the town from door to door and brought all the gentlemen of the city to the bonfire to drink a toast to liberty, property, no stamp duty, and confusion to Lord Bute (a hated Scottish peer King George doted on) and his adherents. After each toast the crowd gave three huzzahs. Having obtained the approval of the "better sort," "they continued together until 12 of the clock, and then dispersed, without doing any mischief."[14]

Encased in propriety, mock ceremonies also conformed to the procedural protocol honed by the conscientious coverage of the press. Newspapers not only made mock ceremonies a popular form of demonstration, they defined the ceremony and shaped its significance. Serving as heuristic devices, ceremonies had signposts to guide the people along their moral way. The place of execution, the form of the ceremony, the companions of the stamp distributor, and his victims—all colored the nature of the crime, and it was the nature of the crime that patriot leaders wished to drive home. Presenting

14. *Pennsylvania Journal*, 2 January 1766, Supplement.

the political message as a set allegory shifted attention away from the fate of the condemned man to the meaning of his fate.

Executions often took place in front of the courthouse, or, if not, the procession passed by the courthouse on its way from the gallows to the funeral site. Perhaps by staging the demonstration in front of the courthouse the crowd was expressing its defiance of the authorities. In Charleston, the people erected a twenty-foot-high gallows right in front of the courthouse and hanged three effigies: a stamp distributor, the devil, and a boot out of which stuck a head wearing a blue bonnet (the boot and the blue bonnet symbolizing the Scottish peer, Lord Bute). On the back of the stamp distributor was pinned a warning: "Whoever shall dare attempt to pull down these effigies, had better been born with a mill-stone about his neck, and cast into the sea." From morning to evening the effigies swung in the breeze undisturbed, "the court of the general sessions of the peace, oyer and terminer, assize, and general jail delivery, sitting all the while; nor was there the least riot or disturbance, tho' a great concourse of people incessantly resorted to the place of exhibition."[15] The effigies swaying, the court droning in the background, the curious observers milling about: the whole presented a pleasing blend of defiance and order.

But although the courthouse offered a handy butt for the crowd's defiance, it also served a positive function in the iconography of resistance ceremonies. Given the efforts at soliciting approval from leading citizens and the emphasis on order and decorum, it seems likely that the demonstrators, by carrying on their proceedings in the vicinity of the courthouse, were seeking the countenance of the law, a tacit agreement with the proposition that resistance to unconstitutional law is legal. The freemen of Talbot County, Maryland, assembled in front of the courthouse and passed a series of resolutions. To draw attention to their political work, they "[e]rected a GIBBET Twenty Feet high, before the Court-House Door, and hung in Chains thereon, the Effigy of a Stamp-Informer, there to remain in *TERROREM* till the *Stamp Act* shall be Repealed."[16] Then the leader read the resolutions publicly: that the Stamp Act was unconstitutional; that colonists were entitled to British rights, including the

15. Ibid.

16. *Maryland Gazette,* n.d., "Apparition."

right to a trial by jury; that colonists could not be taxed except by
their legal representatives in assembly, and that the freemen intended
to preserve and transmit these rights and liberties to their posterity.
(They also resolved to have no communication with "stamp pimps"
except to upbraid them for their baseness, a resolution that suggests
that the scaffold was a sign of detestation but not a threat of execution.) On one occasion, the crowd did not allow the local magistrates
merely to condone the proceedings but demanded they approve of
them explicitly. In Wilmington, North Carolina, a crowd who had
hanged an effigy of a stamp distributor in front of the courthouse
required the lawyers to come out, drink damnation to the stamp
distributor, and express the wish that he and all his generation "may
be forced to take up with the scrapings of the Pott." But for the most
part the courthouse acted as a silent partner. By casting its shadow on
the proceedings, it justified the mock executions as legitimate expressions of resistance as long as order was maintained.

Ceremonies commented on their own validity and legitimacy, but
they also had a message to impart. On one level—the rational one—
the visual message of the mock ceremonies coincided with the written arguments against the Stamp Act that appeared in newspaper
editorials, in petitions and memorials to the king and Parliament,
and in political pamphlets. Colonists argued that government by
consent and trial by jury were political rights that protected liberty.
By executing effigies of men who denied these rights to colonists
they vindicated the rights. On another level, somewhere in the psychological and emotional ether, the mock ceremonies and the written
arguments both were examples of a sense of colonial disorientation
occasioned by the passage of the Stamp Act. In written documents
colonists talked about this disorientation, and in mock ceremonies
they demonstrated it. People conduct funerals as a way of dealing
with loss. When a person dies, the community is in a small way
threatened (were deaths to be multiplied without counterbalancing
replenishment, the community itself would die). By gathering together to honor the deceased, the community expresses its cohesion
and reaffirms its values, and the funeral serves a regenerative function. In 1765, colonists turned funeral psychology on its head. The
death of a stamp distributor did not threaten a community; it saved
the community. People attended the funeral to rejoice in a death that
had averted communal destruction. Mock funerals and executions

differed from real funerals and executions in the nature of the corpses and victims, in the response of participants, and in the performance of the rites themselves. Exposed corpses rotting in the sun and sacrificial funeral pyres were not part of colonial mortuary rituals. Corpses were not resurrected; mourners did not rejoice. The mock funerals and executions were ironic by virtue of their inversions and discrepancies. The shock involved in recognizing the inversions and discrepancies allowed people to participate emotionally and dramatically at the same time that they maintained a distance from violence—it was all make-believe, after all. In the make-believe ceremonies, people released emotions that would have been wildly inappropriate at real funerals or executions: joy and vengeance. All of which is to say that the structure of mock ceremonies—the discrepancy between the serious version of funerals and executions and the ironic version—conveyed a message quite apart from the explicitly articulated message of the allegory itself.

The colonists also saw the political crisis as an inversion, and in resisting the Stamp Act with joyous funerals and vengeful executions they met one topsy-turvy situation with another. The political inversion presented by the Stamp Act disoriented the colonists. In rejecting the Stamp Act, they pointed out the contradictions that were manifest to them but that the British refused to recognize.

> For example, they [the British] will tell you gravely, that the subjects in the colonies are *freemen;*—that they hold their lands, their lives, and liberties, under the security of the laws of England;—that they have a right to justice administered in the same form, and by the same rules, as in England; and that their courts, where justice is administered, derive their existence from the same source, have the same powers, & stand in the same degree of subordination to one another, as the courts of justice do in England. But they assert, that the representative body of the people, a court, by the laws of England, superior in rank, in power, and in importance, to all those courts, is in this colony (by a strange inversion of the constitution) placed below them: that is, in plain English, "You are freemen, entitled to all the rights and privileges of Englishmen, but your constitution wants the only fence, which, in your mother country, secures the subject those invaluable blessings."[17]

17. *Pennsylvania Journal,* 13 February 1766.

Colonists thought the Stamp Act inverted the British constitution in the colonies. Colonists were called free men, but they were to be denied the rights that made them free. In Great Britain, Parliament, the legislative body, was also the highest court in the land. In the colonies, the legislative bodies, which should also have been the highest courts in the respective colonies, were to be subject to inferior courts (especially the Admiralty Court). "Can there, in the name of GOD, any honest reason be given, why the order of things, in this colony, ought to be thus inverted? Or why the representatives of the people should be so degraded, in our constitution, from the rank which they hold in that of our mother country?" colonists wanted to know.[18] In the colonies, the courts, which enforced the laws, were to be superior to the assemblies, which made the laws. In demonstrating against this inversion and in favor of the representative assemblies whose power was threatened by the courts and by Parliament, people in the colonies became representatives of their own representatives.

Newspapers reproduced the colonial sense of inversion visually as well as verbally by flaunting insignia of telling import (such as a skull and crossbones) where the official stamp was supposed to have been affixed. One paper, the *Halifax Gazette,* reached a peak of heraldic insolence. In the place reserved for the stamp, there appeared an escutcheon rich in political implications—a veritable labyrinth of symbolic inversions that enchanted the editors of other colonial newspapers.

> The devise seems to be an empty regal crown, topsey-turvey, in a *field gules* with two *Turkish daggers* or *Highlander dirks* pierced thro' its center, and forming nearly a *St. James'* Cross. Between the points of the *daggers,* but untouched by either, is, AMERICA, with *Capitals inverted.* Between the hilts or handles of the daggers is printed also in Capitals inverted, FOR A HALF PENNY. The exargue also in Capitals is HONI SOIT QUI MAL Y PENSE!"[19]

Mock funerals and executions that scrambled established patterns contributed to a more general upheaval in which social, economic, and political relations had all gone askew: courts overthrew legisla-

---

18. Ibid.

19. *Pennsylvania Journal,* 13 March 1766.

tures; free men were taxed without their consent; consumers tried to become producers; corpses leapt up and frolicked with mourners; law enforcers succumbed to lawless executions. The irony of mock ceremonies depended on inversions, and these inversions mirrored other inversions that the Stamp Act, having churned up life at all levels, drew in its wake. In this formal sense, the mock funerals and executions were not a remedy for the Stamp Act crisis but an expression of it.

The structure of protest pageantry also undercut one of the British justifications of the Stamp Act. In answer to the colonial protest that Parliament could not legally tax colonists because colonists were not represented in Parliament (and subjects of the British Empire could not be taxed without their consent, granted either in person or by their representatives), defenders of the Act claimed that colonists were "virtually" represented in Parliament. The members of the House of Commons, while they were elected by the people of England and not by the colonists, were representatives for the whole British Empire. Caught up in the general responsibilities of representation, they would be bound to consider the good of all members of the empire. Colonists were skeptical. Those virtual representatives, after all, were levying real taxes, and taxes, for that matter, that neither they nor their actual constituents would be subject to. Colonists noticed that their interests, when it came to the question of a colonial tax, differed from the interests of Englishmen, and they doubted that the representative of a Cornwall borough would take to his bosom the interests of New Yorkers or Virginians, Bostonians or Philadelphians. Virtual representation seemed to the colonists an airy abstraction. They felt that only their own representatives could tax them. And so, when they protested the Stamp Act, colonists indulged in a little virtual representation of their own. An effigy of a stamp man or a British minister that could be tried, hanged, burned, or blown up made a nice virtual representative. Mock ceremonies indirectly underscored the ludicrousness of the British reliance on the notion of virtual representation. In Lebanon, Connecticut, the townspeople put an effigy of the former agent for Connecticut on trial.

> He made his appearance at the bar of said court, in the person of his VIRTUAL representative, and was denied none of those just RIGHTS

of Englishmen, being allowed the sacred privileges of a trial by his Peers, &c. After a full hearing, he was sentenced to be taken from the tribunal of justice, placed in a cart, with a halter about his neck, carried in procession through the streets of the town to expose him to just ignominy and contempt, and then to be drawn to the place of execution, and hanged by the neck till dead, and afterwards to be committed to the flames, that if possible he might be purified by fire.[20]

Virtual representation was to representation and a virtual representative was to a representative as a mock trial was to a trial or an effigy to a man. Colonists knew that the vertebrae of a virtual representative did not snap when the shoot of the gibbet was released, and they also knew that a virtual representative did not actually represent anybody. In all their frenzy of demonstrations, colonists, unlike the English, did not blur the distinction between abstraction and reality. They did not execute real men, and they pointed out that their effigies were virtual representatives—quite different from the genuine product.

Mock ceremonies corresponded to written arguments thematically as well as structurally. Writers, of course, could instruct and persuade their readers by rational discursive arguments; whereas an effigy who tried to make political arguments by means of placards would not, chances were, have held a turbulent audience spellbound. Still, pamphlets and pageants shared a moral domain. They presented compliance with the Stamp Act as betrayal; they identified victims; and they depicted the physical and moral consequences of betrayal for the betrayer himself. The allegorical pageants of mock executions often took the form of a domestic tragedy: a mother (Liberty or America), betrayed for gold by her son (a stamp distributor), calls out for vengeance. The executioners satisfy a blood debt, and the crowd, like a Greek chorus, chants moral condemnation of the crime and approval of the punishment. Of course, these pageants were far cheerier than their Greek counterparts or the family set-to's of Shakespeare and Webster and their diluted imitations that trickled down into the eighteenth century and held British and colonial audiences in thrall. In the pageants generated by the Stamp Act, vengeance was taken on the villain, and the innocent victim of the crime that incited ven-

20. *Pennsylvania Journal,* 19 September 1765.

geance in fact escaped unscathed. In the view of the world presented by the pageants, evil motives, not crime, blighted society. Moral balance was restored and the community saved by executing men who wanted to destroy liberty even though they had failed in their attempt.

Similarly, the written arguments against acquiescing in the Stamp Act were conducted in the language of posterity, betrayal, and piety and impiety. Although writers for the most part avoided the fanciful reaches of shattered families and communal bloodletting and framed their argument in terms of contract law (debts and obligations) and moral philosophy (gratitude and fidelity), their message did not differ from the message of the pageants. Resolutions of towns, counties, committees, private societies; editorials; pamphlets: all extolled the bonds that existed, or should exist, between generations of the family of man. "[I]t would be rank ingratitude to the memory of our forefathers, and an offence, in the highest degree to posterity, should we neglect the means, divine Providence has put in our power, of preserving inviolate, these sacred rights," declared one Pennsylvania town.[21] "We have received our liberties as an inheritance from our fathers, and we are bound to transmit them to our children unimpaired. If we do so, we shall do our duty; if we do otherwise, we shall act with the basest treachery and impiety: We shall deservedly incur the censure, the contempt, the abhorrence of all honest men, and intitle ourselves to the curses of posterity," proclaimed an editorial.[22] Political tracts brimmed with arguments, while the elaborate displays of mock ceremonies dazzled the senses; but both expressed the same attitude towards political rights. Colonists not only believed in the rights guaranteed by the British constitution, they believed in their inviolability. Rights that protected liberty (government by consent and due process of law) should not vary with time or place or be transmuted at the whim of a particular ministry. Under constant threat by the ravages of time and men, these rights had to be protected. Such was the moral message transmitted in writing and in pageant. The gratitude that the present generation owed the past generation (or a son owed his mother) and the duty that the present generation owed the future generation (or a parent owed his child)

---

21. *Pennsylvania Journal,* 13 March 1766.
22. *Pennsylvania Journal,* 13 February 1766, from the *Newport Mercury.*

were expressions of a belief in the moral necessity of the transcendence and permanence of rights that guaranteed liberty.

The scenes of family discord reinforced the themes embedded in colonial condemnation of the Stamp Act and its promoters: unnaturalness, greed, and betrayal. In a pageant of effigies in Lebanon, Connecticut, the stamp distributor stood between the Devil, who waved a purse of gold under his victim's nose and hissed a tempting proposition—"Accept this Office and Enslave your Country, and 400 £ per Annum Shall be your Reward"—and his mother (his injured country) dressed in sable with chains rattling at her feet, who begged her son not to betray her by accepting this sordid bribe.

> "My Son! remember that I have treated you with the utmost Tenderness, and bestowed on you my highest Honours, pity our Country, and put not on me those Chains" To which her ungrateful, degenerate Son replied, in a Label proceeding from his Mouth, "Perish my Country, so that I get that Reward."[23]

When arguing against the Stamp Act, colonists claimed their rights not only by the British constitution, but also by the law of nature. They nosed their claim to no taxation without representation from the murky region of precedents, laws, and charters out into the sunshine of universal rights based on a universal morality. Pageants that cast stamp distributors as ungrateful, degenerate sons willing to sell their mothers into slavery portrayed the Stamp Act as a monstrosity that violated the law of nature. When the Lebanon mother heard her son denounce her, she pronounced an "awful, prophetic and parental Curse."

> " . . . . Heaven crush those Vipers,
> Who, singled out by a Community,
> To guard her Rights, Shall for a grasp of Ore,
> Or paltry Office, sell them to the foe."

The parental curse underscored the impiety of a son's betraying his mother and lashed the crowd into a fury. Such was their "Abhorrence and Detestation" of the stamp distributor's "crime" that a strong guard was necessary to protect the effigy from mutilation.

23. *Maryland Gazette*, 26 September 1765.

Stamp distributors broke the law of nature; they also put private gain above public good. Rarely did the stage directors of protest pageants leave out the sack of gold that drove home the selfishness and greed of the stamp distributor, a man without principle. Ironically, the American colonists themselves have been condemned, both by the British in the eighteenth century and by progressive historians in the twentieth, as tax-evaders who tried to hide the selfishness of their motives under the guise of highfalutin principles—men unwilling to give of their wealth in order to support the very empire that made the wealth possible. The Americans were fighting taxation, and, although they were not lining their pockets as were the office-holders in the imperial system, they were keeping a tight grasp on their gold. But supporting principles that materially benefit the supporters does not make people unprincipled.[24] In the eighteenth century, people linked life, liberty, and property. Indeed, life and liberty were types of "property"—that which people had a right to possess and enjoy; and the "British constitution," which colonists were defending when they protested the Stamp Act, was designed to protect property—not only life and liberty, but material possessions as well. People should not be taxed without their consent. The colonists could on principle defend the British constitution and remain principled even though British law protected their property.

Still, a certain poetic justice rings in the condemnation of colonists on the grounds that they profited from the position they took, since colonists themselves linked gain with moral impurity. Patriots did not take seriously the notion that a stamp distributor might really believe in good conscience that sovereignty was indivisible, that it lay with Parliament, and that taxation was a function of sovereignty; and they did not admit that such beliefs would make it morally impossible for men to defy parliamentary legislation, whether or not they benefited from it as stamp distributors. Stamp distributors, according to the colonial opinion, were scoundrels, pure and simple, and they were scoundrels because they were willing to wreak havoc on the public good rather than forego their own profit. Hence the ever-present bag of gold and the Devil, the great tempter and seducer of

---

24. Edmund S. Morgan, "Revisions in Need of Revising," in *The Challenge of the American Revolution* (New York, 1976), 56.

humans. If men took the office of stamp distributor out of greed, they could not appeal to principles that justified their decision.

Greed also denoted treachery. Colonists saw British ministers in general, but especially stamp distributors, less as enemies than as traitors, and they acted out their sense of betrayal in the violence they visited on the executed effigies. In Baltimore the people "diverted themselves with Carting, Whipping, Hanging, and Burning the Effigies of a Distributor of Stamps."[25] In Boston the people cut down effigies of George Grenville and John Huske, (the latter a colonist thought to be sympathetic to the Stamp Act), and "tore them in pieces and flung their limbs with indignation into the air."[26] And the inhabitants of Dumfries, a small town in Virginia, put an effigy of George Mercer, the man appointed stamp distributor, on a horse with his face towards the horse's tail, fastened a halter around his neck, and tied the Stamp Act to it. As the effigy rode through town, it "receiv'd the Insults of the Congregation, by Caneing, Whipping, (the Mosaic Law) Pillorying, Cropping, Hanging and Burning; &c &c"[27]— somewhat tantalizing "&c"s which make one wonder what else this unfortunate effigy could have sustained. The colonists may have been acting out executions, but the effigies of political figures suffered brutalities that condemned criminals were spared. These scenes of mutilation bore more resemblance to Greek myths than to colonial executions. The Theban king Pentheus was torn to pieces by the Bacchae for the sacrilege of spying on the Eleusinian mysteries. Penthesilea tore apart her lover Theseus for playing false. While colonists hanged effigies of British ministers and stamp distributors to express the idea that people who passed and upheld the Stamp Act had broken the (fundamental) law, they mutilated the effigies as an expression, not of legal condemnation, but of anger and frustration—the anger and frustration that comes from feeling betrayed. The dismembered bodies and scattered limbs, in giving public expression to the sense of betrayal, indirectly testify that in 1765, colonists still saw themselves as Englishmen. If the colonists had thought of themselves as a people distinct from the British, they would not have felt betrayed by the Stamp Act—persecuted, harassed, threatened, perhaps, but not

25. *Massachusetts Gazette and Boston News-letter,* 26 September 1765, Supplement.

26. *Connecticut Gazette,* 8 November 1765.

27. *Maryland Gazette,* 12 September 1765.

betrayed. Betrayal presupposes a common bond that has been broken. The colonists thought of themselves as Englishmen who were being treated by Englishmen as if they were not English.

Colonists felt betrayed and needed a nondestructive vent for their anger at being betrayed; they also felt impotent (a Parliament in which they had no representatives was levying taxes on them) and needed a way of overcoming the frustrations of impotence. In turning the British ministers and stamp distributors into effigies and then dealing with them as criminals with all the formality of a real ceremony, colonists transformed a political issue into an ironic farce. The tranformation did not diminish the issue; it diminished the men who had initiated the crisis and the men who proposed to benefit from it. The ceremonies allowed the colonists to come "face to face" with their enemies and betrayers and treat them with contempt and ridicule. Other measures of resistance that the colonists took, such as economic boycotts, petitions, and the intercolonial congress, put them in a fighting stance; but none of these measures would have given them a feeling of superiority. In mock ceremonies colonists could ridicule and deride their enemies. Ridicule is a means of feeling superior; and feeling superior is a means of overcoming a sense of impotence. Colonists confronted political repression with economic boycotts; they confronted the psychological effects of political repression with irony.

iii

In 1765, colonists seemed to have hit on a form of resistance that fulfilled their needs. Through mock executions, colonists intimidated stamp distributors and prevented them from executing their office while limiting violence to the imaginary realm. Furthermore, mock ceremonies worked their charms on the colonists themselves. By giving people a chance to participate in a structured demonstration, they involved large numbers of people in resistance and made public the colonial response to the Stamp Act. Having participated in a demonstration, people became conscious of the existence of a crisis, identified a threat, and, with the help of the ceremonies that spelled out the political message, defined their position. Even the children dancing in the streets alongside a funeral procession became patriots. In Middletown, Connecticut, "young Children, that can hardly speak, have already learnt this lesson well: Liberty, Property and no Stamps; which they sing along the streets"; and in New London, Connecticut, children followed a condemned effigy, crying "there hangs a *Traitor,* there's *an Enemy to his Country.*"[28] Mock ceremonies seem to have catered to the psychological needs of a people buffeted by constitutional surprises and the political needs of a people trying to consolidate in resistance.

But if mock ceremonies so successfully made colonists aware of a crisis and formed a community of resistance, why did they dwindle in the turbulence of subsequent constitutional storms? In later crises, mock executions appeared here and there, but they did not sweep the colonies the way they did in the Stamp Act crisis. The Townshend Acts of 1767, which sought to raise a revenue in the colonies by taxing certain imports, brought forth a battery of written protests, but Townshend and his cronies, the colonial customs officers, did not dangle in effigy from scaffolds up and down the Atlantic seaboard; and when the Coercive Acts—undisguisedly repressive legislation—struck in 1774, colonists rallied to the cause of resistance with economic boycotts, petitions, letters, and resolutions of moral rectitude, but they did turn out *en masse* to bury Liberty. Isolated mock ceremonies took place, but no organized program developed like that of the Stamp Act crisis. In part, the circumstances of the potential victims had changed. The Stamp Act offered a unique opportunity for colonists to put pressure on the administrative machinery of the British Empire, because the men appointed as stamp distributors responsible for carrying out the provisions of the Stamp Act were themselves colonists, men with property in the colonies who lived in a community and had a stake in that community. Men who owned property that was vulnerable to the rampages of a crowd did well not to incur communal hostility. But while the men responsible for carrying out the Townshend Acts and the Coercive Acts were for the most part Englishmen whose property was tucked safely away in England, these administrators still had their lives to consider. Mock executions might have suggested to them certain inconveniences in carrying out the terms of the acts. And yet no other storm of mock executions broke over the colonies, a relative calm that suggests that mock ceremonies were primarily attuned to the needs of the colonists themselves and that

28. *Connecticut Gazette,* 15 November 1765, 13 September 1765.

these needs had changed. Colonists evidently saw mock executions as a symbolic expression of hostility and defiance and as a means to an end, but they seem to have had no intention of translating the implied threat into reality. In 1767, when life, not property, was the only card to be played in the game of coercion, colonists backed off. Subtler currents may also have been at play as mock ceremonies drifted into the background of colonial resistance. Mock ceremonies worked in 1765, but they left a trail of inconsistencies that might well have pricked the colonial sense of ease.

Familiar ceremonies that had their own set of rules, such as funerals or executions, when applied to a political issue, unified people by giving them the formal means of construing the issue in the same way. The mock ceremonies provided a way of processing a political crisis that encouraged uniformity of response. But irony, while it might have had its political assets, had also its social liabilities. In manipulating for political purposes two social ceremonies designed to reinforce community values, colonists risked degrading the ceremonies themselves. Such a risk ran counter to their purpose of using these two ceremonies to shore up community morality. In New England, patriot leaders urged funeral restraint at the same time that they staged elaborate mock funerals. In the summer of 1765, Bostonians, for example, planned a lavish funeral for Liberty. Although Bostonians were at this time emphasizing their Puritan heritage with calls for frugality and distorting this heritage with idealized accounts of their forebears as preservers of liberty, they announced a full Anglican funeral for Liberty. The funeral was to take place at night and the body was to be buried in "the Family Vault under King's Chapel." And at the very time Bostonians started a movement to eliminate mourning in funeral services, they lifted their own ban when burying Liberty. The burial of Liberty, "being an Extraordinary Case, DEEP MOURNING will be allowed of."[29]

Colonists had the problem of resisting political oppression without letting the potential violence underlying resistance disrupt their own society and mangle their own values. Funeral, sartorial, and dietary regulations made colonists self-conscious about routine behavior and helped them relate their daily life to the political cause.

29. *Pennsylvania Journal*, 12 September 1765, from the *American Chronicle*, 19 August 1765.

But in staging mock funerals, patriot leaders undermined their own regulations. They found themselves promulgating one set of standards for "real" ceremonies and another set for mock ceremonies. Irony depends on exaggeration for its effect, hence the elaborate ceremonial trappings. But the ceremonial trappings necessary to underscore the essential incongruity (the incongruity between the event, a funeral; and the response, joy) were not themselves the subject of irony. The ceremony was not meant to draw attention to the discrepancy between elaborate mock funerals and simple real funerals. For irony to work, the foot of the compass has to be implanted in non-ironic soil. Otherwise the attention of the spectator would be torn apart; his laughter and ridicule would twist this way and that, uncertain where to settle; and in the emotional dissolution the quarry would slip away. Spectators at a funeral for Liberty or the Stamp Act or a stamp distributor were not expected to criticize the funeral ceremony itself. They were meant to focus on the resurrection or the death and on the emotional response.

Similarly, the irony of the mock execution provided a growing miasma that could stifle the very values that formed a bulwark against social chaos. State and church authorities made every effort to purge real execution ceremonies of irony and to make moral lessons of them. Magistrates wanted to improve the spiritual condition of the condemned man (they went out of their way to lead him to remorse and conversion), but they also wanted to maintain social order. As a means of maintaining social order they encouraged spectators to participate emotionally by identifying with the criminal (all people stood in need of Christ's forgiveness, and if Christ, who was innocent of all sin, could forgive sinners, then sinners should be able to forgive each other), and they took all possible measures to increase the solemnity of the occasion in order to frustrate any temptation of the multitude to jeer at the condemned man. But irony untuned the moral mechanism of the execution. As effigy after effigy went to its death, spectators cheered and expressed their approval and pleasure. "Nor did a weeping Eye or relenting Heart hinder or allay any Demonstration of Joy."[30] Spectators dissociated themselves from the condemned effigies. The danger loomed that spectators might learn to dissociate themselves from condemned men, and callousness unravel the moral

30. *Maryland Gazette*, 26 September 1765.

fabric of society. When Henry Halbert was hanged for murder in October of 1765, a Philadelphia paper ended the account of the execution, not with a comforting confession of guilt and remorse on the part of the criminal, but with an ironic moralism. "He will never pay any of the taxes unjustly laid on these once happy lands," sighed the reporter, mulling over the benefits of extermination.[31]

Colonists called routine social customs to the assistance of the political cause, but in using the funeral and execution ceremonies ironically, they ran the risk that the political cause could disrupt routine social customs. Mourners at real funerals and mourners at mock funerals received conflicting commands concerning proper behavior. Spectators at the execution of effigies were expected to behave in just the way spectators at executions of criminals were encouraged not to behave: with ridicule, scorn, contempt, and joy—emotions that distanced the spectator from the condemned and filled him with spiritual complacence and superiority. Condemned effigies, unlike condemned men, were not expected to repent, nor indeed could they repent within the terms of the ceremony, because repentance of the victim would deprive the ceremony of its justification. The effigy was being executed not only for his crime, but for his attitude. Intransigence and extermination ruled the day, and had to rule the day for the show to go on. But leaders of colonial resistance did not want colonists to waste money on extravagent funerals; they did not want colonists to be complacent in their superiority; and, most of all, they did want to win stamp distributors over to their cause and avoid internal dissension. If colonists wanted to combat extravagance, complacence, and dissension, mock funerals and executions might prove dangerous waters through which to chart their course.

The irony of the mock execution worked in complicated ways. Colonists followed the prescribed execution ceremony—the trial, the gallows' cart, the halter around the neck of the condemned, the last words and dying speech—in order to emphasize the lawfulness of the proceeding and the criminal guilt of enforcing the Stamp Act. But they also deviated from the traditional execution, and these deviations provide a context for understanding the psychology of colonial resistance. Real executions were conducted as the fulfillment of state

31. *Pennsylvania Journal,* 24 October 1765.

justice, tempered, if possible, by religion. The religious motif protected the community from the sin of vengeance. The community
had to be purged of excessive and persistent sin and protected from
crime, but it took action against the sinner-criminal with reluctance
and sympathized with him for his fate. The mock execution, on the
other hand, was conducted as a sacrifice, a sacrifice in which the
community dissociated itself from the sacrificial victim. Real executions did not include a funeral procession and did not end with the
immolation of the corpse; mock executions did. In the Boston demonstration of August 14, 1765, the crowd hanged an effigy of Andrew Oliver and a boot with a devil crawling out of it. After cutting
down the corpses, parading them through town (with a short pause
in front of the courthouse), they marched to Fort Hill, where they
kindled a "noble" fire. Here "they made a Burnt-offering of the
Effigies for those Sins of the People which had caused such heavy
Judgments as the Stamp Act, &c. to be laid upon them."[32] Now the
ceremony was as much a mock sacrifice as it was a mock execution.
But the participants were putting a symbolic construction on their
exercise.

In transforming an execution into a sacrifice made to expiate their
own sins, colonists revealed an ambivalent attitude towards the significance of the Stamp Act and the appropriate way of responding to
the threat. On the one hand, the Stamp Act was presented as the plot
of evil men who could be executed. On the other hand, it was
presented as a punishment inflicted on a sinful people by an angry
God. This interpretation of the Stamp Act would lead to calls for
moral reformation by the afflicted, in the old Puritan tradition. In
1675, when the Algonquin chief known to the colonists as King
Phillip had attacked the western towns of Massachusetts Colony, the
Massachusetts legislature had responded to the crisis—seen as a
providential punishment for the sins of the people—with laws to
remedy moral laxity. The "burnt offerings" of 1765 and 1766, even
given the mockery in the "sacrifice," showed a similar tendency of
Bostonians a century later to look inward and ascribe responsibility
for their plight to their own style of living. In 1765, the ascription
had more to do with the economics of the situation than with reli-

---

32. *Pennsylvania Journal,* 29 August 1765.

gion. Colonists, when their rights were threatened, realized that a taste for luxury and extravagance (which of necessity fed on British imports) had fostered dependence. And economic dependence weakened the will and prepared the colonists for political enslavement, should the British wish to enslave them. To guard against a threat that they had in part brought upon themselves, colonists felt a need to reform. One such moral reformation was the retrenchment of funeral expenses and the forsaking of mourning dress. These types of ascetic measures would gain in popularity as the imperial crisis crested.

Self-examination as a response to a crisis stretched back into the Puritan past. But Puritans, whether the Puritans of 1675 or their lukewarm descendants of 1765, would not have offered God a sacrifice to expiate their sins. What in the world were Protestants doing conducting their mock executions as sacrifices? In part, of course, they were being ironic. The sacrifice was no more real than the execution, and with its implications of Catholicism and paganism it cast further aspersions on the effigies who were its victims. But even as the execution of effigies bore a relation to the execution of criminals, so the sacrifice of effigies bore a relation to real sacrifices. Sacrificial victims assume the sins of the people; their death purges and saves the community. Colonists in the Stamp Act crisis concentrated all their resentment and frustration on a few isolated men, men who had been designated by the British ministry as stamp distributors or men who associated themselves with the ministry's position.

The English did not have a tradition of burning ordinary criminals. Even traitors were not burned. Burning had been reserved for heretics and witches. Fire consumed the body; the ashes were scattered in the winds; and no gravestone marked the resting place of the corpse. Burning the effigies suggested that stamp distributors were not just morally depraved like criminals, but spiritually depraved like heretics. The people of Lebanon, Connecticut, committed their effigy to the flames, "that if possible he might be purified by fire." The Devil (in effigy) attended this funeral. When the condemned effigy had been hanged until dead, he was cut down "and delivered into the Power of his false Friend and Seducer, who according to his usual Practice, changed from a Tempter to a Tormentor: plunged his Prisoner headlong in a huge Pyramid of Fire, and followed him immediately himself, with his mighty Paws barring fast the Gates of this suitable Habitation."[33] In this interpretation of the funeral pyre that closed mock executions, burning was associated both with the purification of the victim and society and with the endless flames and torments of hell.

Mock executions sent forth various messages in what at times appears to be a random bombardment. Mock executions seemed to place the blame for the Stamp Act on British officials, while mock sacrifices seemed to shift the blame onto American colonists wallowing in sin. The execution-sacrifice presented three possible remedies: destruction of the perpetrators of evil, moral reformation of a sinful people, and sacrifice of deviants to purify society and propitiate an angry god.

iv

Mock ceremonies threatened to undermine the social validity of non-ironic ceremonies, and the layers of meaning embedded in mock ceremonies complicated the political message and sometimes even contradicted each other. But irony also had dangers as a political strategy. In mock executions, colonists destroyed stamp distributors, who were depicted as traitors (men who had forfeited their claim to belong to a community by betraying that community) and heretics (men whose false beliefs led to spiritual depravity and corruption of conscience). But in real life colonists attempted to convert the offenders and embrace them once again within the community bosom. The men chosen by the British ministry to hold the office of stamp distributor were for the most part men of local prominence. Such men, by allying themselves with the British position, threatened the dissolution of their own communities. Colonists who wanted to prevent the exercise of the office but who also wanted to keep the community from splitting into factions tried to maneuver the stamp distributors into resigning their office in such a way as to preserve the harmony of the community. Thus colonists dealt with the internal threat to their society in two potentially contradictory ways. In mock ceremonies stamp distributors were reviled, vilified, mutilated, executed, and burned; they were identified with the office they had been appointed to; and they were depicted as obstinate men unsusceptible to

33. *Maryland Gazette,* 26 September 1765.

reason and persuasion. In the ceremony, the colonists exterminated the men who held the office and thereby exterminated the office. But in real life, colonists who wanted to nullify the office by rendering the job unacceptable had to deal with the stamp distributors as men capable of making a choice, or, if they had already made the wrong choice, capable of reform and moral development. Therefore they emphasized the distinction between the office and the men appointed to it. It was the office that colonists found objectionable, and they asserted again and again that they entertained no animosity towards the men who had been appointed to it (provided, of course, that they resigned). The very elements that made the mock ceremonies effective politically and emotionally—the satisfaction of violent urges, the personification of evil, and the elimination of evil by the destruction of people—pitted the mock ceremonies against the procedures the colonists were developing for dealing with the real stamp distributors.

Take the case of Zachariah Hood, the stamp distributor for Maryland. In Frederick Town, Maryland, an effigy of Hood attended the funeral of the Stamp Act and, as the sole mourner, delivered a speech at the gravesite. Ostensibly this speech was a funeral oration for his friend the Stamp Act. But Zachariah Hood, the effigy, did not spend much time eulogizing his friend. Instead he dwelt on his own material deprivation, brought on by his friend's demise. Then, about three-fourths of the way through, overcome with the thought of lost riches, he himself developed symptoms of dying.

> Dear Object of my warmest Wishes! —thou art now expired under the Hand of Justice! —The same Spirit animated us both, and the cold Grasp of Fate is now upon me! —My Faculties, sink together with thee, and Death freezes my stagnating Fluids! —Let me be buried together with thee, and one Grave receive our breathless Remains! —I hope, Good People, you will not refuse this last Request of a dying Person."[34]

Suddenly the funeral oration had metamorphosed into the last words and dying speech of a condemned criminal. And yet, from the beginning, the speech had been more like a confession than a eulogy:

34. *Maryland Gazette,* n.d., "Apparition."

> Pardon, Good People, this last Testimony of my Affection to the De-
> ceased [the Stamp Act] —For her I despised Country, Humanity,
> Friendship, Kindred, and all the Ties of Honour, Nature, Gratitude
> and Honesty —For her was every Motive of Justice, Benevolence, Pity
> and Compassion banished from my Breast —For her could I have
> sacrificed the Good of the Public, the Happiness of Individuals, and
> (encircled in her Embraces) have smiled at the Curses of the Poor, the
> Tears of the Orphan, the Cries of the Widow, the Groans of the op-
> pressed; and without one Pang of Remorse, have viewed the Land of
> my Birth gnashing her Teeth under the Load of Bondage, whilst I
> enjoyed the Sunshine of Ministerial Influence, and decked myself in the
> Spoils of the Wretched and Unfortunate!

What really changed at the end of the speech was the status of the
speaker, from mourner to dying man.

The speech of Zachariah Hood, the effigy, was a confession, but it
was a confession only from the point of view of the audience and not
from the point of view of the speaker himself. It was presented as if
the speaker did not understand the significance of his own words,
words that were highly colored to the disadvantage of the speaker.
Zachariah Hood began his speech: "Good People—for Country
Men I dare not call you—having forfeited all Claim or Title to that
Appellation—Wonder not at my Hesitation of Speech, or my Sighs
and Groans on this sad Occasion—The Powers of Utterance being
in a great Measure taken from me by the Sight of that mournful
Object." The word "forfeited" makes it sound as if he was going to
confess and repent. But he did not. Instead, he was overcome with
grief at the sight of the corpse of the Stamp Act. He did not curse the
day the Stamp Act was passed or the day it went into effect; he
cursed the day the people of Frederick Town decided to ignore the
Act and resume their business without stamps. Zachariah Hood the
man, even though he advocated the Stamp Act, would not have said
what his effigy said. The language of the effigy reveals not Hood's
(either the real Hood's or the effigy Hood's) view of himself, but the
audience's view of him.

> And must all my Hopes perish, my Schemes for advancing my Fortune
> at the Expence of my Country be blasted, and public Emolument tri-
> umph over private Gain! —Shall *Maryland* freely export her Wheat and
> Corn, and find out Markets for her Flour and Provisions without my

Participation in the Fruits of the Toil and Sweat of her laborious Sons!
—Shall the Press continue Free, and exist only to publish my Disgraces, and instill Notions of Constitutional Rights and Liberties into the Minds of *North-Americans*! —Shall the Power of Taxing the Poor (who are chiefly involved in the Duties of the Stamp-Act) by imposing an arbitrary Price on stamped Paper be wrested from me; and instead of Lording it over my country-men, must I needs be reduced to the State of an Exile, a Fugitive and a Vagabond on the Face of the Earth!

A man who saw nothing wrong in backing the Stamp Act would not have used words like "scheme" and "arbitrary" and would not have talked of taxing the poor (even if that was what he was doing) or of lording it over his countrymen. Instead, he would have talked of sharing the expenses of the Empire and would have mentioned the sovereignty of Parliament, the indivisible nature of sovereignty, and taxation as a function of sovereignty. There can be no power within a power, he might have said, and he might have given authority to the argument by saying it in Latin, *non imperium in imperio*. By having the last words and dying speech of a recalcitrant stamp distributor written from the perspective of the colonial audience, the designers of the mock ceremony managed to juxtapose the refusal to repent with a confession of guilt. The effigy said, not what Hood thought, nor what the crowd thought he thought, but what the crowd thought he *should* be thinking and revealing about himself, given his "immoral" approval of the Stamp Act. The parody served to reveal Zachariah Hood's character to the public. Because the form and language of the speech contradicted the message of the speech, the speech of the effigy exposed the self-deception of the man.

Effigy stamp distributors were men with no life story. Questions such as why they had been appointed, why they had accepted, and would they resign, never arose. The mock execution functioned as a modified form of the medieval morality play, in which personified abstractions vied for the soul of "Everyman." In the colonial version of good versus evil on the battleground of man, the protagonist was the stamp distributor who, instead of representing Everyman, represented "the Wicked Man." The Wicked Man was seen with his counselors—but only the evil counselors: the British ministers and the Devil—and usually he was not seen in the throes of a decision, wavering between good and evil, but after the decision had been made. (Even when he was depicted in the act of rejecting Liberty, he was not seen torn between conflicting allegiances: his heart was already hard.) Because the Wicked Man had made the wrong choice, his good counselors—Patriotism, his Country, Liberty—melted away, and he was left to consort with the evil counselors and reap on the scaffold the consequences of succumbing to temptation. The drama did not lie in the decision, but in the consequences of the decision.

At the same time that colonists presented generic stamp distributors as the embodiment of evil, villains by definition, they took pains to treat individual stamp distributors as men of honor and reason who could be persuaded to resign their office. In real life, Zachariah Hood was one of the most intransigent of the stamp distributors. Fearful of bodily injury, afraid for his life, but not willing to resign, he fled Maryland and made his way as a fugitive northwards through New York City and on to Long Island. Here local patriots discovered him at the town of Flushing, and a delegation waited on him to urge his resignation.[35] Hood turned out to be a bit of a whiner. Twisting and turning, he tried to avoid any irrevocable act that might deprive him of future profits in better times. He excused his acceptance of the office by telling the delegation of all the services he had rendered to his colony, services he presumably thought entitled him to the rewards of a lucrative office, and he tried to arouse their sympathies by dwelling on his expectations and disappointments. He had been long absent from Maryland and his friends, working for their advantage, and naturally he had expected "an agreeable and endearing reception" together with "the pleasing prospect of a genteel Subsistence for Life." In every way he had been totally disappointed, and therefore, he wailed, he should be the object of compassion and not resentment.

If Hood hoped to wriggle out of resigning by this display of self-pity, he missed the mark. The delegation, though they treated him with "as much tenderness as the case would permit," said that if he did not resign they would hand him over to the emotional crowd, and he would be passed from one town to another, like a criminal,

---

35. The following account comes from the *New-York Mercury*, 9 December 1765, and the *Pennsylvania Journal*, 5 December 1765, 12 December 1765.

with labels signifying his office and designs, until he was delivered into the hands of the people of Maryland. Hood did not find the prospect appealing, but he seems to have taken a narrowly personal view of his situation and failed to comprehend the issues involved. Realizing that he would have to resign, he tried to stipulate conditions for his resignation, and the conditions he stipulated indicate that he saw the office as a piece of property he did not wish to relinquish. Therefore, while the delegation was urging him to resign absolutely a commission that would enslave the colonies, Hood asked permission to have first dibs on the office if it were ever later to go into effect after the crisis subsided. Clinging to his sense of personal injury, dwelling on his personal losses, he seemed unable to wrap his mind around the idea that the object of popular protest was not to persecute him but to annihilate the office.

Hood made one last stab at cutting his losses by proposing to make a declaration upon his honor, a strategy that would relieve him of swearing an oath. He pointed out that Peter De Lancey of New York had given his word of honor only, which patriots had accepted as a valid resignation. But the delegation, far from satisfied with Hood's proposal, insisted on an oath given before a magistrate in public. Although they did not come right out and say that their confidence in Hood's sense of honor was limited, they did point out the difference between De Lancey's situation and Hood's. De Lancey had been ready and willing to give up the office and had resigned among his friends and relations. His respect for his friends and relations and his need to maintain their respect served as security for his behavior, since he could not break his word without dishonoring them as well as himself. In other words, De Lancey still had a stake in the community, which he would forfeit if he broke his word. Zachariah Hood, on the other hand, was a stranger in New York who could lay no claim to the trust of the inhabitants. He had been obstinate in holding onto the office and had fled his own colony without resigning. At eight o'clock in the evening, Hood finally acquiesced in the demands of the delegation. He was then put in a chair and carried four or five miles to the nearest magistrate, who lived in Jamaica. A hundred people accompanied him from Flushing to Jamaica "in regular order," some in carriages, others on horseback or on foot. At Jamaica he took his oath.

> I Do, hereby, with the utmost Cheerfulness and Willingness promise to resign the said Office of *Distributor of STAMPS;* and Do, without any Equivocation or mental Reservation, solemnly declare, that I never will, directly or indirectly, either by myself or any other Person, serve in the said Office.

Of all the stamp distributors, Hood seemed to have conformed most closely to the generic stamp distributor of the pageants—a man motivated by greed, oblivious to the plight of his country. And yet the New York delegation treated him "tenderly," listened to his excuses and self-justifications, and tried to reason with him and explain the offensiveness of the office. And although they made clear the consequences of his refusal to comply, they did not propose to hang him. After the resignation, all was good will and harmony. Instead of exulting in victory, the crowd complimented Hood on his decision, showered him with loud "Huzzas," and invited him to an entertainment. Hood, for his part, thanked them for their politeness and humanity but excused himself from the festivities on the grounds that "he was in such a Frame of Body and Mind that he should be unhappy in Company." The delegation, assuring Hood that the people of New York bore him good will and that he could appear anywhere in the province with safety, put him in a carriage, and he was escorted back to his lodging by a jubilant crowd who drank constitutional toasts and went off into the night with great humor and joy.

The resignations of stamp distributors had common features: they took place in public; the man resigning professed his "cheerfulness" and "willingness" and denied any "equivocation or mental reservation"; and the ceremony ended in a public demonstration of reconciliation and joy. Almost all the men who had been appointed stamp distributors publicly promised not to exercise their office. Although some (De Lancey of New York and William Coxe of New Jersey) promised on their honor neither to accept nor to execute the office, most took an oath very similar to that of Zachariah Hood. If stamp distributors swore with "cheerfulness and willingness," they could not later be absolved on the claim of coercion. If they swore "without any equivocation or mental reservation," they could not later appeal to a higher authority. (English Catholics in the seventeenth century who, in spite of the official policy of their country, still maintained that the pope was the head of the church, avoided the spiritual consequence of their oath of allegiance to the King of England, who was the head of the Church of England, by later claiming a mental reservation to the oral or written oath they had taken.) Stamp distributors were denied any mental maneuvering to escape the impasse. The oath of resignation was designed to entrap the conscience of the appointee and restrict his future action. By designing a "voluntary" oath with no room for mental finger-crossing, patriots tried to eliminate the office of stamp distributor without eliminating the men who had been appointed to the office. Luckily for the effectiveness of this policy of distinction between person and office, no stamp distributor stood on his conscience and refused to take a voluntary oath under compulsion.

Yet surely colonists must have seen the futility of coercing stamp distributors into taking a voluntary oath. The resignation ceremonies may have prevented the appointed stamp distributors from exercising their office, but the colonists would have been naïve indeed to treat these ceremonies as evidence of harmony restored. The clue to this colonial complacence lies in the mock funerals. When the effigy Zachariah Hood presented his own case in the condemnatory language of the colonists, the language of the speech served as a confession, while the speaker persisted in his unrepentance as if he did not understand his own words. The patriots were making use of an old Puritan device for dealing with people whose theological views did not jibe with the accepted doctrine of the community. Ministers tried to persuade heretics of their errors, but if they failed in their efforts at persuasion, they claimed that the heretic was in fact sinning against his own conscience. In the resignation ceremonies, the stamp distributor was handing over his conscience to the community. He was not acting under duress, because he was acting according to his "true" conscience, and the community was not coercing him but saving him. They could therefore take heart in the fiction of his willingness and cheerfulness.

Stamp distributors took an oath of resignation in public and took it "cheerfully" and "willingly." The patriot leaders, for their part, made every effort to protect the character of the men who resigned. James McEvers, the man appointed stamp distributor for New York, appeared before Governor Cadwallader Colden and the Governor's Council and declined to accept the office. The Sons of Liberty, however, desired McEvers to make a further public resignation, but they protected McEvers' character by announcing that their request for a further resignation was "not in consequences of any kind of Jealousy in the *Sons of Liberty,* of his having an Inclination to act at any Time in the said Office."[36] They just wanted the proper procedure to be followed, and the proper procedure was a public resignation. At the same time, then, that patriots were blackening the character of stamp distributors in mock ceremonies and making a personal effigy the embodiment of evil, they insulated the character of stamp distributors in actual confrontations; and even as they identified the office with the man in mock ceremonies, they distinguished between the office and the man in real life.

Resignation ceremonies ended in a public demonstration of joy in which the former stamp distributor was treated like a hero. The outward display of respect put a seal on unity. Even someone so much disliked and so little trusted as Zachariah Hood received approval when he resigned. The respect with which New Yorkers treated Hood after his resignation put a formal end to his life as a fugitive. In most cases, however, stamp distributors resigned in their own colony and were reincorporated into their own community. Jared Ingersoll, the stamp distributor for Connecticut, was intercepted by a crowd on his way to Hartford to plead his case before the Assembly and pressured into resigning on the spot. At the suggestion of the crowd, Ingersoll said "liberty and property" three times, while the crowd cheered. "Mr. Ingersoll then went to a Tavern, and dined with several of the Company."[37] The resignation ceremony bore witness to restored harmony. In Wilmington, North Carolina, around four hundred citizens waited on the stamp distributor, William Houston, with drums beating and flags waving and asked if he intended to carry out his office. He answered evasively that "[h]e should be very sorry to execute any office disagreeable to the people of the province."[38] The crowd, less interested in his sorrow than in his intentions, carried him off to the courthouse to sign an official resignation. Now, Houston had not exactly clapped his hands with glee at the opportunity to resign. A certain reluctance and ambivalence might have been detected in his behavior. Yet still, when he did

---

36. *Pennsylvania Journal,* 12 December 1765.

37. *Massachusetts Gazette and Boston News-Letter,* 26 September 1765.

38. *Pennsylvania Journal,* 2 January 1766, Supplement.

resign, the crowd was overjoyed and treated him like a hero. They put him in an armchair and carried him around the courthouse, stopping at every corner to give three huzzahs. Then they carried him home and deposited him on the doorstep, formed a circle around him, and once again gave three huzzahs. Still they could not bear to leave him. So they accompanied him into his house and poured him the finest liquors. Throughout they treated him with extreme gentility.

In mock executions, the effigies of stamp distributors were treated as criminals, traitors, and heretics—men who had forfeited their membership in the community by betraying it. Hanging the stamp distributors along with British ministers and the Devil, the crowd pitted them against their own country and transformed them into foreigners, strangers, and exiles as a justification for execution. The community was executing an outsider, not one of its own members. In the resignation ceremonies, on the other hand, the real stamp distributors were treated as members of the community who had gone astray but whom the community wanted to reincorporate. By taking an oath not to execute an office the community disapproved of, they were reinstated in the community and harmony was restored. Stamp distributors resigned in such a way as to prove their allegiance: publicly, cheerfully, and willingly. The act of resignation was an act of naturalization, an avowal that the affinities of the stamp distributor lay with the colonies and that he was once again a member of the community.

The political success of mock ceremonies draws attention away from the plight of stamp distributors, but from their point of view, of course, the danger of the situation, the potential for violence, was not mock danger and was not dissolved by ritual. They could never be sure that they would not follow their effigies to the scaffold. At the center of the make-believe ceremonies, real people endured real suffering. All the stamp distributors were subjected to intimidation; several suffered property damage; some were roughed up physically; and a few were victims of brutality. Nonetheless, none was hanged and the majority were treated with formality.[39] While stamp distribu-

---

39. For the treatment of individual stamp distributors, see Edmund S. Morgan and Helen M. Morgan, *The Stamp Act Crisis: Prologue to Revolution* (1953; New York, 1963), 180–204; for the intimidation practiced by the Sons of Liberty in Connecti-

tors, caught in the throes of uncertainty, with their lives at stake, could not predict the outcome, the outcome in fact, given the intensity of feeling, was relatively benign. It certainly could have been worse. The mock execution, seemingly so provocative, had set procedures and a defined goal that limited the action of the crowd and controlled violence.

*   *   *

In 1764 and 1765, colonists, new to the business of organized political resistance, tried three different approaches: economic, moral, and ironic. Economic measures, such as reducing importation and consumption of British goods, were designed to pressure English merchants to lobby in Parliament for repeal of the Sugar and Stamp Acts. These economic measures, in turn, launched a moral movement. Colonists justified abstention and asceticism on moral as well as economic grounds. Measures such as reducing the cost of funerals by eliminating mourning paraphernalia and mementos made colonists feel more virtuous and less susceptible to corruption. In addition to reviewing their own behavior, colonists fingered people whom they held responsible for taxation measures and people who approved of the measures because they stood to benefit from them personally. Having identified the victims, colonists contained violence by liquidating them in effigy, rather than in the flesh. The moral mode of resistance and the ironic one worked together in uneasy alliance. If colonists cast the blame for the political crisis elsewhere, they did not need to put themselves under intense scrutiny, and if they could identify specific people who were bringing ruin on the colonies, in the long run real people, not effigies, would feel the rub of the noose.

Mock executions and funerals served a purpose: they encouraged stamp distributors to resign and they swaddled colonial sensitivities. Feeling themselves victims, colonists created victims of their own and asserted control over a situation that threatened to swamp them. They could arrange the outcome of ceremonies to their liking, untrammeled by any restrictions that reality might impose. But fear and dissension might tear apart a society cluttered with victims. Mock

---

cut, see Lawrence Henry Gipson, *American Loyalist: Jared Ingersoll* (New Haven, Conn., 1971), 149–228.

ceremonies in fact presented acts that colonists did not want to happen. They did not want to execute stamp distributors; they wanted stamp distributors to resign. They did not want recalcitrance; they wanted conversion.

In 1765, when the British Parliament passed the Stamp Act, the American colonists thought themselves wronged. In 1774, when Parliament passed the Coercive Acts, American colonists again thought they had been wronged. A sense of injustice is often allied with a sense of powerlessness. In 1765, colonists dealt with their sense of powerlessness ritualistically and ironically. They buttonholed an elusive ministry and demanded of it intimacy and personal contact by creating surrogate victims who, unlike real people, could be mutilated, hanged, and immolated with impunity. In the make-believe world of 1764 to 1765, stamp distributors died, and their death, like the deaths of the giant in "Jack and the Beanstalk" and the witch in "Hansel and Gretel," solved the problem of moral evil. But ceremonies that fulfilled wishes of colonists also relieved them of responsibility both for their actions (the executions were not really executions) and for their situation. The ceremonies rallied colonists to the cause and offered an emotional outlet that was not too destructive, but the ceremonies centered attention on aggressors (Englishmen and their allies) and not on the colonists themselves—on resentment, not on reform. In 1774, colonists responded to the Coercive Acts in much the same way that they had responded to the Stamp Act ten years earlier: by holding a continental congress, sending petitions to England, and organizing economic boycotts of English goods. But they did not depend so heavily on irony, and they modulated their practical measures with intensive self-scrutiny, a characterological examination that went well beyond the scope of the immediate political crisis. This time around, colonists confronted parliamentary aggression, less with mockery (an admission of their own impotence), than with unadulterated moral reformation. They took measures to resist corruption and slavery by strengthening their own will, rather than dissipating energy on ceremonies that exposed the corruption of others but did not solve the problem of a parliament intent on establishing its sovereignty.

The moral movement of 1774 burst the confines of economic pragmatism. Members of the First Continental Congress, meeting in October of 1774, set aside a parcel of time amidst the hurly-burly of petitions, letters, and boycotts to consider the question of a national character. Although the political activity of the Congress focused on the publicity of self-justification and on economic measures designed to bring about repeal of the Coercive Acts, tucked away between forbidden exports and imports there appeared a list of renunciations that were to hold sway throughout the colonies. With the exception of funeral regulations, these measures were not designed to affect England. A ban on mourning apparel might put pressure on English merchants to lobby in Parliament against legislation offensive to the colonists, but a colonial ban on cockfighting and horse-racing would not close down the "Royal Cockpit" or prevent the horses from running or the bets from flying at Newmarket. News of American morality would not break up English faro games. The dice would still roll and the cards fall at White's, and the earls and the gentlemen would continue to stake bets of 1,000, 2,000, or even 3,000 guineas on a cock main or a horse race or a hand of macao, unruffled by the congressional fiat. But though Englishmen would not feel the pinch of the colonists' renunciations, the renunciations did bear reference to England. The members of Congress selected the activities to black-list while looking over their shoulders at England. In fastening on cockfighting, horse-racing, and theater attendance (all activities far more popular and widespread in England than in the colonies), Congress was indirectly presenting colonists with a package of English life against which they could measure their own moral strength and feel superior by virtue of their own renunciations. Together, the activities added up to English life in the raw, a life of unbridled sensuality that was threatening to suck the colonists down in the same undertow of corruption. Even within the lifetime of the members of Congress, these English activities were rapidly gaining in popularity in the colonies. In renouncing horse races, cockfights, theater, cards, dice, and extravagant funerals, the colonists were stepping out on their own. They preened a bit and bustled about, but the course they followed, however trivial the steps appeared, dissociated them as a people from the English as a people and prepared the ground for a declaration of independence.

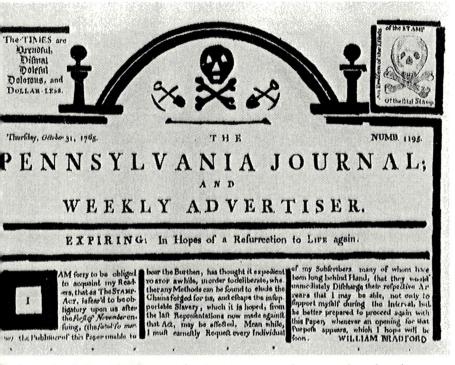

The Pennsylvania Journal and some other newspapers went into mourning when the
Stamp Act was to go into effect. *Library of Congress*

In this mock funeral, British officials, heavy with grief, carry a child's coffin containing Miss Americ Stamp, who was born in 1765 and died in 1766, to the vault of British traitors. A dog urinates on the officiating minister, who holds the burial service and funeral sermon. Two of the mourners carry black flags bearing the stamp. The ships in the background are named after British ministers who opposed the Stamp Act. After the death of Miss Americ Stamp, commerce begins again. America ships bales of unused stamps and mourning materials to England. "The Repeal. or the Funeral Procession, of Miss

People of all classes and occupations were swept up in the furor of betting on cock-fights. Hogarth suggests the moral corruption of the activity by depicting several of the participants as physically deformed. *William Hogarth, "The Cockpit"*

Cocks were specially cut out for fighting and silver spurs were fastened to their legs. "Cock Fighting," *The Sportsman's Cyclopedia* (London, 1831). *Special Collections Division, Michigan State University Libraries*

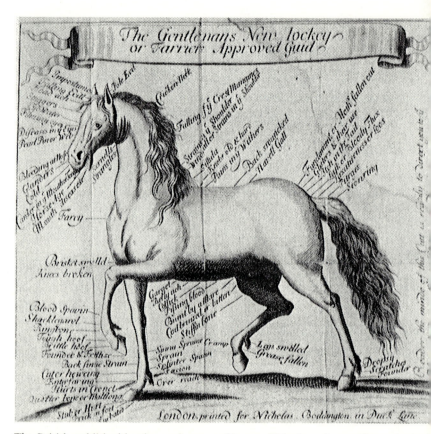

The British published books on the care of horses. This chart shows where a horse might develop health problems. The British also bred horses for different tasks. *The Gentleman's New Jockey or Farrier's Approved Guide* (London, 1687). *Special Collections Division, Michigan State University Libraries*

The British used draft horses for many purposes. *Essays on Husbandry* (London, 1764). *Special Collections Division, Michigan State University Libraries*

An *Englifh* HARROW, in the year 1669.

The British on their farms practiced animal husbandry. This print shows several fat animals gathered in a courtyard. R. W. Dickson, *A Complete System of Improved Live Stock and Cattle Management* (London, 1822). *Special Collections Division, Michigan State University Libraries*

The British were encouraged to feed their hogs in a central courtyard. In the American colonies, hogs ran wild and foraged for themselves. *A Compleat Body of Husbandry* (London, 1756). *Special Collections Division, Michigan State University Libraries*

British farm life was concentrated on a central yard. British farmers, therefore, could easily collect dung to be used as fertilizer. This picture shows the design for a dung pit in the middle of the farm yard. *A Complete Body of Husbandry* (London, 1756). *Special Collections Division, Michigan State University Libraries*

This detail from a post–Civil War print illustrates the association of slavery with the hoe and freedom with the plow. Detail from "Family Record." *Library of Congress*

In this mezzotint, a group of North Carolina women cluster around a document that reads "We the Ladys of Edenton do hereby Solemnly Engage not to Conform to tha Pernicious Custom of Drinking Tea, or that we the aforesaid Ladys will not promote the wear of any Manufacture from England untill such time that all Acts which tend to Enslave this our Native Country shall be Repealed." At the left, a woman dumps tea from a caddy into the hat of a man standing in the doorway. At the bottom right a dog pisses on a tea caddy. "A Society of Patriotic Ladies, At Edenton in North Carolina" (London, 1775). *Library of Congress*

A loyalist in Virginia has been "persuaded" to sign a patriotic document (probably the Association or Resolutions drawn up by the Williamsburg Convention). The documents on the makeshift table are entitled *The Resolves of the Congress* and *Non Importation*. To the left, another loyalist is being dragged toward the gallows, labeled "A Cure for the Refractory." From one arm of the gallows swings a bag of feathers; from the other, a barrel of tar. One of the loyalist's captors brandishes a pair of scissors to cut off his victim's hair prior to tarring and feathering him. In the upper left a statue of Botetourt, a governor who was popular with Virginians, points towards the gallows. "The Alternative of Williams-Burg" (London, 1775). *Library of Congress*

In England, communities branded moral deviants by parading them through the streets in public rituals called "skimmingtons." Participants made noise and ridiculed and dehumanized the victim. Here one man brandishs horns on a pole with a nightshirt. To the left a boy slings a dead dog, while a man urinates on the wall. In the Revolutionary period, Americans developed a political version of the skimmington—tarring and feathering. Victims were marked off as political deviants. William Hogarth, "Hudibras XII: Encounters the Skimmington."

Tarring and feathering, brutality that stopped short of murder, both intimidated and dehumanized the victim. Here five patriots, jerking John Malcolm's head back, pour tea down his throat until he vomits. A noose is tied around his neck and held by one of the patriots. Another noose hangs from a branch of the liberty tree. The Stamp Act is tacked upside down to the tree. In the lower left a liberty cap on a pole rests beside the tar bucket. "The Bostonians Paying the Excise-Man, or Tarring & Feathering" (London, 1774). *Library of Congress*

This depiction of tarring and feathering accentuates the dehumanization of the victim, who is thrust forward on all fours in a position to be served by the devil, himself part beast. Mezzotint (177?). *Library of Congress*

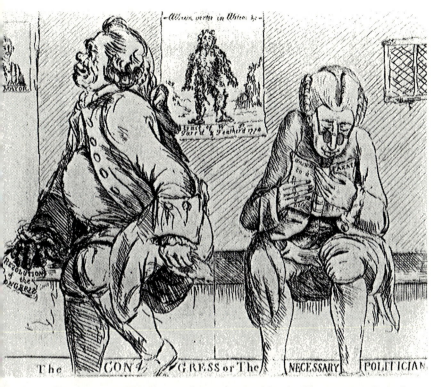

The CON GRESS or The NECESSARY POLITICIAN

Members of Congress, caught in an embarrassing position in "the necessary," are degraded even as they themselves degraded the man in the print on the wall. One uses the resolutions of his own congress as toilet paper, while the other pores over a patriot pamphlet answering Samuel Johnson's *Taxation no Tyranny*. Excrement was used in prints and in public rituals to defile victims. "The Congress or The Necessary Politicians" (1775?). *Library of Congress*

The Grafton administration is attacked and defiled by its enemies. The Chevalier D'Eon, with a head like an ape, vomits on the Earl of Bute, while a doctor prepares to prime another weapon. To the left an Indian, representing America, shoots an arrow at a fallen minister, probably the Earl of Hillsborough, Secretary of State for the North American Colonies, who is being trampled by his colleagues. "The Chevalier D" . . . a producing his Evidence against certain Persons" (August 12,

is pro-British print ridicules America and her allies. France, a seasick fop, vomits on
merica, a fallen Indian with a feathered headdress. Spain bleeds from one eye. Holland
fat and impotent. "Jack England Fighting the Four Confederates" (London, 1781).
rary of Congress

British ministers abuse a half-naked America. Lord North forces tea down her throat, while she vomits in his face. Sandwich lewdly peers up her skirt, while England, the only other female, turns away in horror. A petition from Boston lies in shreds in the foreground, while Boston is being cannonaded in the background. "The able Doctor, or America Swallowing the Bitter Draught" (May 1, 1774). *Library of Congress*

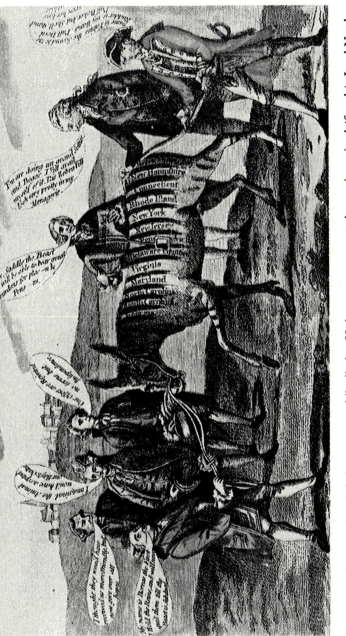

An exotic animal, a zebra, is being put on public display. Various men act upon the passive animal (female). Lord North holds the reins and says he "will never quit them till the Beast is subdued." To his left, three peace commissioners try to lure the zebra with hay and oats. George Grenville is putting a saddle marked "Stamp Act" on her back. To the right, France says she will look very pretty in his menagerie. Beside him, George Washington pulls her tail and says "Pull Devil—Pull Baker, but She'll Stand upon her legs at last." "The Curious Zebra, alive from America! walk in Gem'men and Ladies, walk in" (London, 1778). *Library of Congress*

Above: Dogs pee everywhere in the political prints. This one is defiling the British lion. Detail from "A Picturesque View of the State of the Nation for February 1778." *Library of Congress*

Right: The devil is usually depicted as half beast and half human. The great seducer, his sexual prowess is often stressed. Detail from "A Political, Anatomical, Satirical, Lecture on Heads and No Heads; as Exhibited at St. J___s's 1766." *Library of Congress*

I hand them off

★ 7 ★

Animals and Politics

W H E N Josiah Quincy, a dyed-in-the-wool New Englander, arrived in Charleston, South Carolina, in 1773, people in mourning
dress seemed to swarm everywhere. When he went to a public assembly, half the people there, both men and women, came in mourning
dress. Quincy had been eleven years old when the Stamp Act crisis had
dampened New Englanders' enthusiasm for a costly and showy response to death. Lavish funerals featuring fashionable mourning dress
and numerous gifts would have been only a childhood memory to
him. So all the black crepe, bombazine, and silk darkening the general
hue of social gatherings must have impinged on his consciousness.

Quincy noticed other things besides mourning: the quality of the
dancing, the elegant appearance of the food (its taste impressed him
less favorably), the sensibility of the toasts. But he did not come to
South Carolina to be overawed. Quincy was neither one of those
who favored everything strange over his own culture nor one who
denigrated foreign customs and thanked God for the blessed superiority of his own. The food, while elegantly disposed, was ruined by
improper dressing; the wines were indifferent; and the dancing, no
matter how graceful, could not disguise the music.

Quincy was not to be swept off his feet. But South Carolina did
offer him one completely new experience. Quincy arrived in time for
the biggest horse race of the season. And this year patriotism added
to the tension of competition. Flimnap, an English-bred stallion, was

185

matched against Little David, native-born, who had won his last sixteen races. By the end of the afternoon, Little David had lost, 2,000 pounds sterling had changed hands, and Quincy had picked up some equine parlance. He now knew a little of the "singular art of the Turf," and he had seen a "prodigious fine collection of excellent, though very high-priced horses."[1]

As Quincy made his way up the coast, he continued to hear much talk of racing, French horns, bassoons, and violins. But in Virginia he encountered a far more unpleasant activity than watching horses run or listening to out-of-tune quartets: "the vile practice of cock-fighting equally degrading sense, sentiment, and humanity." Quincy read three or four advertisements of cockfights in the Williamsburg paper; he witnessed five matches in his journeys from Williamsburg to Port-Royal; and near the Potomac he spent an afternoon with some rich young Virginians who could talk of nothing but the pit and the turf.

When Congress banned cockfighting and horse-racing, it banned activities that had become part of life in the colonies south of New England.

i

In England in the seventeenth century, but more especially in the eighteenth century, enthusiasm for cockfighting penetrated cities, towns, and countryside. Critics responded with an assault on the sport. From the standard criticisms of cockfighting we can glean values that members of Congress sought to reinforce by banning cockfighting. An analysis of the sport and the criticism it engendered enhances our understanding of the self-perception of the embattled colonists, who felt threatened by more than the political acts of Parliament.

Critics objected to cockfighting as a sport because of what men did to cocks and because of what cockfighting did to men. It was admitted that cocks fought each other naturally, but this natural disposition to fight did not justify putting cocks together in order to make them fight, betting on the outcome, and in general deriving pleasure from the suffering of animals. First of all, men themselves were

1. Josial Quincy, Jr., "Journal," in MHS, *Proceedings* 49 (1915–1916): 451.

responsible for the cock's disposition to fight, because it was Adam's fall that had introduced sin into the world. "[T]he Antipathy, and Cruelty, which one Beast sheweth to another, is the fruit of our Rebellion against God, and should rather move us to mourn than to rejoice."[2] Critics pointed to the cruelty of arranging fights that had no use other than entertainment. Animals preyed on other animals for food and fought each other to protect their families. Such behavior, while violent, served a purpose. But men had made killing into an art to be enjoyed by spectators. "[I]t *scandals* me extreamly, to see *Christians,* those who professe to have their Bosomes a Nest for the *Heavenly Dove,* to be Companions of the *Lamb of God,* to *Recreate* themselves in *Blood,* though it be of the meanest Creatures."[3]

Modern studies in animal behavior show that animal aggression in nature is a ritualistic behavior that rarely ends in death unless the species is exerting too much pressure on the environment. Animals do not prey on members of their own species, and when they prey on other animals they are not manifesting symptoms of aggression. Animal aggression serves a purpose in nature. Eighteenth-century Englishmen may have lived before scientific studies of red-bellied sticklebacks, but they knew that cockfighting as it was practiced in the pit was unnatural.

The defense of cockfighting on the grounds that cocks fought each other naturally seemed feeble in view of the elaborate preparation that breeders took to turn their cocks into vehicles of destruction and in view of the rules of cockfighting, which were designed to prolong fights as long as possible and increase the chances that the fight would end in death. Even the environment, the confinement in a rimmed pit that offered no escape, virtually ensured the destruction of one of the two cocks.

Cocks usually did not fight until they were two years old, although occasionally one-year-olds were entered in a contest. A cock's training would begin two weeks to one month before the fight. He would be taken from his walk and put in a pen where for four days he would be fed on crumbs of old manchet, a white bread made with wheatmeal and oatmeal kneaded into a stiff paste with ale, egg

---

2. Edmund Elys, *The Opinion of Mr. Perkins, and Mr. Bolton and others concerning the Sport of Cock-fighting* (Oxford, 1660), 5.

3. Elys, *Cock-fighting,* 4.

whites, and butter. After the manchet had purged the cock of corn, worms, and gravel, he would begin a regimen of sparring and chasing. When cocks sparred, their heels were covered up with a pair of "lots made of rolled-up leather." After sparring, the cocks were given a diaphoretic or sweat bath. The trainer would take deep straw caskets, fill them a quarter full with straw, put one cock in each basket, and then fill the baskets the rest of the way up with straw. "Let them sweat, but do not forget to give them first some sugar-candy, chopt rosemary and butter, mingled together; let the quantity be about the bigness of a walnut; by so doing you will cleanse their grease, increase their strength, and prolong their breath."[4] The trainer alternated sparring with chasing. On chasing days the trainer held a "dung hill" cock in his arms and enticed the fighting cock to follow. The training encouraged a cock to follow his opponent even when not himself threatened. Four days before the match, all training stopped while the cock rested.

Cocks were turned into death machines. Their own spurs were sawed off to about a quarter of an inch, and artificial spurs, or "gaffes," were fastened to their legs and bound on with waxed thread. Silver spurs were preferred to steel spurs, because they were less deadly and the fight would therefore last longer. Besides being armed, the cock was "cut out" for the fight: his comb was cut down short, so that the other cock could not so easily grab hold of it and rip off the whole scalp. The wing feathers were trimmed at a slope to make them sharp, and the hackle and rump feathers were shortened so that the other cock would have less to get his beak into. The bird that appeared in the pit was man's invention to amuse himself. He bore little resemblance to a cock defending his hens and his territory from intruders.

Breeders challenged each other to "mains," a series of fights. Short mains would last two to three days; long mains, four to seven days. Usually around six to eight battles took place each day. A breeder might "show" forty-one cocks for a set amount for each battle—five to ten guineas was a usual bet; and for a set amount for the main— anywhere from twenty guineas to a thousand. In England, mains

---

4. Nicholas Coxe, *The Nobleman and Gentleman's Recreation* (London, 1812), 85. Coxe has for the most part copied Gervase Markham's *The Pleasures of Princes* (London, 1635).

might take place between two individuals, two towns, two counties, a county and an individual, etc. And of course spectators could place their own bets. These wagers bore no relation to the official stakes. Cocker manuals that offered advice on breeding and printed the rules and regulations for fights often devoted three-quarters of their space to betting odds.

The rules of cockfighting were designed to keep cocks fighting to the death, if possible. "Setters on" put the cocks into the pit and could not touch the cocks again except to extricate them from the matting. If a cock refused to fight, the setters-on would pick up the two cocks and face them breast to breast. If one refused to fight, the other eventually was declared the winner. But elaborate rules made this outcome of the fight extremely unlikely. When a bird refused to fight, the "law was told" by a man counting twice twenty. If he reached forty and the fight had not recommenced, both birds were taken up and placed beak to beak in the center of the pit. They could not be touched again until one or both had refused to fight for as long as it took the teller of the law to tell ten, at which point both birds were again picked up and set beak to beak. A cock was "told out" only after he had refused to fight ten times in succession. If, having refused nine times, he even so much as pecked the other cock, the "long law" had to be told all over again. The ten refusals had to follow each other with no fighting, motion, or aggression between the tellings before a cock could lose a fight and still remain alive.

Cockers went to great lengths to keep the fights going until the death. For example, cocks were meant to be set bill to bill, but when they were "far spent," exceptions were made to this rule. "[I]f either be blind, then the *blind* COCK *to touch;* if either be drawn neck'd, then his *Head to be held fair,* and even with the other Cock, so that the Party do his best in setting too, to make his Cock fight."[5] In short, men took a natural phenomenon, the aggression of cocks, and made it into something unnatural. And unnatural pursuits, critics argued, corrupted men.

Cock-breeding threatened community cohesiveness by generating suspicion. In the cockpit itself men learned to cheat. Although some manuals in their enthusiasm for the sport denied the existence of cheating, most warned their readers to beware, "for there are cer-

5. Reginald Heber, *An Historical List of Horse-Matches Run* (London, 1752), 150.

tainly many who bubble the ignorant and credulous, and purchase money and good apparel with everlasting shame and infamy."[6] The high stakes and cheating of the English cockpit impressed a visiting Frenchman at the end of the seventeenth century. "Cock-fighting is one of the great English diversions: they build Amphitheaters for this," he observed. But "a man may be damnably bubbled if he is not very sharp."[7] Cheating could take many forms. Because cocks could be crippled so easily (quick pressure exerted by the thumb and finger could strap a thigh), anyone who handled the cock was a target for bribery. Sometimes the man responsible for feeding a cock, if bribed, would mix the food with food taken out of the crop of another cock sick with the roop. Fraud could take place during weighing. Weighers could use weights filled with wax to falsify a cock's weight. Sometimes cocks were exchanged during trimming, after bets had been placed. Or a breeder might rub the face of his cock with flour and grease to make him look "stale" or with blacking to make him look "rotten." Illegal spurs might be used. During the fight, crafty setters could make a difference in the outcome. When the spur of one cock became lodged in the other cock, the setter for the victim cock was allowed to dislodge it. If he had been bribed he might twist the spur around and yank a big hole in the cock which would result in heavy bleeding. Or a setter could pretend he did not notice that the spur of his cock had been lodged in his opponent's cock, and might grab hold of his own cock to separate the two, holding his cock up in the air and letting the other cock be ripped with the spur and fall with great force. If a cock had been blinded in one eye, the opposing setter might try to put his own cock on the blind side of the other cock. When both cocks were refusing to fight, one setter might slip his hand under his cock's head and make it appear as if the cock had pecked when he had not.

Cockfighting undermined the Christian concept of community by turning neighbors against neighbors, and friends against friends. Christians promulgated generosity and openness; cock-breeders, suspicion. Christians taught honesty; cheating abounded in the cockpit. While the preacher in the pulpit urged men to give to those in need and to love neighbors, manuals for cock-breeders recommended that

6. Coxe, *Gentleman's Recreation,* Introduction.

7. Misson, quoted in Sir Walter Gilbey, *Sport in Olden Time* (London, 1912), 42.

breeders should regard neighbors as potential enemies. As soon as a breeder could distinguish his pullets from his cocks, he should kill all the pullets, suggested one manual.

[F]or was you to be visited by any of your friends, their seeing so many pullets, might induce them to solicit one, and if they are persons you wish to oblige, you cannot deny their request; the consequence of which will be, if ever any of these gentlemen should take part in a match against you, your cocks will have to fight against their own relations: which leads me to think, that gentlemen who follow this diversion should live with their friends as if they would one time or another become their enemies.[8]

In 1759, William Hogarth drew a picture of a cockfight, which he presented as a satanic version of Leonardo da Vinci's "Last Supper."[9] In place of the quiet and stability of the Last Supper, all is noise and confusion at the cockfight. A man taking snuff in the outer ring spills some on the man below him, who is about to shower the whole company in a colossal sneeze. Everywhere people are lunging over other people or clawing at each other in frenzy to place bets. To the right a man pressed forward by the throng is bent over double, his head forced into the pit and his wig tumbling off, exposing a shining bald pate. His own dishabille is mirrored in the nakedness of the cocks, whose plucked bodies gleam in the pit. Hogarth has presented cockfighting as an activity that perverts communion—the love that binds people together in fellowship. In the cockfight everyone is isolated in his own passion. A blind nobleman occupies the central position of Christ, but in contrast to Christ, whose hands are extended in a gesture of giving, the nobleman is grasping the money that has been put on the fight. Physical deformities underscore spiritual isolation and lack of communication. The blind duke leads the spiritually blind crowd. Over the tumult in which no one can talk to anyone else, a deaf cripple, grabbing his hearing horn in one hand and a crutch in the other, strains to hear someone who is screaming into his horn. It is an environment in which no one can communicate

8. *Directions for Breeding Game Cocks* (London, 1780), 26.

9. For an explanation of the iconography of the print, I have relied on *Hogarth's Graphic Works*, compiled and with a commentary by Ronald Paulson (New Haven, Conn., 1965) 1:239–41.

with anyone. The lame, the halt, and the blind, maimed by their own greed, pursue their own damnation in the pit of hell.

In Leonardo's picture, Christ, who can see into the hearts of men, has just said, "One of you will betray me," and the apostles express surprise and incredulity and protest their personal innocence. But all around the gambling nobleman, acts of betrayal are taking place, and are expected. Cheating is the norm. Under the cover of a tricornered hat a young man is stealing a bill from the duke's betting pool. To the right of him a man is eavesdropping on a conversation, trying, perhaps, to get a betting tip. On the near side of the pit, a thief, using a cane, is about to pluck a purse from a drunk victim. The shadow of a man falls across the pit to the right of the fighting birds. He had been suspended in a basket over the pit because he was unable to pay his debt on the spot or satisfy his creditors. The rules and orders for cocking set the penalty for this offense.

> If any Man lay more Money than he hath to pay, or cannot satisfy the Party with whom he hath laid, either by his credit or some Friend's Word; the which if he cannot do, then he is to be put into a Basket, to be provided for that purpose, and to be hanged up in that Basket in some convenient Place in the *Cockpit*, that all Men may know him, during the time of Play that day: and also, the Party so offending never to be *admitted* to come into the *Pit*, until he hath made Satisfaction.[10]

Hogarth shows the shadow dangling a watch fob in the vain hope of placing another bet. Obsessed with gambling, he is heedless of his shame, careless of his reputation.

Hogarth associates cockfighting with crime by showing a man with a gallows chalked on his back (perhaps the hangman or perhaps a criminal destined for the gallows) and with horse-racing, another arena for betting, by depicting a famous hunchbacked jockey waving his crop. Another man, perhaps an ardent bettor, displays a band with horseshoes galloping across his back. While jockeys and criminals might be considered fringe elements of society, Hogarth conveys the impression that all of England congregates in the cockpit. It is possible to identify in the picture, besides the nobleman and the setters, a butcher, a carpenter, a newspaper

10. Heber, *Horse-Matches,* 151–52.

vendor with his Mercury helment, a post boy with his crop, a black footman, and a clergyman. (The clergyman has struck an ambiguous attitude. He may be exhorting the sinners to repent, or he may be straining to see the fight, or he may be about to sneeze.) People with useful occupations dissipate time and money. All classes mingle in a chaos that drowns decorum. While the rich man's wig tumbles into the pit, a chimney sweep, covered with soot and hugging his broom, dips snuff in the background.

The gambling that took place at cockfights turned men inward and made them oblivious of the pain and suffering of the birds. Gambling had long been recognized as an escape. Because it distracted people, gambling had been allowed at funerals. Men who were condemned to die gambled, as did men who were dangerously sick. But in eighteenth-century England, gambling distracted people from life itself. It created an artificial world in which men, distraught with anxiety, had no thought but for the outcome of a bet, no thought but for themselves. James Boswell described the numbing effect that betting had on men's sensibilities, the sharp contrast between the activity of the cockpit and the emotions that were generated in the crowd.

> The uproar and noise of betting is prodigious. . . . I was shocked to see the distraction and anxiety of the betters. I was sorry for the poor cocks. I looked round to see if any of the spectators pitied them when mangled and torn in a most cruel manner, but I could not observe the smallest relenting sign in any countenance, I was therefore not ill pleased to see them endure mental torment.[11]

Apologists for cockfighting had argued that the spectacle of two birds fighting to the death would inspire courage. (Themistocles, they pointed out, in besieging Dalmatia, had staged a cockfight for his army the night before a big battle to teach men how to fight to the death—a well-learned lesson that had resulted in glorious victory.) Cockfighting, they also argued, would arouse pity and bring men to repent their sins. But these theories ignored the effects of gambling. Gambling, in creating a situation of tension, does arouse

11. James Boswell, *London Journal,* 1762–1763, F. A. Pottle, ed. (New York, 1950), 87.

emotions, but not a sensibility that reaches out to other people and creatures; it arouses self-torturing passions. Boswell's observations are borne out by Hogarth's picture. Of the thirty-nine poeple in the picture, only four are watching the fight, and pity would not be the word to describe their emotions. That gambling undermined benevolence, the will to do good, was particularly evident in the cockpit, where men were unmoved by bleeding and pain and rejoiced in death.

Gambling offered an ironic rivalry to the religious ardor of Puritanism. In a sense Puritans and gamblers endured similar psychological tensions. Puritans, even when they had saving grace, could never be quite sure they had saving grace. If they were sure, then they were examples of the security that deadens, and were not saved. Puritans, like gamblers, put themselves on the rack. They needed to be tortured. But Puritans, unlike gamblers, clung to their insecurity because they believed in their utter helplessness before an all-powerful God. To admit to any power of their own limited the power of God. Puritans responded to their position of utter heiplessness with a frenzy of activity. They sought to control themselves, their society, and their world; not because they thought they could, but because it was God's will that they should try to. If they were saved, they loved God and would want to do his will, even though they never could. If they were not saved, they could not love God, but they would want to love God and so would still try to do his will.

Gamblers, however, take the opposite course. In order to secure their insecurity, they remove themselves from the world. They put themselves in an artificial win–lose situation, they give up all social relationships (gambling absorbs all their interest), and they play until they lose. By putting themselves in a situation over which they have no control, they reduce all the values of society to an absurdity; and yet, even though they subject themselves again and again to chance, this subjection, instead of leading them to a realization of their own helplessness, reinforces their sense of control. Gamblers keep playing until they lose, because when they are winning they think that they are responsible for winning and that therefore they will be able to win again.[12]

12. Robert D. Herman, *Gamblers and Gambling: Motives, Institutions, and Controls* (Lexington, Mass., 1976), 93–99; Edmund Bergler, *The Psychology of Gambling* (New

In the political crisis of 1774, colonists, claiming they were acting together in a common cause, depended on unanimity, dedication, and participation. Cockfighting posed a threat to values needed to make resistance successful. Community action constituted the core of resistance. Cockfighting isolated men in suspicion; gambling isolated them in passion. Colonists claimed they were being enslaved by legislative tyranny. Gambling enslaved the will. Sentiment and benevolence adorned political documents and reinforced the colonists' public stand against Great Britain. Cockfighting hardened men's hearts. The economic boycott depended on frugality and industry. In attending cockfights, people with useful occupations dissipated money and time.

ii

Formal horse-racing took hold in the colonies in the 1750s, although local informal racing had long since established itself as a form of entertainment. In Virginia in the 1720s, planters raced their horses. "The common Planters leading easy Lives don't much admire Labour, or any manly Exercise, except Horse-Racing, nor Diversion, except Cock-Fighting, in which some greatly delight."[13] Planters who came together to race or watch a race used the opportunity to discuss business and pass on news. But horse races were not regularly announced in the newspapers until the 1750s. In the New York papers, announcements appeared about once a year in the fifties and early sixties and then increased dramatically in the late sixties and early seventies to about six a year. In 1774, nine racing items were reported. Different kinds of races took place: subscription races for thoroughbreds, subscription races for non-thoroughbreds, matches between horse breeders, races at local fairs. Smaller races offered purses of twenty to fifty pounds; larger races—at Newmarket (Long

---

York, 1957), 17–18. Dostoevsky's wife described Dostoevsky's obsession with roulette. He "borrowed" his wife's money, convinced that he would win. He pawned shoes, an overcoat, his wife's jewelry—anything he could get his hands on—and then played until he lost everything. *The Diary of Dostoyevsky's Wife,* René Fülöp-Miller and Dr. Fr. Eckstein, eds., translated from the German edition by Madge Pemberton (New York, 1928), 217–404.

13. Hugh Jones, *The Present State of Virginia* (London, 1724), 48.

Island), Philadelphia, Annapolis, and Charleston—offered purses of 100 pounds. Match races were run for greater amounts: 300, 400, or even 1,000 guineas.[14] The variety of races meant that a broad spectrum of the population could participate. A young woman on her way from Philadelphia to New York in the spring of 1759 found the road crowded with country people going to a fair: "Young beaus on race horses—the girls putting on all their airs and graces to captivate, so that it was hard to find out which made the deepest impression on the young fellows' minds, horses or women."[15] A Scottish merchant on his way up from Virginia to Rockhall to catch the ferry to Annapolis stopped off at a fair. He saw two horse races and refreshed himself with punch.[16] Newspapers announced a race for three-quarter bloods for a silver tankard worth twenty pounds; a race for a saddle worth five pounds "no horse of more than ¼ blood to qualify;" a race for a bridle, saddle, and saddle cloth; a race for any horse who had never won a plate, match, or purse over ten pounds. The paper set the tone for this last race. "It is to be hoped no gentleman in Possession of a full-blooded horse will spoil sport for the value of 30 pounds."[17] Nor did all match races involve large sums. Two Philadelphians raced their horses for a quarter cask of wine.[18]

People who did not race themselves could, of course, participate by watching and betting. New Yorkers attended *en masse* a race on Hempstead Heath in Long Island in 1750. Seventy chairs and chaises came over by ferry the day before, and "it was thought the number of Horses on the Plains at the Race far exceeded a thousand."[19] In 1768, 1,000 people attended a small race at Beaver Pond, New York, for a

14. *New-York Gazette; or the Weekly Post-Boy,* 18 April 1765; *Rivington's New-York Gazetteer,* 6 September 1773.

15. "Extracts from the Diary of Hannah Callender," *Pennsylvania Magazine,* Vol. 12: 437.

16. William Gregory, "Journal, from Fredericksburg, Virginia, to Philadelphia, 30th of September, 1765, to 16th of October, 1765," *William and Mary Quarterly* XIII (1905): 228.

17. *New-York Gazette; or the Weekly Post-Boy,* 31 October 1763, 3 April 1766; *New-York Mercury,* 28 September 1767, 5 October 1767, 7 October 1771.

18. Jacob Hiltzheimer, entry for 12 May 1769, *Extracts from the Diary of Jacob Hiltzheimer, of Philadelphia, 1765–1798,* Jacob Cox Parsons, ed. (Philadelphia, 1898), 17.

19. *New-York Gazette; or the Weekly Post-Boy,* 4 June 1750.

purse of twenty pounds.[20] In the two years before the Continental Congress convened, horse-racing flourished. Virginians challenged each other to match races for hundreds of guineas. In September 1773, more horses were entered for the Annapolis Jockey Club Sweepstakes than had ever been entered before. In October a group of gentlemen from Virginia, Maryland, and New York planned a race at Hempstead Heath for the next year.[21] A race at Powlis Hook, New Jersey in May 1774 received favorable publicity. "The spectators were very numerous, the weather was extremely fine, the sport was excellent, but the most confident in the betting branch were grievously disappointed."[22] In June the papers announced that the Maryland horses had arrived in Philadelphia for the sweepstakes.

Yet despite the increased racing activity, Congress' recommended ban had an immediate effect. On November 4, 1774, the Jockey Club of Annapolis published its decision to cancel its race.[23] This decision set a precedent for other jockey clubs, and no major races were held during the Revolution. Nor does it appear that many individuals violated the ban. In April 1775, a New York judge was called to decide the case of a disputed horse race at Rye. He summoned a number of inhabitants to appear to serve on the jury, but they "unanimously refused to be sworn, declaring, that as Horse racing was contrary to the Association of the Congress, they would never serve as Jurors in any such cause, and that if the Justice thought proper to commit them, they would go to gaol."[24]

Horse-racing could have appealed to members of Congress as an appropriate activity to ban for several reasons. Horse-racing, which had grown in popularity so dramatically in the two decades preceding the Congress, was associated with England. Englishmen in the eighteenth century were revolutionizing horse-racing. They started importing stallions from northern Africa and the Near East and breeding horses for the track. Often the sons of the rich of South Carolina, Virginia, and New York went to England for their educa-

20. *New-York Gazette and Weekly Mercury,* 6 June 1768.

21. *Rivington's New-York Gazetteer,* 26 May 1774, 16 September 1773, 30 September 1773.

22. *Rivington's New-York Gazetteer,* 26 May 1774.

23. *New-York Gazette and Weekly Mercury,* 14 November 1774.

24. *New-York Journal,* 6 April 1775.

tion.[25] Many attended Cambridge University, right near Newmarket, the center of English racing, and came home with an interest in importing English thoroughbreds, breeding, and racing for high stakes.[26] Colonial newspapers listed the English-bred horses running in colonial races.[27] These English imports, who consistently outran native-bred horses, stirred up English–colonial rivalry and reinforced colonial feelings of inferiority. In 1765, a breeder challenged any horse that could be produced in America to beat his horse, True-Britton.[28] In Charleston a challenge match for 1,000 guineas between Noble, a native, and Centinel, bred by the Duke of Lancaster, aroused a great deal of fervor. Out of national pride, Noble was favored. People bet great sums, but the "foreigner" won.[29] Later the same spring the English Figure beat Salem, the "gallant American."[30]

Horse-racing was associated with a style of high living. Often racing events lasted three days and ended with a sumptuous ball.[31] The horse breeders and racers fancied themselves to be English gentry. John Baylor, who decided that participating in racing was too expensive and took too much time away from more worthwhile business, imported and bred racehorses to sell, a lucrative venture that earned him a profit of 1,537 pounds in one year. With an appreciation of the self-image of Virginian horse breeders and racers, Baylor preferred that his imported horses come from "a noble stud," because a "pedigree at full length and certificate of age under a nobleman's hand would be looked on here in a much higher light."[32]

Josiah Quincy, having spent a day with some wealthy young Vir-

25. Fithian, 26; Lord Adam Gordon, "Journal," in Newton Mereness, ed., *Travels in the American Colonies* (New York, 1961), 398, 405.

26. John Tayloe of Richmond County, for example, and John Baylor of Caroline County, who named his plantation Newmarket, both received some education in England.

27. *New-York Mercury,* 15 October 1764.

28. *New-York Gazette, or the Weekly Post-Boy,* 17 January 1763.

29. *New-York Gazette and Weekly Mercury,* 18 April 1768.

30. *New-York Gazette and Weekly Mercury,* 16 May 1768.

31. Anne Manigault, "Journal," *South Carolina Historical & Genealogical Magazine* XX:61; *New-York Gazette and Weekly Mercury,* 23 February 1767.

32. The citation is in Fairfax Harrison, "The Equine F F Vs," *The Virginia Magazine of History and Biography* (October, 1927) 35:362.

ginians engrossed in cockfighting and horse-racing, criticized the young men for their obsession with activities that detracted from intellectual pursuits. "The ingenuity of a Locke or the discoveries of a Newton were considered as infinitely inferior to the accomplishment of him who knew when to shoulder a blind cock or start a fleet horse."[33] Horse-racing and cockfighting, however, threatened more than philosophy and the spirit of inquiry; the sporting activities struck directly at agriculture and husbandry. Colonists banned gambling in general, but they singled out horse-racing and cockfighting. The political crisis probably made them more aware of the role of animals in the colonial economy and the incongruity of breeding racehorses and fighing cocks at a time when Americans needed to concentrate on productivity.

iii

Horse-racing and cockfighting undermined the values in which colonists grounded their resistance to England. Both activities seemed frivolous and extravagant. They diverted people from work; they produced nothing of benefit to society; and, by encouraging competition and gambling, they weakened community cohesiveness. The ban on horse-racing and cockfighting made sense as part of Congress' program to resist tyranny by strengthening the virtue of American colonists. But the ban also functioned as a political strategy in the context of Southern agriculture. Southern planters—men who grew tobacco in Virginia and rice in South Carolina—imported racehorses from England, bred them in the colonies, and arranged big racing events. In Virginia, the planters growing tobacco in the Tidewater were surrounded on the north, west, and south by farmers growing wheat, hemp, and diversified crops; in South Carolina, the rice planters were surrounded by farmers growing indigo, hemp, and wheat. In the back country of South Carolina, stockmen rounded up cattle and once a year drove them to markets on the coast. The culture of plantations differed from the culture of farms—differed in ways that related to the political struggle between colonists and the British. Planters and farmers could work together to build an integrated society, or they could let tensions between the two types of

33. Quincy, *Journal*, 467.

agriculture fester. The ban on horse-racing worked as a political strategy in planter societies surrounded by farming societies.

British and European visitors who toured America in the eighteenth century were appalled at the slovenliness of agriculture and, in the South, at the indolence of the planters. Americans in general did not treat their soil with either organic or inorganic fertilizers; they did not grow fodder for animals or grasses that could be plowed under as green manure; they let their animals run wild, even in winter, rather than building barns, stables, pens, and fences. Most did not rotate crops, but planted the same crop again and again until the fertility of the soil was depleted. Then they let the field go fallow. Weeds sprang up everywhere.[34]

Foreigners, while severe on American agriculture in general, particularly condemned the indolence of Southern planters. Planters, as one English observer phrased it, did not "much admire labour."[35] The daily routine of the Virginia planter, according to a Scottish observer, was nothing but sloth and indolence; the planter whiled away his existence in near-comatose lethargy.

> The gentleman of fortune rises about nine o'clock; he perhaps may make an excursion to walk as far as his stables to see his horses, which is seldom more than fifty yards from his house; he returns to breakfast, between nine and ten. . . . He then lies down on a pallat, on the floor, in the coolest room in the house, in his shirt and trousers only, with a negro at his head, and another at his feet, to fan him, and keep off the flies; between twelve and one he takes a draught of bombo, or toddy, a liquor composed of water, sugar, rum, and nutmeg, which is made weak, and kept cool: he dines between two and three. . . . Having drank some few glasses of wine after dinner, he returns to his pallat, with his two blacks to fan him, and continues to drink toddy, or sangaree, all the afternoon: he does not always drink tea; between nine

34. *American Husbandry* (London, 1775), I:77–79, 81, 126–29; II:123–24 (hereafter cited as *AH*); Johann David Schoepf, *Travels in the Confederation, 1783–1784* (New York, 1788), translated from the German by Alfred J. Morrison, ed. (Philadelphia, 1911; reprinted New York, 1968), I:165; II:32, 48, 89, 108–11; David Ramsay, *History of South Carolina* (Charleston, S.C., 1853), 288, 294, 296, 303.

35. Hugh Jones, *The Present State of Virginia: From Whence Is Inferred a Short View of Maryland and North Carolina* (London, 1753), 48.

and ten in the evening, he eats a light supper . . . and almost immediately retires to bed, for the night.[36]

In presenting a picture of Southern planters, foreigners (and Americans from the Northern colonies) sometimes commented on their predilection for cockfighting and horse-racing.[37] These diversions underscored the indolence, frivolity, and extravagance of planters that resulted in deplorable agricultural methods. "Such a country life as they lead, in the midst of a profusion of rural sports and diversions, with little to do themselves, and in a climate that seems to create rather than check pleasure, must almost naturally have a strong effect in bringing them to be just such planters, as foxhunters in England make farmers."[38]

These condemnatory and dismissive evaluations of American agriculture and of planters in the South are a bit puzzling. Planters in Virginia and Maryland exported tobacco whose average annual value from 1768 to 1772 was 756,128 pounds sterling, and many tobacco planters were also growing some wheat, which they exported not only to Great Britain, but to southern Europe and the West Indies as well. In South Carolina, rice exports surged upwards in the late 1730s and again in the early 1750s, and then expanded steadily from 1760 until the Revolution. Planters exporting their rice to Great Britain, southern Europe, and the West Indies prospered. From 1768 to 1772, the average annual value of rice exports was 305,533 pounds.[39] Clearly, Southern planters had more competence and energy than outside observers were willing to grant them. Nor did Southern planters rely on overseers to run their plantations. In South Carolina, planters might escape to Newport, Rhode Island, at the end of the summer or spend some time in Charleston, but, unlike the sugar planters of the Caribbean, they still managed their plantations.

36. John F. D. Smyth, *A Tour in the United States of America*, vol. 1 (London, 1784): 41–43.

37. Jones, *Virginia*, 48; Quincy, *Journal*, 467.

38. *AH* 1:238.

39. John J. McCusker and Russell R. Menard, *The Economy of British America, 1607–1789* (Chapel Hill, N. C., 1985), 129–30, 174, 176; James F. Shepherd and Gary M. Walton, *Shipping, Maritime Trade, and the Economic Development of Colonial North America* (Cambridge, Mass., 1972), 213–15, 218–19, 221–22, 224–25, 227.

Virginia planters stayed in residence all year round. Surely an incongruity exists between the accounts of planter indolence and the reality. Virginia and Maryland planters could hardly have been producing 756,128 pounds' worth of tobacco if they were too tired or full of rum to keep their eyes open. It is difficult to imagine Landon Carter, Robert Beverley, George Washington, or Thomas Jefferson lying on a pallet all day, drowsy with bombo, too languid to brush away a fly, let alone stroll to the stables. Where do these derogatory and uncomplimentary pictures come from?

Maybe some planters did succumb to heat prostration, although the picture seems to emerge more from conditions in the Caribbean than from those on the mainland. Maybe also planters, while they had visitors, did not engage in plantation work and therefore gave the impression of leading a life with no responsibilities.[40] Two clues to the incongruity between perceived indolence and agricultural productivity survive in the texts of journals. When visitors to the South, whether European, British, or American, waxed eloquent on the indolence of planters, they were apt to slip in a reference to climate and slavery. Hugh Jones, an Englishman who arrived in Virginia in 1717, commented of the planters, "the Heat of the Summer makes some very lazy, who are then said to be climate-struck."[41] Sixty years later another young Englishman echoed the same sentiments and made explicit a connection between climate and slavery. "The great number of negroes they have, the warmth of the Climate and the very easy manner in which a comfortable subsistence is procured in this plentiful country all conspire to make the inhabitants exceedingly indolent."[42] According to the "scientific" notion of the day, white people, unlike black people, could not function in the hot sun and humidity. They needed black slaves, and having slaves exacerbated the climatically induced indolence of masters.

---

40. Gregory A. Stiverson attributes the anomaly to a distinction that Virginia planters made between time devoted to work and time devoted to play. When at play, Virginians were conspicuous in their frivolity. Stiverson, " 'Gentlemen of Industry, Skill, and Application': Plantation Management in Eighteenth-Century Virginia," Research Report, Colonial Williamsburg Foundation (1975), 9–10. (microfiche)

41. Jones, *Virginia*, 48.

42. Nicholas Cresswell, *The Journal of Nicholas Cresswell, 1774–1777*, ed. A. G. Bradley, 2nd ed. (New York, 1928), 268.

Planters who owned slaves did not, in fact, have to do physical labor. The work that planters did was managerial and therefore not highly visible to an outside observer. Planters had to operate their plantations in such a way that they not only made a profit but supported a large labor force. They had to decide how much land to put in the production of food as opposed to the staple crop. They had to oversee a work force that had no motivation to work. They had to plan each stage in the production of the staple crop and coordinate the agricultural schedules of the staple and subsistence crops. They had to train slaves as carpenters, coopers, sawyers, blacksmiths, tanners, curriers, shoemakers, spinners, weavers, knitters, and distillers, and then plan and direct the manufacture of necessities for the plantation. They had to secure agricultural instruments and keep them in repair. They had to get their crop to merchants and arrange for the marketing of it. They had to decide what land to clear, what land to buy, what crops to experiment with.[43] All these managerial tasks, however, did not count as work. Slaves were visible, as was the work they did. British and Northern observers must have mentally compared planters with farmers, who were known for their physical labor, and, reinforced by racial theories of climate, concluded that planters lay around all day on their pallets.

British observers had to digest the slave economy, and they did so according to the accepted theory of climatic determinism. But they also had set notions of proper agricultural procedures. In the eighteenth century, the British were generating theories of agriculture and husbandry and disseminating these theories in books, tracts, and instruction manuals. American agriculture in general and the production of tobacco and rice in particular did not conform to British ideas of proper agricultural methods. Hence the scathing view of plantation agriculture. But in fact conditions in Britain differed markedly from conditions in the colonies, and British crops differed from the staple crops of the South. Agricultural methods appropriate to England were not necessarily appropriate to the plantation economies of Virginia and South Carolina.

British farmers grew grains and practiced husbandry. They were

43. For an excellent account of plantation management, see Stiverson, " 'Gentlemen of Industry' "; for the self-sufficiency of the plantation, see Kate Mason Rowland, *Life and Correspondence of George Mason, 1725–1792* (New York, 1892) I:101–2.

concerned with maximizing productivity since land was limited, but they were not concerned with conserving labor. Indeed, some British agriculturalists condemned labor-saving machinery. "Hence it is that all inventions which perform the work of twenty people, with one pair of hands, are, upon the whole, detrimental rather than useful, in a well-peopled country."[44] British farmers were encouraged to undertake any tasks and routines that increased productivity, regardless of the labor costs (transplanting seedlings, hoeing many times, weeding constantly, setting, drilling, meliorating barren lands, draining bogs, cutting peat, making compost dunghills, etc.) because they would "gain much money by such undertakings, and employ more work-people at the same time."[45]

British agricultural theory emerged from British agriculture. British farmers grew grains—oats, wheat, and barley—and practiced husbandry. The "new" agriculture focused on planting methods that increased productivity and employment opportunities, on care of animals, and on the integration of planting and husbandry. The farm was divided into field, yard, and stable. In the fields, drill plows regularized planting. Seeds were drilled in straight lines, at regular intervals, and set depths. Cereals were to be rotated with legumes, grasses, and clover. Live fences (usually locust) kept animals from destroying crops, without putting a strain on dwindling timber resources. The yard was chiefly for animals who were kept in stables and pens, bedded down with straw, and, in the winter, fed on grains, hay, turnips, etc. Because of the arrangement of the farm around a yard and because of the proximity of market towns, British farmers had access to organic fertilizers. They often dug a pit in the yard where dung could be collected and treated (beef broth, urine, and soapsuds were treatments highly recommended), and from market towns they obtained oxen and sheep offal, blood, hair, wool-nippings, cattle hoofs, refuse of rabbit skin, and "every other kind of rejected matters."[46] British farmers had access to organic fertilizer, and they also had an incentive to maintain the fertility of their lands, because they had nowhere to expand. British agriculturalists, keen on maintaining fertility, encouraged farmers to develop a nicety of judge-

44. Walter Harte, *Essays on Husbandry* (London, 1764), 38.
45. Ibid.
46. Thomas Hale, *A Compleat Body of Husbandry* (London, 1758), 133–38.

ment in the application of dung—to discriminate between pigeon dung and hog dung, between the dung of carnivores and the dung of herbivores. Each kind of dung was to have its appropriate use.

Now, suppose an Englishman, attuned to this kind of farming and sensitized to the minute distinctions agriculturalists were making, came across a Virginia tobacco plantation. The Englishman would be used to the precision of drill planting, to the symmetry of the yard and stables, to a pristine agriculture in which the farmer was like a gardener constantly turning the soil and keeping it weed-free. The manuals pronounced a message: "One of the principal objects, in our new method of culture, is to recommend industry, neatness, and the extirpation of weeds." The plantation had no central yard. Weeds choked the fallow fields and even appeared in the tobacco and corn crops; two crops were often grown together in one field to save the labor of preparing two fields. There were no live fences (not only did growing and maintaining live fences require skill and labor, live fences were ineffective against rooting hogs), and animals foraged for themselves. In most plantations there were no ploughs or wagons. The plantation would have some riding horses, but an Englishman would have noticed the scarcity of draft animals and their harsh treatment. British travelers, when they criticized Southern agriculture, were in fact calling on planters to be farmers.

Many of the methods and reforms advocated by the British agriculturalists actually did not make sense for a staple economy based on slave labor and plentiful land. In Virginia, planters practiced exploitative agriculture. It worked to their advantage to clear new land for production of the staple crop rather than to use expensive labor to grow meliorating crops that would neither yield a profit nor feed the labor force. Plantations did not, and could not to any great extent, integrate agriculture and husbandry. Planters had to devote the land that was not planted with the cash crop to subsistence crops to feed the labor force. They could not spare acreage and labor for raising fodder for livestock. Even draft animals strained the resources of the plantation. Landon Carter preferred to have his slaves roll hogsheads of tobacco and corn by hand to spare him the expense of feeding draft horses.[47] He resented what he considered an excess of carts and

47. Jack P. Greene, ed., *The Diary of Colonel Landon Carter of Sabine Hall, 1752–1778* (Charlottesville, Va., 1965) 2:1,039.

plows, which required horses and oxen, and he extolled the productivity of his father, who had never used plows and had only one cart.

Horses were expensive to maintain. They needed pasture and supplemental feeding, particularly if they were to serve as draft horses. English agriculturalists felt that each horse needed two tons of hay in the winter. It would take an acre mown twice to produce the two tons. In the summer, four horses needed six acres of green clover. Thus, to support four draft horses for a year would require planting ten acres in grass and clover.[48] Planters who owned a large slave force whom they had to feed felt they could not afford to take this kind of land and labor out of the production of corn and tobacco. To feed 100 slaves, half of whom were adults, a planter had to devote 150 acres to the production of corn—a hundred and fifty acres that could not be used for tobacco. Furthermore, the labor required for tilling and weeding the corn during the growing season was labor taken away from tobacco.[49]

Surrounding the plantations were farms. Growing crops that were less labor-intensive than tobacco and rice, farmers needed fewer slaves than planters did and could spare more land to crops for livestock. Unlike plantations, farms integrated agriculture and husbandry.[50] Jefferson, contrasting tobacco planters with wheat farmers, recognized that farms were more oriented towards animals than plantations were. Tobacco planters raised little food, "so the men and animals on these farms are badly fed." Wheat farmers, on the other hand, raised "great numbers of animals for food and service."[51] Farmers, whether indigo farmers or wheat farmers, depended on draft horses. A traveler in Georgia described a farm on Jekyll Island: "a very Large Barnfull of Barley not inferior to the Barley in England, about 20 Ton of Hay in one Stack, a Spacious House & fine Garden, a plow was going wth. Eight horses, And above all I saw Eight Acres

---

48. *Rural Œconomy* (London, 1770), 15–16.

49. Stiverson, " 'Gentlemen of Industry,' " 93.

50. Compare the inventory for setting up a 2,000 acre tobacco plantation with the inventory for setting up a 500-acre farm: *American Husbandry,* 235–36; *The Journal of Nicholas Cresswell, 1774–1777,* 195–96.

51. Thomas Jefferson, *Notes on the State of Virginia,* in *The Writings of Thomas Jefferson,* Andrew A. Lipscomb, ed. (Washington, 1903) 2:232.

of Indigo. . . ."[52] An indentured servant in Virginia described his master's new machine for threshing wheat. "The Machine is drawn round by 4 Horses and beats out 100 Bushels of wheat every day."[53]

The draft horse was an integral part of farm culture. Farmers relied on draft horses and oxen for preparing the soil, planting the seeds, and covering the seeds. Horses pulled plows, rollers, harrows, drill plows, and occasionally even threshing machines. Unlike tobacco and rice seed, cereal and grass seed were for the most part sown broadcast. Broadcast sowing required the ground to be well pulverized. Relying on draft animals, farmers plowed the land at least once and then went over it with a heavy harrow or drag to break up the clods. Farmers interested in the new agriculture might use drill plows, drawn by draft animals, to plant the seed. Robert Beverley, Landon Carter, and George Washington all experimented with drill plows. Washington tinkered with his, trying to make adjustments for different kinds of seeds.[54] Once the seed was planted, whether by broadcast or drill plow, the farmer again harnessed his horses and harrowed the ground to cover the seeds. Washington used a brush harrow to cover grass seeds and a fine-toothed harrow to cover grain seeds.[55] After wheat was harvested, horses and cattle were used to tread out the grain. Draft horses were essential to the production of the farm. Besides pulling plows, drills, harrows, and threshing machines, horses also pulled carts and wagons. Farms developed in the back country away from water transportation. Therefore farmers were more dependent on horses and wagons for transportation than planters were.

Farmers in the back country of Georgia and the Carolinas also

52. *The Colonial Records of the State of Georgia* (Atlanta, Ga., 1915) 25:97.

53. Edward Miles Riley, ed., *The Journal of John Harrower: An Indentured Servant in the Colony of Virginia, 1773–1776* (Colonial Williamsburg, 1963), 60, 107. See also Cresswell, *Journal*, 56.

54. Patricia Gibbs, "Agricultural Implements And Vehicles Used on Plantations in Tidewater Virginia, 1700–1776," Colonial Williamsburg Research Report (December 1976), 112–16; John C. Fitzpatrick, ed., *The Diaries of George Washington, 1748–1799* (Boston, 1925) 1:211; Donald Jackson, ed., *The Diaries of George Washington* (Charlottesville, Va., 1976) 1:337-38; Landon Carter, *Diary* 1:276, 287, 294, 298.

55. Gibbs, "Agricultural Implements," 86–87; *The Diaries of George Washington*, Fitzpatrick, vol. 1:154–55, 178; vol. 2:361–62; vol. 3:314 (hereafter cited as *Diaries*).

depended on horses and raised them for market. Here hunters and farmers clashed. Hunters raided farms and often stole horses. A Georgia law noted that hunters "do also Trafick much in Horses which there is great Reason to believe are frequently stolen." South Carolina farmers, petitioning for redress of grievances, insisted that "numbers of Idle Vagrant Persons . . . after the season of hunting is over, Steal Cattle, Hogs and Horses." Regulators described the theft of valuable horses, and a law in North Carolina, like the Georgia law, accused hunters of horse-stealing.[56] In the back country, the clash between hunters and farmers revealed the value of horses and their importance for farm agriculture and transportation.

In the South, plantation culture was juxtaposed with farm culture, and each bore symbolic freight. The farm with its horses and plows was associated with freedom, in contrast with the plantation with its slaves and hoes. According to the prevalent notions of the day, if white men were going to engage in agriculture in hot climates, they would have to use black labor. (No one questioned that black labor meant slave labor.) But people who opposed slave labor looked to the horse. Using draft horses to pull plows, they reasoned, would allow white men to function in hot climates and free them from the necessity of depending on slave labor. John Bolzius in 1745 argued against the introduction of slavery into Georgia. Perhaps, he admitted, it was too hot in the summer months for white people to work in the fields with a hoe, but surely they could plow the fields in the early morning and late afternoon and grow European grains. "If the poor white people in this Colony could be Supply'd with a Horse each or 2 families, or a Couple of broke Oxen, or with Convenient tools for Agriculture, I am sure, they would not make Complaints of the great Heat of this Climate."[57] Others, too, saw the plow and the horse liberating southern farmers from a dependence on slaves. A French traveler noticed that Virginians did not plow their land but worked it with hoes and made little holes to drop the seeds into. He could not understand why they did not plow. "There being no stones, a single horse could be used to plough anywhere." He felt

56. Rachel N. Klein, *Unification of a Slave State: The Rise of the Planter Class in the South Carolina Backcountry, 1760–1808* (Chapel Hill, N. C., 1990), 56.

57. *The Colonial Records of the State of Georgia* (Atlanta, 1915) 24:360–61.

certain that if he settled in Virginia he could make a profit by relying on plows, horses, and oxen rather than on slaves. "I would like to state & aver that were I settled there, provided I had two servants, a plough with two cows & another one with two horses, I could boast of accomplishing more work than anyone in the country with eight strong slaves."[58] The plow, symbol of independence, stood in opposition to the hoe, symbol of slavery. In 1745, when Georgia still prohibited slave labor, a promoter of Georgia looked forward to the introduction of more plows into the colony. "Plows will (in 2 or 3 years) be in fashion here, if not sooner, for Hoes are looked on as Badges of Slavery among the labouring English."[59] Instead, slaves became the fashion.

In Virginia the racehorse became caught up in the complex of agricultural symbols. Many people, both foreigners and Americans, noticed the sorry state of American draft horses. Landon Carter compared them unfavorably to slaves. Carter was constantly grumbling that the weather was too wet or too hot for plowing, that the horses were too weak, that the plows only scratched the weeds. Six slaves working with hoes, he calculated, could do more work in four days than two plowmen, two plowboys, eight steers, four horses, and two plows could do in five days.[60] George Washington, too, often brooded that his horses were not strong enough for plowing. He ordered a special light plow from Europe that he thought might accommodate his feeble horses.[61] But the farmers who relied on draft horses, even those who were caught up in the new agriculture and experimented with crops and planting methods, neither bred draft animals nor took care of them. While in Britain farmers recognized

---

58. Durand of Dauphiné, *A Huguenot Exile in Virginia, or, Voyages of a Frenchman exiled for his Religion with a description of Virginia and Maryland,* from the Hague Edition of 1687 with an Introduction and Notes by Gilbert Chinard (New York, 1934), 117.

59. Ellis Merton Coulter, ed., *The Journal of William Stephens, 1743–1745* (Athens, Ga., 1959), 210.

60. Jack P. Greene, ed., *The Diary of Colonel Landon Carter of Sabine Hall, 1752–1778* (Charlottesville, Va., 1965) 1:432, 445. Carter writes, "5 women and man does more work in 4 days. . . ." He could mean six slaves or ten slaves.

61. Washington, *Diaries* 1:395; idem, *Writings* 2:421, 28:512.

many different kinds of horses (racehorses, hunters, coach horses, riding horses, draft horses, packhorses) and bred them for different characteristics, Virginians distinguished only between race horses, riding horses, and draft horses, and they bred only racehorses.

Americans did not take good care of their animals, including their horses. Compare the lot of a colonial horse with that of an English horse. Colonists rode their horses hard and then turned them loose to fend for themselves. In England, farmers, if they followed the instructions of the agricultural manuals, not only pampered their horses, but established a personal relationship with them. Horses were to be watered two miles before the end of a journey and then put in a warm stable, well littered, where they were to be rubbed down. They were to be fed hay daily and once a week, warm grains and salt. Agriculturalists suggested that farmers give their horses a variety of foods (oats, peas, beans, bread) so they would not lose their appetites, and, should loss of appetite occur, they particularly suggested white wine, salt, and vinegar as restoratives. Care of the horse included rubbings, swims, and bleeding. No wonder that British visitors were shocked at the American treatment of animals. One Englishman claimed that he did not know any country in which animals were treated in a worse way. "Horses are in general, even valuable ones, worked hard, and starved: they [Americans] plough, cart, and ride them to death, at the same time that they give very little heed to their food; after the hardest day's work, all the nourishment they are like to have is to be turned into a wood, where the shoots and weeds form the chief of the pasture."[62]

Racehorses, however, unlike draft horses, did receive care and attention. After the Revolution, when racing came back into vogue, a German doctor commented on what must have been obvious to Virginians before the Revolution.

Horses are a prime object with the Virginians; but they give their attention chiefly to racers and hunters, of which indubitably they have the finest in America, their custom formerly being to keep up and improve the strain by imported English stallions and mares. The pedigree of their horses is carried out with great exactitude. . . . But the province has no good draught and work-horses, and their teams, in the

62. *AH* I:80.

low country at least, are in general extremely sorry. One sees every-where little, thin animals, hitched to wagons.[63]

Racehorses took a privileged place among Virginia's animals. They escaped the neglect and harsh treatment awarded other animals, and they stood out as fine specimens of horseflesh in an agricultural society that otherwise neglected breeding. These fine horses, marked for a privileged life of little work by privileged men who themselves did no work, could become symbols of what was wrong with planta-tion agriculture.

In Virginia, the racehorse, an exotic import financed by agriculture that did not use draft horses, was caught in a society in agricultural transition. The boundary between wheat agriculture and tobacco agri-culture blurred as tobacco planters in times of depressed prices set aside more of their land for wheat or changed over to wheat com-pletely. In this agricultural flux, planters, who had to consider the advantages and disadvantages of wheat and tobacco and also had to confront the condemnation of outsiders and their own self-doubts about tobacco and slavery, encountered an agricultural world orga-nized by symbols: the hoe, symbol of slavery; the horse and plow, symbols of independence; and the racehorse, symbol of English and planter decadence and extravagance.

In the imperial crisis, when Americans focused on their inadequa-cies, the racehorse symbolically had to bear the responsibility for the sorry life of the draft horse. After the Revolution, Jefferson tried to eliminate the gap between the unbred draft horses who did useful work and the bred racehorses who ran simply to amuse spectators. Convinced that Virginia offered the best climate for raising horses and that wheat farmers should put part of their land into pasture, he encouraged wheat farmers to raise Arabian horses (the best race-horses) both to work on Southern farms and to be sold in Northern markets. "Their [the Arabian horses'] patience of heat without injury, their superior wind, fit them better [than the native draft horse] in this and the more southern climates even for the drudgeries of the plough and wagon. Northwardly they will become an object only to persons of taste and fortune, for the saddle and light carriages."[64]

63. Schoepf, *Travels,* 2:65.
64. Jefferson, *Notes on the State of Virginia,* in *Writings* 2:234.

Jefferson wanted to harness the "decided taste and preference" of Virginians for Arabian thoroughbreds to productivity and profit. The racehorse was to become part of the farm, both as a workhorse and as a marketable product.

At the time of the imperial crisis, Southern planters were besieged. They had to confront a negative public image. The climate allegedly enervated them; slaves induced tyranny and indolence; and their plantation agriculture did not conform to the "new" standards based on farm agriculture. Planters did not reject assumptions about climate and slavery and did not deny the validity of the criticism of their agriculture, however inappropriate it was in many respects. But by banning cockfighting and horse-racing they overcame the moral deterioration imposed on them by plantation agriculture on the one hand and slavery on the other.

Planters were engaged in raising a staple crop with slave labor, but in a political crisis that forced articulation of values, it became clear that planters held values associated with farm agriculture: work, frugality, and independence. The wheat farmers in the South, like the planters, used slaves, but they escaped the poor image that slavery entailed because they were performing the same type of agriculture that farmers without slaves performed: farmers in England, New England, New York, and Pennsylvania.[65] Planters did not use horses in agricultural production; instead they bred racing horses. Horses for them were a diversion, and a diversion that related them to English decadence. Wheat farmers, on the other hand, used horses to pull plows, drills, harrows, rollers, carts, and wagons; they bred "the staff of life," not a "stinking weed"; and they were associated with work and independence. No matter that the laborers on the wheat farms of the South were still slaves; the agriculture comported with accepted notions of hard work and independence. In banning horse-racing, planters were publicly stating that they embraced farm values, and, while they did not abandon tobacco or slaves, symbolically dissociated themselves from the moral contamination of plantation agriculture.

The planters of Virginia at the time of the friction with Britain

---

65. Timothy Breen discusses the good image of wheat and the bad image of tobacco in *Tobacco Culture: The Mentality of the Great Tidewater Planters on the Eve of Revolution* (Princeton, N. J., 1985), 185, 199–201.

feared the moral effects that slavery was having on them. They saw themselves, as masters, succumbing to indolence on the one hand and tyranny on the other. Cockfighting and horse-racing—expensive, nonproductive pursuits—encapsulated the image of the indolent and frivolous planter who did not work himself and who lavishly wasted the profits reaped by the labor of slaves. The image of the indolent planter sprang from popular conceptions of the effects of climate and slavery. Southerners, of course, could not change their climate, and they were not about to give up slaves. They could, however, cleanse themselves of the debilitating effects of slavery. The moral reformation symbolized by the abandonment of cockfighting and horse-racing proved to them and to the observing world that they were not slaves to slavery.

The ban on horse-racing was a public statement that Virginia planters would not waste their time and money on frivolous pursuits and would devote themselves to work. Virginia planters cleaned up their image and confronted their own insecurity about the debilitating effects of slavery by dissociating themselves from expensive "English" pursuits and by identifying themselves with the hard-working farm culture. Virginia planters were making a statement to themselves and to the world; they were not, however, trying to solidify their relations with wheat farmers. They did not have to, because many wheat farmers had been tobacco planters. In Virginia the class distinction between gentry and yeoman farmers did not correspond to the agricultural distinction between tobacco and wheat production. Growing wheat occupied farmers both large and small.

In South Carolina the situation was different. Setting up a rice plantation required substantial capital. Planters who grew rice, considerably richer than the farmers who surrounded them, constituted a separate and distinct society. In the back country, farmers trying to establish themselves searched for crops they could market. They had interest in agricultural experimentation, but not the capital to perform it. Sometimes back country farmers felt bitter towards the Eastern planters and their lavish style of life, a style made visible in extravagant horse-racing events. The money dissipated at horse races could, they felt, be far better invested in testing different crops on the frontier: hemp, flax, wheat, barley, oats, rye, mulberries, logwood, braziletto and orange trees, and cochineal. (Optimism often outran the limitations of climate and soil.) "Instead of throwing away *Five*

Hundred Pounds annually to spoil good Horses, suppose this Sum was yearly raised by Subscription, for the Encouragement of [agriculture and manufactures]."[66] (Racing not only wasted money, it "spoiled" horses for productive work.) The premiums raised by diverting money from horse-racing could serve as prizes for producing beer, potash, grains, tar, oxen, calves, and various exotic crops.

Back country farmers and cattlemen wanted to build a South Carolinian economy they could take part in. They urged that bridges be built across creeks and roads improved so they could have access to Eastern markets. They wanted to raise cattle and plant crops that cattle could feed on, and they reasoned that the development of this type of economy would benefit the East. The farmer who argued his case in the newspaper for diversified agriculture and livestock management pointed out that if back country farmers could sell Easterners grains, cattle, and beer, it would save "the Colony much Specie, which now travels to the Northward for these Articles."[67] Back country farmers had more active needs than rice planters, who were well established and satisfied with the status quo. While rice planters bought imports (including British racehorses) with their profits, back country farmers wanted some of the money earned from South Carolinian exports to be invested in the development of an economy that integrated the back country and the coast. They did not want money wasted on racehorses.

An Easterner answered the proposal of the back country farmer. He agreed that agricultural experimentation should take precedence over horse-racing and other expensive "diversions" and suggested that a society for the improvement of agriculture should be formed to operate with the library society.

> The Arts and Sciences would no longer live as Strangers among us. The Plates given annually for such useful Purposes, would remain to Generations, as Memorials of the Industry and Wisdom of their Ancestors: But if Horse-Racing and other expensive Diversions are encouraged, the Descendents of many of them, may have little else left in time, but their Plates to show; to show, not as marks of Honour and Fortune,

66. *South-Carolina Gazette*, first issue of 1758.
67. Ibid.

but Monuments of the Folly and wrong Application of the Talents of those who obtained them.[68]

In South Carolina, tensions between the back country and the coast threatened to fragment society. As the conflict with Great Britain gathered momentum, colonists reevaluated internal tensions. The ban on horse-racing and cockfighting, by its symbolic significance, might well have eased social tensions in South Carolina. The rich were to join the not-so-rich in directing their energy towards productivity, a productivity that bound people together rather than forcing them apart.

*   *   *

Cockfighting and horse-racing, both in full flush in eighteenth-century England, gained steadily in popularity in the colonies in the 1750s. Cockfighting, like the theater, towed in its wake a heavy cargo of moral outrage that swelled many a pamphlet. Cocks clawed cocks even as people involved in cockfighting clawed each other: owners, breeders, setters, gamblers. Deceit and cheating mangled community spirit and pitted people against people. Cockfighting and horse racing were condemned for undermining the very values that later assumed political importance during the imperial crises. The resistance movement depended on community solidarity, which activities such as cockfighting ripped apart. Horse-racing also engendered competition rather than cooperation. Furthermore, as an activity it was closely associated with England, an irritant exacerbated by the continual triumph of British-bred horses over American ones.

For years, foreigners had criticized American farmers in general and Southern planters in particular for their emphasis on exploitation over conservation, for their harsh treatment of animals, and for their indolence. Virginia planters scrutinized themselves and saw a need to reform; for South Carolinians, curtailment of extravagance improved their relations with the back country farmers. The political crisis heightened the colonists' awareness of the importance of agriculture and husbandry. The very method by which they resisted British legislation—boycotts of English products—forced them to look more closely at their own economy and to become aware of its deficien-

68. Ibid.

cies. In the political crisis the emphasis on industry and frugality impinged on agriculture; the crisis brought into existence societies for the improvement of agriculture and manufactures. Breeding horses for racing and cocks for fighting did not suit a society suddenly made aware of the importance of productivity and self-sufficiency.

★ 8 ★

Enforcement

i

T H E First Continental Congress passed the "Association" in which they established economic boycotts and a moral code of behavior. Congress branded violators of the boycotts and moral code as "enemies of the people," prescribed social ostracism as the punishment, and left enforcement up to local communities. Communities were to establish committees of inspection to publish the names of violators in the newspapers, and everybody was to "break off all dealings" with them. When the system went into effect, committees in fact punished two kinds of offenses: violations of the Association on the one hand; and on the other, slander and libel—usually criticisms of the Continental Congress or the Association itself.

Slander and libel seemed to be an even more serious offense than violations of the Association, probably because words were harder to control than acts and because the extent of their damage was difficult to ascertain. One man addressed some questions to a committee of inspection.

> Whether the person who publickly avows opposition to their [Congress'] measures, and so warmly calls upon the people to refuse obedience to them, is not as wicked and dangerous an enemy as any Merchant who should import Goods contrary to their Resolves?

Whether it does not, therefore, appear to be part of your duty to use every proper method of discovering the author [of *A friendly Address to all Reasonable Americans*], and publishing his name in the several newspapers on the Continent, as an enemy to AMERICA?[1]

The Continental Congress had no legal authority. Nor did it operate as a government. It did not legislate, adjudicate, collect revenue, or allocate resources. The legally constituted governments of the colonies still consisted of the governors, the general assemblies, and the courts. The Continental Congress, an extralegal congress, drew up the Association that regulated economic and moral behavior and recommended it as the best way of resisting British tyranny, but the Association, bearing no legal authority, had to be adopted at the local level. The effectiveness of the Association lay in the perception people had of Congress' authority. Any attacks on the Congress—on its legitimacy or the legality of its recommendations—endangered the whole resistance movement.

Some people did question Congress' authority. They failed to recognize the distinction between laws and recommendations and claimed that Congress was passing laws. "The late Congress, (which even if it had been regularly chosen, yet, from its very nature was only to advise and consult upon the proper mode of obtaining redress of our grievances,) swelled with the idea of its own importance, erected itself into the Supreme Legislature of *North America*."[2] Others argued that since the recommendations of Congress were not laws, they could not be enforced. "If what is generally said be true, that the Congress made no laws, then it can be no transgression to trample upon and contemn the Association. For where there is no law, there can be no transgression."[3] Some condemned the Association itself: the regulations and the methods of enforcement. The regulations overturned established laws, they argued, and Congress and committees bypassed and rendered ineffectual the established institutions of government: the executive, the legislature, and the courts.

1. *American Archives,* ed. by Peter Force, series. 4 (Washington, 1837), I: 1,011 (hereafter cited as *AA*).

2. Ibid., 1,292. Gage, the military governor of Massachusetts, did recognize the distinction. Ibid., 1,245.

3. Ibid. II:37.

The Association, which with some is every thing, is calculated for the meridian of a *Spanish* Inquisition; it is subversive of, inconsistent with, the wholesome laws of our happy Constitution; it abrogates or suspends many of them essential to the peace and order of Government; it takes the Government out of the hands of the Governour, Council, and General Assembly; and the execution of the laws out of the hands of the Civil Magistrates and Juries. The Congress exercises the Legislative, the Committees the Executive Powers.[4]

Failing to grant a distinction between social ostracism and punishments imposed by courts of law, they condemned the members of the committee that enforced the Association. "These men, at the same time they arraign the highest authority on earth [Parliament], insolently trample on the liberties of their fellow-subjects; and, without the shadow of a trial, take from them their property, grant it to others, and not content with all this, hold them up to contempt, and expose them to the vilest injuries."[5] In fact, the Association did protect property, and committeemen were careful to abide by the regulations. While they did not conduct formal trials (since the Association was not law and violations of it were therefore not illegal), they did conduct hearings. And when they encountered a recalcitrant violator, they did mete out the punishment set forth in the Association: social ostracism.

Because of the vulnerability of Congress, committees of inspection set up to enforce the Association punished critics of Congress, the Association, and the committees, as well as violators of the Association. Someone who publicly damned the Congress or its recommendations threatened the unanimity of resistance more than someone who secretly imported goods from England. Laughlin Martin of Charleston, South Carolina, drank a toast: "Damnation to the Committee and their proceedings." He was tarred and feathered. Another man was brought before a committee "for calling upon the Supreme Being, in a most Solemn manner, to d--n the Congress, and all that would not d--n it." He barely escaped being tarred and feathered and was drummed out of town. An indiscreet Virginian said to a negro, "Piss Jack, turn about my Boy and sign [the Association]." He had to

4. Ibid. I:1,212. See also Ibid. I:988, 1,095, 1,141, 1,157, 1,212, 1,230, 1,292; II:37.

5. Ibid. I:988.

apologize publicly for his "unhappy Perverseness of temper." Another Virginian said he looked upon the Committee of Inspection "as a pack of damn'd rascals," and a captain said "Damn the buggers," when a member of a committee boarded his sloop. Both offenders were censured as enemies of the people.[6] Committees particularly went after people who not only criticized Congress, but were in a position to influence others: ministers, schoolteachers, officers in the militia.[7] John Saunders of Virginia refused to sign either the Virginia Association or the Continental one. He was held up to public censure because "he hath had the advantage of a liberal education, and for some time past hath studied the law." After much pressure he signed. "But, behold! at the end of his name he added the negative *no,* with a Capital N!"[8]

To declare someone an enemy of the people for calling committeemen damned rascals or buggers seems like a drastic overreaction. But the response of the committees to slander and libel was not an anomaly. Seventeenth- and eighteenth-century Englishmen and colonists were very concerned about defamation, and a body of precedent had developed defining the limits of both slander and libel. Calling someone a "Buggering Rogue" was actionable, for example. Calling someone a traitor was also actionable, but calling him a traitorous knave was not, since it indicated intention only.[9] Case after case scrutinized the words, the manner of speaking, and the damage done. Lawyers agreed that slander and libel directed at government or its officers deserved the greatest punishment. If a private person were libeled it might incite him to take revenge in action that would break the peace, but if the government were criticized it might lead to sedition.[10] In Virginia in the seventeenth century, the fledgling government responded vindictively to criticism. When the council heard that a man had said "base and detracting" things against the gover-

---

6. Ibid. II:922–23; III:1,550; William James Van Schreeven, comp., Robert L. Scribner, ed., *Revolutionary Virginia* (Charlottesville, Va., 1973) II:161, 223, 235.

7. *Revolutionary Virginia* II:34, 308–09, 314–15; *AA* I:970–72; Ibid. II:77, 107.

8. *AA* II:76–78.

9. *Siderfin's King's Bench Reports* 1:373; *Bulstrode's English King's Bench Reports* 1:145; Edward Coke, *English King's Bench Reports,* 4:19; Giles Jacob, "Action on the Case for Words," *A new law-dictionary,* sixth edition (London, 1750).

10. Coke, *King's Bench* 5:121, 125; Jacob, "Libel," *A new law-dictionary.*

nor, they ordered that he "be disarmed, and have his armes broken and his tongue bored through with a awl. shall pass through a guard of 40 men and shalbe butted by every one of them, and att the head of the troope be kicked downe and footed out of the fort."[11] In England, a man who claimed Lord Bacon had done an injustice was fined 1,000 pounds and forced to ride on a horse with his face to the tail from Fleet to Westminster with the offense written on his head, to acknowledge his offense in all the courts of Westminster, to stand in the pillory, to have one of his ears cut off at Westminster, the other at Cheapside, and to be imprisoned for life.[12] By the middle of the eighteenth century, seditious libelers were less likely to lose their ears, but they were still subject to the pillory, fines, and imprisonment. In the American colonies, cases of seditious libel were not often argued in the common law courts after a New York jury in 1735 acquitted John Peter Zenger on the grounds that printing truth could be no libel, but colonial legislatures, even more suppressive than the courts, protected their reputation by vigorously prosecuting seditious libel as a breach of privilege.[13] In cases of libel, not only the author, but the publishers, printers, and booksellers as well were subject to indictment. When *North Briton* No. 45 attacking the king was published in April 1763, forty-eight arrests were made.[14] In the American crisis, committeemen, sensitive to the political dangers of slander and libel directed at the Continental Congress, responded as vigorously as they could. The Continental Congress was not part of a legally constituted government, and the committeemen could not inflict the punishments of courts and legislatures. But they could and did brand people who criticized the Continental Congress as enemies of the people, subject to the same ostracism and vilification as violators of the Association.

Committees of inspection also punished violations of the Association. Some merchants violated the import-export regulations or raised the price of goods to take advantage of the scarcity. A few

11. Edmund S. Morgan, *American Slavery, American Freedom: The Ordeal of Colonial Virginia* (New York, 1975), 124.

12. *Popham's King's Bench Reports*, 135; Jacob, "Libel," *A new law-dictionary*.

13. Leonard W. Levy, *Emergence of a Free Press* (New York, 1985), 16–61.

14. Robert R. Rea, *The English Press in Politics, 1760–1774* (Lincoln, Nebr., 1963), 44.

people violated the moral regulations. Some gambled. William Lewis won from Anthony McKenley a silver watch, two pairs of leather breeches, and two fine men's hats. Some drank tea. Some were suspected of horse-racing. Usually violators wrote a confession and an apology, which were then published in the newspaper along with the committee's recommendation for forgiveness. Forgiveness, it was made quite clear, proceeded from mercy, not condonement. "It need scarcely be added, that this mitigation of the punishment prescribed in the eleventh article [of Association] proceeds from a desire to distinguish penitent and submissive from refractory and obstinate offenders." If a violator refused to cooperate, he was condemned as an enemy of the people. All communication with him was to cease. He could not buy or sell goods. A recalcitrant tavernkeeper might find his license revoked. A recalcitrant landlord might find his tenants refusing to renew their leases. A recalcitrant schoolteacher might find himself with no schoolhouse or pupils.[15]

While the Continental Congress made recommendations, the force of the political movement before independence was declared lay in the communities, which appointed committees to put into effect the recommendations of Congress, build consensus, and control violence.[16] Local committees employed two strategies for building consensus. On the one hand, the committees strove for the allegiance or at least compliance of as many people as possible; on the other hand, they publicly and dramatically censored, ostracized, and expelled those deemed beyond reconciliation or intimidation. Committees concentrated on the first objective. First, as many people as possible were called upon to serve on committees. Once they were serving on committees they would be actively engaged in the politi-

---

15. *Revolutionary Virginia* II:290, 196, 302; *AA* I:1,178–79; *Revolutionary Virginia* II:220, 300; *AA* I:984, 970–72.

16. For an excellent overall discussion of committees, see David Ammerman, *In the Common Cause: American Response to the Coercive Acts of 1774* (Charlottesville, Va. 1974), esp. 103–24. For detailed discussions of committees in particular colonies and states, see Richard D. Brown, *Revolutionary Politics in Massachusetts: The Boston Committee of Correspondence and the Towns, 1772–1774* (Cambridge, Mass. 1970); Edward Countryman, *A People in Revolution: The American Revolution and Political Society in New York, 1760–1790* (Baltimore, 1981); and Richard Alan Ryerson, *"The Revolution Is Now Begun": The Radical Committees of Philadelphia, 1765–1776* (Philadelphia, 1978).

cal cause. John Ferdinand Dalziel Smyth, a Tory from Maryland, described how the committees politicized people. Committees, he claimed, became bigger and bigger until anyone of any influence was elected, whether he approved or disapproved of the committee's action. The size of the committees, often over 100 members, did not impede their effectiveness, because while the committees were large, the forum was kept small, sometimes only five men out of a committee of 100. Smyth himself was nominated to a committee, even though he had always "openly and publicly disavowed and detested the whole of their proceedings," and he was also appointed to command two troops of light horse. Although Smyth did not find power so "alluring" as to "fascinate" him out of his loyalty to the Crown, he recognized the effect it might have on others.[17]

Committees, whatever the private opinions of the members, publicly assumed that people of the community were patriots and then courted them as such. Even when presented with evidence of disaffection, committees tried to give offenders a chance to retreat from their position. The committee of Orange County was informed that the Reverend John Wingate had in his possession several pamphlets containing "obnoxious reflections on the Continental Congress" that were calculated "to impose on the unwary." The committee requested "in the most respectful manner" that the pamphlets be delivered to them and professed not to have "the least suspicion" that Wingate intended "to make an ill use of them." They could not have been more surprised, so they professed, when Wingate absolutely refused to deliver them.[18] Committees were constantly being "shocked" or "dismayed" when they encountered violations or recalcitrance—the very last things they would have expected. When a person refused to join a committee or to sign the Association, then committeemen tried to persuade him to change his position. Committees stressed their own reasonableness and, when reasonableness failed, their reluctance to publicize the offender. A litany appears again and again in the committee reports that were published in the newspapers. The committee of

17. *Narrative or Journal of Captain John Ferdinand Dalziel Smyth of the Queen's Rangers, taken Prisoner by the Rebels in 1775, lately escaped from them, and arrived here in the Daphne* (New York, 1777–1778), in Catherine S. Crary, ed., *The Price of Loyalty: Tory Writings from the Revolutionary Era* (New York, 1973), 74–78.

18. *Revolutionary Virginia* II:377.

Norfolk Borough, Virginia, was "fully sensible of the great caution with which public censure should be inflicted" and was at all times "heartily disposed to accomplish the great design of the association by the gentle methods of reason and persuasion." But they were obliged to publish as an enemy of the people John Brown, a merchant who had been importing slaves in violation of Article Two of the Association. They bemoaned Brown's "proneness to unmanly equivocation" and regretted that this fault, together with his violation of the Association and some "very unjustifiable steps taken to conceal his disingenuous conduct," precluded the "milder methods" they would have preferred to adopt.[19]

Committees wanted to reduce the potential for conflict and preserve communities intact. Informers who could not produce evidence were chastized. The Richmond County Committee investigated two storekeepers accused of engrossing goods. They were able to clear themselves, and the committee reprimanded the informer and published the account in the paper "to discourage and stifle such ungenerous, as well as unjust Accusations against any Individual of a Community so sacredly engaged to preserve its Liberties."[20] Committees, however, did not want to alienate people who were trying to do their duty by reporting violations. William Triplett, a merchant of Fredericksburg, was accused and acquitted. The committee publicly cleared both the accused and the accuser. "In justice to the gentlemen who lodged the said complaint, as well as to the said Triplett, we further certify that there was good ground for the accusation, but the said Triplett has fully acquitted himself, and, in our opinion, has sold his goods on very reasonable terms."[21] Sometimes committees intimidated dissenters who were driving them to distraction. Someone might mention the tar barrel or write a letter of warning. The committee of Caroline County, Virginia, commissioned Edmund Pendleton to write to some "contumacious" merchants requesting their attendance at the next meeting. In a postscript to his letter to the merchants, Pendleton wrote, "I am authorised to engage the faith of the Committee that no kind of injuries shall be offered to your persons or such of you as may attend to morrow during your atten-

19. Ibid., 307.
20. Ibid., 215.
21. Ibid., 257.

dance coming and returning."[22] Pendleton left open the question of what might happen to those who did not attend. Even when a person actually violated the Association, he could save himself by contrition. Francis Moore, guilty of gaming, "gave such evidence of his penitence, and intention to observe the association strictly for the future" that the committee thought it "proper to re-admit him into the number of friends to the public cause."[23] Committees tried to get offenders to recant so that they could be taken back into the community. The opinion of the community could well mean more to people than their political beliefs. Enoch Bartlett of Haverhill, Massachusetts, acquiesced to the committee and begged the forgiveness of the people of his community. " 'As my comfort does so much depend on the regard and good will of those among whom I live, I hereby give under my hand . . . that I will not buy or sell tea or act in any public' manner 'contrary to the minds of the people in general . . . and will yet hope that all my errors in judgement or conduct will meet with their forgiveness and favour which I humbly ask.' "[24] Only when enticement, persuasion, and reconciliation had all failed did committees publish offenders as enemies of the people.

Some people, however, were both beyond persuasion and impervious to social ostracism. Even when their names were published, they continued to voice their opposition to Congress and the Association. These people received special treatment, sometimes by order of the committees, sometimes by an angry crowd. In 1765, colonists had staged mock executions for stamp distributors and British officials. Stamp distributors who did not resign were marked off symbolically from the community as criminals or as foreigners in their own country. In 1774 and 1775, the style of marking people off from the community changed. Crowds dealt with real people, not effigies, but they did not execute their victims; they humiliated them.

Tarring and feathering came into vogue. The offender was stripped

---

22. Ibid., 233.

23. Ibid., 302.

24. Enoch Bartlett to [the Haverhill, Massachusetts, Committee of Correspondence], 9 September 1774, Miscellaneous Manuscripts, Massachusetts Historical Society; and to Nathaniel Peabody, 23 September 1774, Peabody Papers, New Hampshire Historical Society, quoted in Robert McCluer Calhoon, *The Loyalists in Revolutionary America, 1760–1781* (New York, 1965), 305.

to the waist, sometimes shorn, and daubed with hot tar or pitch. Then a pillow of goose feathers (or sometimes turkey or buzzard feathers, which had a stronger smell) was emptied over him, and he was carted through town.[25] The theme had variations. One Tory was made to walk from New Milford, Connecticut, to Litchfield, about twenty miles, carrying one of his own geese the whole way. He was then tarred, made to pluck his goose, feathered, drummed out of town, and forced to kneel down and thank the crowd for its leniency.[26] A tax collector in Pennsylvania who tried to confiscate two wagons was seized by a group of young men. Tying a grapevine around his neck, they dragged him to a mill, "where they primed him over a little, not having a sufficient quantity of varnish to give him a complete gloss," emptied a pillow of feathers over him, took him into town, and led him "like a victim" to a duck hole where he was dunked for some time. Finally they tied him up with the grapevine and forced him to damn Bute, North, and all their followers and to praise the Americans as a generous, spirited, and much injured people.[27] When a Tory made himself offensive by publishing pamphlets, sometimes the pamphlet had to stand proxy for the unavailable Tory.

> The pamphlet was afterwards handed back to the people, who immediately bestowed upon it a suit of tar and turkey-buzzard's feathers; one of the persons concerned in the operation, justly observing that although the feathers were plucked from the most stinking fowl in the creation, he thought they fell far short of being a proper emblem of the author's odiousness to every advocate for true freedom. The same person wished, however, he had the pleasure of fitting him with a suit of the same materials. The pamphlet was then, in its gorgeous attire, nailed up firmly to the pillory-post, there to remain as a monument of the indignation of a free and loyal people against the author and vendor of a publication so evidently tending both to subvert the liberties of *America,* and the Constitution of the *British* Empire.[28]

25. Frank Moore, *Diary of the American Revolution* (New York, 1860) I:90, 138; *New-York Mercury,* 3 July 1775; "The Alternative of Williams-Burg," (a political print showing the shears).

26. Moore, *American Revolution* I:123.

27. *New York-Gazette; or the Weekly Post-Boy,* 27 March 1775.

28. *AA* II:35. See also *AA* I:1,013; II:15.

Tarring and feathering received much publicity, but in fact the threat of the punishment often sufficed. One Tory, on "being formally introduced to a tar-barrel, of which he was repeatedly pressed to smell, thought prudent to take leave abruptly, lest a more intimate acquaintance with it should take place."[29] A suspected Tory in New Shoreham, Rhode Island, when a crowd hummed with suggestions of tarring and feathering, "frankly confessed he was no tory, had acted only from a spirit of opposition, and despised, and hated a real *Tory* as much as he did a highway robber, or the devil, their principles and practices being exactly similar, and tending to the same end, *viz.* that of plundering and enslaving mankind."[30] A captain carrying a cargo of tea received a letter from the Philadelphia "Committee for Tarring and Feathering."

> What think you Captain of a Halter around your Neck ten Gallons of liquid tar decanted on your Pate with the feathers of a dozen wild Geese laid over that to enliven your Appearance. . . . Let us Advise you to fly without the wild Geese Feathers.[31]

He did not land the tea. A political print of the time—"The Alternative of Williams-Burg"—shows two dapper Virginia Tories surrounded by a crowd of roughly clad patriots. In the background is a pair of shears for shaving the potential victim and a gallows from which a bag of feathers hangs. One of the Tories is using the tar barrel as a desk on which to sign the Association. Reports often turned out to be reports of non-events—the tarring and feathering that did not take place. Samuel Peters of Connecticut and Isaac Hunt of Philadelphia incurred much hostility. Many wanted to give them a "new suit of clothes," but in spite of all the stir, nothing happened. One man censured by a committee filed a suit in a court of law against the members for insulting him. This offense gave rise to talk of tarring and feathering, "but after some hesitation, and much persuasion, [they] were prevented from using any violent measures,

29. *Pennsylvania Packet,* 15 May 1775.
30. *Pennsylvania Gazette,* 8 February 1775.
31. Great Britain, Public Record Office, Colonial Office 5, Vol. 133, 14 (microfilm).

unless beating the drum a few rods, and two boys throwing an egg apiece unknown to the men" could be counted as violence.[32]

The Association set in motion communal mechanisms of enforcement. Traditionally communities, not law courts, forced moral conformity on members of the community and punished moral deviance. A community might hold a "skimmington ride," in which a moral deviant such as an adulterer would be paraded through the town—perhaps on a rail, perhaps dressed as an animal—and exposed to public ridicule.[33] Congress, by adding moral proscriptions to an economic program of resistance, eased the transfer of coercion from officers of the state to members of local communities working together. Disobeying the import-export regulations, which were not laws but agreements, was equated with moral deviance, punishable by community ridicule and ostracism. The process of associating unpopular political opinions with moral deviance reached back to the Stamp Act crisis of 1765. Stamp distributors who failed to resign their office were punished, not as criminals, with flogging, imprisonment, or execution; but as moral deviants, with scorn, mockery, and ridicule. In 1774 and 1775, the style of community response changed. Live men replaced effigies. Disapproving crowds abused the bodies of offenders. Nonetheless, treatment of offenders still

32. *AA* I:711–18; III:170–76, 1,551.

33. On skimmingtons or charivaris, see André Burguière, "The Charivari and Religious Repression in France during the Ancien Régime," in Tamara Harven and Robert Wheaton, eds., *Family and Sexuality in French History* (Philadelphia, 1979), 84–110; Natalie Davis, "Charivari, Honor, and Community in Sixteenth-Century Lyons and Geneva," in John J. MacAloon, ed., *Rite, Drama, Festival, Spectacle: Rehearsals toward a Theory of Cultural Performance* (Philadelphia, 1984); Natalie Davis, "The Reasons of Misrule," in *Society and Culture in Early Modern France* (Stanford, Calif., 1975), 97–123; Martin Ingram, "Ridings, Rough Music, and the Reform of Popular Culture in Early Modern England," *Past and Present* 105 (1984): 79–113; Jacques Le Goff and Jean-Claude Schmitt, eds., *Le Charivari* (Paris, 1981); Ruth Mellinkoff, "Riding Backwards: Theme of Humiliation and Symbol of Evil," *Viator* 4 (1973): 153–76; Henri Rey-Flaud, *Le Charivari: Les rituels fondamentaux de la sexualité* (Paris, 1985); Fabio Sampoli, "A Popular Traditional Punishment in a Revolutionary Context: The Promenade des ânes in Arles," *Proceedings of the Eighth Annual Meeting of the Western Society for French History* (1980), ed. Edgar Newman, 1981, pp. 205–20; E. P. Thompson, "Rough Music: Le charivari anglais," *Annales* 27 (1972): 285–312. For skimmingtons in the American Revolution, see Paul A. Gilje, "Republican Rioting," in William Pencak and Conrad Edick Wright, eds., *Authority and Resistance in Early New York* (New York, 1988), 202–25.

remained within the boundaries of the skimmington. Tarring and feathering displayed offenders as moral monsters, not men. The skimmington model of coercion, applied to regulations undertaken for a political purpose, identified dissent as moral deviance and made the political movement a community affair.

ii

Various rituals of public humiliation ostracized victims by satirizing them. The victims had to endure bodily abuse and physical pain, but the effectiveness of the ritual lay in its ability to ridicule the victim for the benefit of the community. Public punishments—drumming people out of town, riding them on rails, and tarring and feathering them—first marked the victims as abnormal and corrupt, then rendered them ridiculous and contemptible, and finally dramatized their separation from the community. The abnormality and corruption of the deviant heightened by contrast the morality of the community that was condemning and expelling him. In reducing Tories to objects of ridicule, the orchestrators of the public rituals drew on traditional techniques of satire. A symbiotic relationship existed between the public rituals and satiric political prints, so popular in both England and the colonies. Printmakers, for example, readily incorporated tarring and feathering into the political satires and in so doing helped popularize the punishment.[34] For their part, the committees and crowds who devised public rituals satirized the Tory position in ways that the political prints had satirized corrupt and ineffectual politicians. The public condemnation and humiliation of Tories drew on many of the conceits made popular by the prints. Tarring and feathering, an American invention, in a sense enacted some of the satiric conceits of the prints and turned the prints into real life.

Geese, known for being silly creatures with weak intellects, filled the satirical prints of eighteenth-century England. English politicians drove flocks of geese or were themselves depicted as geese. Pitt was shown an "Neck and Giblets a famous Goose belonging to Esqr.

---

34. See, for example, "The Bostonian's Paying of the Excise-man, or Tarring & Feathering" (London, 1774), which depicts five Bostonians pouring tea down the throat of John Malcom, a customs officer who has been tarred and feathered.

Goosecap bred out of Waddle by the Wild Gander Lord Anser who flew all round and Came back again"; a court sycophant as "Sly a famous Goose of Lord Leo's his breed is very low & being fond of Dabbling in the Dirt is turn'd off the Common but is to be kept at the expence of the Farmers round about"; a peer who fancied himself an orator as "Gabble and Hiss an excellent Goose for the High Road he was bred out of Little Tony this Goose has been remarkable in all the Dirty Courses has has waddled thro' for bringing the other Geese on thier way." The prints used classical apothegms to satirize political fools. A goose standing on one leg illustrated Plutarch's story of the stranger who entered Sparta, stood on one leg, and said to a Spartan, "I do not believe you can do as much." "True," replied the Spartan, "but every Goose can."[35]

Colonists in their public rituals created for Tories the character of the goose—a character that had been well established in the prints. Geese waddled. They dabbled in dirt. They gabbled and hissed. They made noise without meaning and they moved without direction or purpose. Geese drew attention to themselves by doing foolish things and tried to get others to imitate their foolishness. Geese did not think for themselves; they recognized other geese and flocked together in some stupid pursuit.

> Birds of a Feather will flock together
> Like to like, as the Devil said to the Collier:

warned one goose print.[36] The stupidity of geese undermined the public good. In another print, Britannia rides in a chariot drawn by geese and turkeys. The geese cry "Hiss," the turkeys cry "Cobble," and Britannia moans, "I cannot bear to be haul'd along in this Ridiculous manner." In case people missed the point, a verbal message reinforced the visual one. The chariot drawn by geese and turkeys, the print informed the public, "plainly indicates the weak Intellects

---

35. Matthew Darley, *A Political and Satirical History of the Years 1756 and 1757* (London, 1757), 23, 25; *Catalogue of Political and Personal Satires Preserved in the Department of Prints and Drawings in the British Museum* (London, 1978) 3:1,024; 5:534 (hereafter cited as *Catalogue*).

36. "The Pleasures of the Turf," in *A Political and Satirical History*, 24.

of those in Power at the Time, who had the Driving of Britannia."[37] Geese and turkeys endangered their country—both stupid politicians in England and stupid Tories in America.

Tarring and feathering produced a "goose." Tories strutted and hissed and flocked together because they could not think. The punishment also made men into something strange. This was an age when the strange and exotic were put on exhibit and called to people's attention. Noblemen in England had menageries where zebras and giraffes fascinated visitors and pheasants were exhibited to effect. Newspapers printed accounts of strange animals and fish and advertised exhibits of monsters. "This MONSTER is larger than an Elephant, of a very uncommon Shape, having, three Heads, eight Legs, three Fundaments, two male Members, and one Female Pundendum on the Rump," announced a New York paper. "It is of various Colours, very beautiful, and makes a Noise like the Conjunction of two or three Voices."[38] In a political print America is represented as a Zebra, an exotic animal. While English politicians saddle and bridle the Zebra, a Frenchman remarks, "You are doing un grand Sottise, and Begar I vill avail myself of it. Dis Zebra Vill look very pretty in my Menagerie."[39] A mangoose carted through town was like an animal in a menagerie or traveling show. He was something strange the crowd could gawk at and dissociate themselves from. Committees of inspection thought it appropriate to "exhibit" Tories as "public spectacles."[40] A newspaper might refer to "those species of creatures called *tories*."[41]

Beasts in menageries, however strange they might be, were nonetheless part of nature. But a man-goose, a mixture of species, violated the law of nature. So did Tories. Colonists who betrayed the colonial cause were "Unnaturals."[42] They may not have broken manmade laws, but they broke the law of nature; therefore they could be punished according to the law of nature.

37. "Needs must when the Devil Drives," in *A Political and Satirical History* 21; *Catalogue,* no. 3518, 3:1,087–88.

38. Caroline Powys, Diaries (microfilm), 1762, p. 13; *New-York Mercury,* 16 February 1761.

39. "The Curious Zebra," *Catalogue* 3:295.

40. See, for example, *AA* III:174.

41. *Pennsylvania Packet,* 15 May 1775.

42. *Pennsylvania Journal,* 25 January 1775; *AA* II:172.

In our present struggle, is it not equally necessary to guard against intestine enemies as foreign foes? But by what law of the land can we do it? By none, and therefore we appeal to the law of nature. By this law, the Representatives of a people in Committee publish an enemy and make him infamous forever; and by this law the people at large tar and feather tories and traitors. The sole object of natural law is justice.[43]

The consignees of the tea in Boston received a threatening letter. "Are there no Laws in the Book of God and Nature, that enjoin such miscreants to be cut off from among the people as Troublers of the whole congregation? Yea verily there are Laws and Officers to put them in execution which you can neither corrupt intimidate nor escape."[44] Tarring and feathering dramatized the violation of the law of nature. The external, visible unnaturalness of a man-goose paralleled the internal, moral unnaturalness of upholding the sovereignty of Parliament and denigrating the Continental Congress.

Tarring and feathering dehumanized the victims by associating them with fowls. Variants of this ritual dehumanized Tories by associating them with animals. In political prints, men were associated with animals to emphasize certain characteristics. The animals that roamed through the political prints that English and American satirists turned out in the eighteenth century each bore their own messages. Asses plodded; vultures exploited. The cow, a passive female, was brutalized. Animals mingled with humans in scenes that portrayed confusion. In a print satirizing British elections, a crowd carried a man who had just won an election through the streets in a chair, while pigs galloped toward an embankment (an animal procession mirroring the human one) and a goose flew overhead. Other prints bustled with figures part-animal, part-human. In a mélange of bestial and human anatomy, a man might sprout asses' ears or a vulture might sport the head and wig of a minister of state.

The public rituals of humiliation also associated the human victim with animals. One Tory was strung up by the seat of his pants together with a dead catamount.[45] Another Tory—Jesse Dunbar of Halifax,

---

43. *AA* III:1,551.

44. PRO, CO 5, Vol. 133, p. 12 (microfilm).

45. Lorenzo Sabine, *The American Loyalists; or Biographical Sketches of Adherents to the British Crown in the War of the Revolution* (Boston, 1817) I:118.

Massachusetts—bought some fat cattle from one of the counselors appointed by the king and drove the cattle to Plymouth to sell. The people of Massachusetts condemned "mandamus counselors"—the men who had accepted the royal appointment—for having violated the charter, and considered them enemies of the country, with whom true patriots should have no commerce. They therefore took their resentment out on Dunbar. Seizing him, they fixed him in the belly of one of his oxen that he had just slaughtered and skinned and hung up for sale. They carted him in the carcass, a noisome and bloody conveyance, for four miles, made him pay a dollar, and handed him over to the people of Kingston. They in turn carted him four miles, forced him to pay another dollar, and delivered him the people of Duxbury, who carted him to the house of the mandamus counselor, forced him to pay some more money, and flung the beef into the road.[46] Aside from the unorthodoxy of the ox carcass, patriots, in escorting Dunbar from town to town and back to his own town, were treating him the way madmen and idiots were treated.

In associating Tories with animals, colonists dramatized another theme of political satires: defilement. The animal imagery of political prints was enhanced by dirt and bodily effluvia: feces, urine, and vomit. Geese dabble in dirt; ass-politicians must bear their burden "through every dirty Slough." One ass, wearing a wig, complains:

> Thro' Dirt & Mire,
> I'm forc'd to plash,
> And patient bear,
> This Beldham's [*sic*] lash.[47]

In the political prints of the American Revolution, dogs piss everywhere. A dog pisses on a lion, symbol of Britannia; on a fashionable macaroni; on a map of America; on a tea caddy. Blood and vomit mingle with rape and lust. A man stabs a cow (America) in the leg with a knife while another man holds out a basin to catch blood that is spouting out of a wound in the cow's neck. A Spanish diplomat

46. *Rivington's New York Gazetteer,* 9 March 1775.
47. *Catalogue,* 3:1,077.

vomits over a fallen Englishman, while Yankee Doodle looks on. An English politician peeks up the skirt of a ravaged woman, America.[48]

In real life colonists not only dehumanized Tories, they defiled them. When they daubed a man with tar, they smeared both his body and his character. One Tory, after he had been tarred and feathered, was drenched with "Newberry rum and water, taken from a duck-hole, until it began to work upwards."[49] Jesse Dunbar, who was pinioned in the carcass of an ox, had tripe and dirt thrown in his face.[50] A Newport committee prepared to smear a Tory with fish gurry.[51] Excrement and sexual abuse played a part in the defilement. An angry crowd might daub a Tory's house with excrement or force a Tory to ride on a rail.[52] One victim of this punishment was "injured in a Manner unfit for Description."[53]

Patriots linked Tories with animals in several ways: by turning Tories into animals in political prints and public rituals and thereby dehumanizing them, by defiling Tories with offal and excrement, and finally, by using Tory animals as scapegoats for community resentment. Sometimes they perpetrated more drastic violence against Tory animals than they could inflict on the Tories themselves. Timothy Ruggles of Massachusetts, for example, had a valuable stallion poisoned. More often, though, Tory animals received the same kind of treatment that Tories themselves received. Ridiculing the animal of a Tory was another way of identifying the Tory with the animal and thus debasing him. A group of patriots got a hold of a horse of Ruggles' one night, painted him, and shaved off his mane and tail.[54] Elisha Foord and John Baker of Marshfield, Massachusetts, a Tory town, went to an auction in a nearby town. Foord had earlier antago-

48. "A Picturesque view of the State of the Nation for February 1778"; "Miss Macaroni and Her Gallant"; "The Wise Men of Gotham and their Goose"; "A Society of Patriotic Ladies"; "The Contrast"; untitled print in Sylvia Dannet, *The Yankee Doodler* (New York, 1973), 55; "The Able Doctor."

49. *New York-Gazette, or the Weekly Post-Boy,* 17 March 1775.

50. *Rivington's New-York Gazetteer,* 9 March 1775.

51. *Pennsylvania Gazette,* 8 February 1775.

52. *The History, Debates, and Proceedings of both Houses of Parliament of Great Britain* (London: Debrett, 1792) VII:89; *Rivington's New York Gazetteer,* 9 March 1775.

53. *New-York Gazette and Weekly Mercury,* 27 February 1775.

54. *Rivington's New-York Gazetteer,* 9 March 1775.

nized patriots by saying that he could take Duxbury minutemen "with an Elder shoot." Despite the protests of the crowd, the auctioneer ruled that Foord and Baker could bid. Tensions rose. When Foord bid on a cable, the crowd hooted that it would serve to hang him by. After the auction, a group emerged from the tavern, the leader with a mug and wineglass, and announced that they were going to christen Foord's horse. While one man held the horse's mouth open, another man poured some rum down the horse's throat, sloshed the rest in his face, and called him "lumber ass." John Baker protested such abuse on an animal. In response, the crowd gave his horse the same treatment and christened him "Tory."[55] Animals served as proxies for Tories. This way of identifying Tories with animals deflected violence away from the Tory himself.

Tories might also be associated with blacks. A Virginia colonel handcuffed a Scottish Tory "to one of his brother black soldiers . . . which is the resolution I have taken shall be the fate of all these cattle."[56] Being handcuffed to a black was meant to degrade the Tory both socially (blacks were slaves) and physically (blacks were thought of as animals—"cattle"). Tories returned the racial favor. A group of Tories in Delaware apprehended Robert Appleton, and, when he refused to preach a Methodist sermon, had him whipped by a black man.[57]

Patriots publicly humiliated the most vociferous Tories in ceremonies that satirized them. They dressed Tories up in a "new suit of clothes" and put them on display in their "gorgeous attire." In a satirical version of the social manuals that were so popular in the eighteenth century, they made Tories into "men of fashion" and instructed them on how to be well received in society. By identifying Tories with animals, patriots made the distinction between animals and humans sharper and used the distinction to define what was

---

55. "The Second Provisional Congress: February 1–April 15, 1775—The Royal Executive, Instructions to Governor Gage—Depositions, British Officers' Reports, and related Documents," in *Province in Rebellion: A Documentary History of the Founding of the Commonwealth of Massachusetts,* L. Kinvin Wroth, ed. (Boston, 1975), 1,996–2,007, F21.

56. *AA* IV:245.

57. Harold B. Hancock, *The Loyalists of Revolutionary Delaware* (Newark, Dela., 1977), 96.

human and what was not and what was natural and what was not. Tories did not simply hold erroneous political notions; their erroneous political notions had robbed them of their humanity and rendered them unnatural. All the ceremonies ridiculed Tories and in ridiculing them rendered them impotent. Less than human, ineffectual, ridiculous—Tories were expelled from their communities but, after they had been degraded in a public ceremony, their threat was nullified and they were deemed not worth liquidating.

iii

The lot of outspoken Tories was definitely not a happy one. No one can envy Jesse Dunbar, bumping for hours in the nauseating carcass of a freshly slaughtered ox, or Joseph Clarke with his penis battered on a sharp rail, or any of the victims of tarring and feathering, their skin blistered by hot tar, later trying to remove the tar without peeling the skin off, too. And yet the debasement and defilement of Tories protected both the victims and the communities. Violating the Association or criticizing Congress either orally or in writing did not result in executions. Although Tories emphasized mob violence, mobs during the political crisis did not lynch victims. In 1775, John Wetherhead, a native of England who had been living in New York for twelve years as a well-to-do importer, served on a grand jury that was to consider whether to indict a handful of men for treason. Wetherhead, who sided with British government and was to be one of fifty-nine loyalists proscribed and banished by an Act of Attainder in October 1779, described the incident as part of his claim for compensation from the British government. Wetherhead intended to condemn the unruly populace who clamored for execution and to extol his own role as the voice of justice. "It required no small degree of exertion," he wrote, "to counteract these wicked designs and persuade 11 men out of 13 to do right." Wetherhead, who won the day, unwittingly showed that when it came to executions, crowd justice did give way to court justice. The men were liberated, and, in Wetherhead's words, "all the wicked and violent intentions of the Faction were happily frustrated."[58]

58. Memorial of 3 October 1783, *Loyalist Transcripts*, Vol. XLIV, 122 ff., in Catherine S. Crary, *The Price of Loyalty: Tory Writings from the Revolutionary Era* (New York, 1973), 44–47.

Later, after the Declaration of Independence, a few Tory civilians were executed, but not by mobs. They were put on trial, and those who were executed were executed not as Tories, for their political beliefs; but as traitors, for serious security offenses such as supplying information to the British or recruiting men to serve in the British army. In the early years of the political crisis, when people were defining a position, concentration on debasement and defilement of dissenters deflected interest from more drastic violence. Once a Tory had been smeared and reduced to something subhuman, an object of ridicule, he was hardly worth executing. The communities, for their part, in targeting a few obnoxious Tories and in dealing with them ritualistically, protected themselves against the division that more violent measures directed at a greater number of people would have catalyzed. Tories were intimidated, yes, often brutally; but slaughtered, no. The public rituals of humiliation forestalled more drastic measures and limited the range of the community's hostility. After all, for a system of social ostracism to work, the victims have to be relatively few; otherwise they can join together and form a community of their own.

The victims of the public rituals were those the committees had given up on. Committees did not expect people who had undergone such an ordeal ever to be reconciled to the community. Tarring and feathering made public and dramatic the expulsion from the community (and in this sense differed from skimmingtons). The committee of Charleston, South Carolina, after tarring and feathering Laughlin Martin and John Dealy, put them onboard Captain Lasley's ship, "lying windbound for Bristol."[59] Whether or not they were actually conducted out of the community, most people who were tarred and feathered or ridden on a rail left the community. Nor, in general, were they counted among those who returned after the Revolution was over. Laughlin Martin did ask to be allowed to stay, and his request was granted, but most victims of crowd hostility had no inclination to stay or later to return. John Malcolm, a customs officer who was tarred and feathered in Boston, stayed in England permanently, leaving behind in Boston his wife and five children, two of whom were deaf and dumb; John Hopkins, a pilot of Savannah who was tarred and feathered, made to stand in a cart with a candle in his

59. *New-York Gazette and Weekly Mercury,* 3 July 1775.

hand, driven all over town from nine o'clock at night until well after midnight, and threatened with hanging, went to East Florida when the British evacuated Savannah in 1782; Thomas Brown, who was tarred and feathered in Augusta, Georgia, left for East Florida where he became a lieutenant colonel of a corps of the King's Rangers and after the war settled in the Bahamas; Seth Seely, a Connecticut farmer who was ridden on a rail and smeared with eggs, settled in New Brunswick, as did Dr. Joseph Clark, who was ridden on a rail in a town near Hartford; Dr. John Kearsley of Philadelphia, who was the center of a violent crowd and barely escaped being tarred and feathered, was later attainted for treason and put in prison, where he died; Isaac Hunt, his fellow victim in the mob violence, settled in England.[60] Whether the violence perpetrated against them turned them into irreconcilable Tories or whether they were singled out because of their recalcitrance, many of the men who were ridiculed in an elaborate, public, often brutal, display left their communities for good.

Did committees of inspection, who arranged for violators of the Association to be published as enemies of the people, also preside over tarring and feathering? No set rules standardized procedures in all the colonies. Certainly committees at times tried to intimidate recalcitrants with the threat of tarring and feathering, and certainly in some cases committees, whether or not they actually participated in the ritual, did condone it. Committees, however, wanted to maintain order and keep their communities from disintegrating into violence. They did not as a rule criticize public rituals of humiliation, but a few cases surface in the documents that reveal the concern of committees that crowd action might get out of control. In Philadelphia a group of patriots who were not members of the committee of inspection put two provocative Tories, Dr. John Kearsley and Isaac Hunt, on display and intended to tar and feather them. They recognized, however, their responsibility to maintain order, and, when they realized that they might not be able to control the crowd, canceled the tarring and feathering. "The people flocked together in such numbers, and

60. Lorenzo Sabine, *Biographical Sketches of Loyalists of the American Revolution, with an Historical essay*, 2 vols. (Boston, 1864), I:260–65, 314, 543, 597; II:43, 273; Gregory Palmer, *Biographical Sketches of Loyalists of the American Revolution* (Westport, Conn., 1984), 106, 156, 400, 413, 451, 581, 772.

were so exasperated at the insolence of his [Kearsley's] behavior, that the men under arms were afraid to proceed to the operation, lest the violence of the people should put it out of their power to protect his person, which they were determined to do at the risk of their lives."[61] Even though the vigilante group did succeed in protecting Kearsley and Hunt, they were reprimanded for their action, which was undertaken without the permission of the committee. In western Massachusetts, a crowd from Lennox tarred and feathered one Stephen Resco, a suspected Tory who had been released from jail, crowned him with a dead owl, and marched him to the county convention at Stockbridge. According to a Tory account of the incident, the convention disapproved of the treatment of Resco. Fearful of the violence of the Lennox group, they remanded him to jail for his own safety.[62]

Whether the public rituals were spontaneous crowd actions or planned events orchestrated by the committees, the accounts that appeared in the papers stressed the decency of the ceremony and the propriety and civility of those who were conducting it. A cooper in New Jersey was tarred and feathered and, according to the account, released in half an hour. "The whole was conducted with that regularity and decorum that ought to be observed in all publick punishments."[63] The committee of Charleston, South Carolina, cleaned up its victims. "After having been exhibited for about Half an Hour, and having made many Acknowledgements of their Crime, they [Laughlin Martin and John Dealy] were conducted home, cleaned, and quietly put on board of Capt. Lasley's ship."[64] The self-appointed vigilante group who wanted to tar and feather Kearsley and Hunt later found themselves under attack for handling the Tories roughly. In their defense they claimed that their design was "to bring a public and notorious offender to public disgrace without danger to his person or life." They had made every effort, they claimed, to eliminate violence from the proceeding. "The gentlemen who planned the affair, and those who conducted it, are far from being mobbish or mobbishly inclined: it was conducted with sobriety, decency and

61. *AA* III:174.

62. Pocumtuck Valley Memorial Association, Deerfield, Massachusetts, no. 242, 8, E-18, in Crary, *Price of Loyalty*, 59–60.

63. *AA* IV:203.

64. *New-York Gazette and Weekly Mercury*, 3 July 1775.

decorum on their part, and with the utmost safety to the persons of the Doctor and Mr. *Hunt,* as is evident from the repeated thanks which they received from both for their kind protection."[65] Patriots did not condone violence, and those who acted without authority or were too rough in their treatment of Tories might privately be called to account. After all, patriots did not wish to arouse sympathy for Tories; they wished to ridicule them.

The victims of public rituals were doubtless less impressed by the propriety of the proceedings than the organizers and the public press. Thomas Brown, a well-to-do young Englishmen who had arrived in Georgia in late 1774 with the intention of settling, received particularly brutal treatment from a group of Georgia Sons of Liberty. Like several other Englishmen who arrived late in the crisis (but dramatically unlike Thomas Paine), Brown seemed to have little understanding of the constitutional issues and every inclination to voice his contempt for patriots and his admiration for the king and Parliament. When Brown, who deemed the Association traitorous, ridiculed the patriots in toasts and helped organize a counter-association, a committee decided to pay him a visit. The accounts of what happened differ drastically. In a letter to his father a few months after the incident, Brown described himself eloquently addressing an angry mob of a hundred people, fifty of whom were so moved by his words that they withdrew. When the rest tried to force him to sign the Association, he defended himself with pistols. He was disarmed, but he drew his sword and held all fifty at bay with his parries and thrusts until he was struck from behind by a "cowardly miscreant." While Brown probably made the most of his own reasonableness and bravery, there seems no reason to doubt the brutal details of his treatment: that he was brought down by a blow to the head, that on the way to Augusta the patriots tied him to a tree and jammed burning lightwood under his feet, burning him so badly that he lost two toes, and that in Augusta they shaved off his hair with a knife, tarred and feathered him, and carted him around town.[66] Brown did

---

65. *AA* III:174.

66. Edward Cashin, *The King's Ranger: Thomas Brown and the American Revolution on the Southern Frontier* (Athens, Ga., 1989), 26–29; Gary D. Olson, "Loyalists and the American Revolution: Thomas Brown and the South Carolina Backcountry, 1775–1776," *The South Carolina Historical Magazine* 68 (October 1968): 207–08.

not make a public statement about his treatment. In a letter to Lord Cornwallis in 1780, five years after the incident, and in a memorial to the commissioners for inquiring into the losses and services of American Loyalists in 1788, he described the brutality in greater detail than he had done for his father. In both cases, of course, the brutality of his treatment would have enhanced his own glory. At no point does Brown mention that he gave in to the demands of the crowd.

Meanwhile, from the patriot account, one would hardly think that violence had occurred at all. "A respectable body of the Sons of Liberty" waited on Brown and "requested" him "in civil terms" to clear himself of accusations against him. When Brown denied their authority, they "politely" escorted him into Augusta (they make no mention of having burnt his feet) and "presented him with a genteel and fashionable suit of tar and feathers." After carting him around town, they brought him to Mr. Weatherford's house, "where out of humanity they had him taken proper care of for the night." The next morning Brown "voluntarily" swore "upon his honour" that he "repented for his past conduct, and that he would for the future, at the hazard of his life and fortune, protect and support the rights and liberties of America." The Sons of Liberty then discharged Brown and "complimented" him "with a horse and chair to ride home." When Brown later retracted his oath, the Sons of Liberty were offended that he had "forfeited his honour" by violating an oath "voluntarily taken," and they vented their contempt for his allegedly dishonorable act with a sarcastic postscript: "The said Thomas Browne is now a little remarkable; he wears his hair very short, and a handkerchief tied around his head in order that his intellects this cold weather may not be affected."[67] Brown, an arrogant young man who delighted in taking public stances and parading his self-righteousness, goaded the Sons of Liberty into vindictive brutality. They did not, however, take pride in their excesses, and in presenting the incident to the public they purged it of brutality, dressed it in decorum, politeness, and propriety, and shifted responsibility for the incident to Brown himself.

Tories, for their part, stressed the violence and lawlessness of the public rituals. Sometimes they spoke of the mob being out of control. Sometimes they tried to associate mob violence with the leaders of the community. Each side, patriot and Tory, was concerned with

67. *Georgia Gazette,* 30 August 1775.

self-presentation. One Tory was furious with the way patriots treated the wife of Sir John Johnson. Sir John had fled to Canada, leaving his wife behind on their estate in the Mohawk Valley. Lady Johnson was conducted from Sir John's seat to Albany, "guarded by a parcel of half-clothed dirty yankees and squired by a New England officer, by trade a cobbler, as dirty as themselves, until he had decorated himself with a suit of Sir John's clothes, and a clean shirt, and a pair of stockings, stolen at the Hall." It is unclear whether this reporter was more concerned with the class disparity between Lady Johnson and her escorts or with the robbery. There can, however, be no mistake about his indignation at the virtuous self-presentation of patriots and the vilification of Tories. "And yet these were the people who during the whole war boasted of their humane, generous, behaviour and taxed the British and Loyalists as butchers, cut-throats, and barbarians."[68] Both patriots and Tories strove to maintain a public image of courtesy, propriety, decency, and reasonableness, and in doing so, whatever the reality of specific confrontations may have been, publicly and piously condemned violence. Each side seemed to agree that violence jeopardized its cause.

Tarring and feathering, ironically, was a sign of community strength. The public ritual of humiliating and banishing a deviant showed that the community had coalesced in a common political and moral position and could agree on the identification and expulsion of deviants. As long as communities remained politically unified, they could control violence. Where community consensus was shattered or where neighboring communities disagreed, civilian violence in the war years became uncontrolled—robberies, lootings, and even murders—in Tryon County, New York, for example, or in Ninety-Six District in South Carolina, or in the swamps of Cape Fear in North Carolina. And when the armies clashed in areas where communities had not been powerful enough to enforce consensus or at least compliance, the bitterness was so great that both patriot soldiers and loyalist and British soldiers committed barbarities, executing prisoners of war, sometimes without a trial.

The ritual violence targeting a few vociferous Tories strengthened

68. Thomas Jones, *History of New York during the Revolutionary War,* Edward F. Delancey, ed. (New York, 1879), 76–77, in Crary, *Price of Loyalty,* 79–80. See also F. W. Halsey, *The Old New York Frontier, 1614–1800* (New York, 1901).

the solidarity of communities and in the long run made the Revolution less divisive than it might have been. Neutrals and unobnoxious Tories stayed in their communities and after the war were easily absorbed into the republic. It had been estimated that half a million out of a population of two and a half million were Tories at some point in the war.[69] Eighty thousand to one hundred thousand emigrated, but the rest remained at home and after the war lived in peace among neighbors who had taken the opposite side.[70] Everywhere, once the war was over, Tories were taken back into their communities with minimum or no penalties. A few incidents mar the general atmosphere of clemency. Mathew Love, a Tory who had committed atrocities in the back country of South Carolina during the war, returned to Ninety-Six District and was arrested on the grounds that the peace treaty could not apply to people who had committed acts as barbarous as his. The judge held that the peace treaty did cover Love, and Love was released, but the relatives of Love's victims seized him and, bearing him off into the woods, lynched him.[71] Even in the back country of the Carolinas, however, where the revolution had disintegrated into civil war, most people who supported the British resumed normal lives after the war.[72] And elsewhere Tories had an even easier time. The vast majority of Tories did not flee their communities and were simply reabsorbed. Even the more active Tories who had left during the war and wanted to come back were generally allowed to do so.[73]

69. Paul Smith, "The American Loyalists," *William and Mary Quarterly,* Vol. XXV, no. 2 (April 1968), 269.

70. Crary, *Price of Loyalty,* 9.

71. Robert Stansbury Lambert, *South Carolina Loyalists in the American Revolution* (Columbia, S. C., 1987), 297.

72. Ibid. 286–302; Rachel N. Klein, *Unification of a Slave State: The Rise of the Planter Class in the South Carolina Backcountry, 1760–1808* (Chapel Hill, 1990), 114–23; Jerome J. Nadelhaft, *The Disorders of War: The Revolution in South Carolina* (Orono, Me., 1981), 71–85; Robert Weir, " 'The Violent Spirit,' The Reestablishment of Order, and the Continuity of Leadership in Post-Revolutionary South Carolina," in Ronald Hoffman, Thad W. Tate, and Peter J. Albert, ed., *An Uncivil War: The Southern Backcountry during the American Revolution* (Charlottesville, Va., 1985), 70–124; A. Roger Ekirch, "Whig Authority and Public Order in Backcountry North Carolina, 1776–1783," in ibid., 99–124.

73. Robert M. Calhoon, "The Reintegration of the Loyalists and the Disaffected," in

The American Revolution was in part a civil war and like all civil wars generated bitterness and personal violence. But what makes the American Revolution remarkable is the limited extent of the civilian violence, which did not escalate into slaughter, and the relative ease with which Tories were absorbed into the new republic. The Association that Congress drew up in 1774 immediately thrust the responsibility for resistance onto local communities. Communities organized resistance to Britain and sought to politicize people, but they did not strive for too much purity. People who sympathized with England, as long as they did not voice their opinion and as long as they acquiesced in the Association, were tolerated. On the other hand, vociferous Tories who tried to divide the community were identified as deviants, humiliated, and driven out. Community leaders had two goals: to organize resistance and to preserve the community.[74] The general success of communities in maintaining their integrity while accelerating revolutionary momentum kept the Revolution directed toward Britain and prevented wholesale internal disintegration. The American Revolution escaped the civilian massacres of the European religious wars that had preceded it and the institutionalized terror of the revolutions that succeeded it.

Jack P. Greene, ed., *The American Revolution: Its Character and Limits* (New York, 1987), 51–74.

74. Edward Countryman documents the extraordinary strength of community and family ties in Schodack, a small New York village. Edward Countryman, *A People in Revolution: The American Revolution and Political Society in New York, 1760–1790* (Baltimore, 1981), 122.

Epilogue

I N 1774, the colonists formed an association to protect themselves from tyranny. They took economic measures to put pressure on England and moral measures to strengthen their own character. The moral measures—proscriptions of specific activities and types of behavior—rested on values: frugality, industry, and dedication to the common good. Congress, in the ascetic moral provisions of the Association, shifted attention from perception to behavior, devised a highly specific code of behavior, and identified compliance with the code as a statement of resistance to Britain and deviance from the code as a statement of sympathy for Britain. Congress simplified morality, limited its scope, and standardized it. The simplification and limited scope made it possible for many people to perform the same acts defined as moral, and the standardization made it possible, however arbitrarily, to invest community action with political significance.

The colonists devised their program to achieve a specific goal, the repeal of Acts dealing with the colonies and a return to the status quo of 1763. The failure of the program on a practical level assured its success on a psychological level. As long as the British did not respond, the Americans remained bound together in a common course of action. They continued to abide by their economic and moral regulations, and in the process they came to think of themselves as a people with a will and a character. Their awareness of their virtuous character automatically led them to choose a type of government— republican government,—that, according to the notions of the time, suited a virtuous people. They established thirteen republican governments. But another notion of the time, that republics could not operate over extensive areas, blocked the formation of a strong central government.

Moral proscriptions have an ephemeral quality. They can bring people together in a crisis, but they cannot hold them together. In 1783, right after the peace treaty, Johann Schoepf, a German doctor who had served in the British army, made a tour of the colonies. In Virginia he visited the Assembly and found that the members had much on their minds besides lawmaking. The main room was a buzz of noise and a stir of movement. "In the Ante-room there is a tumult quite as constant; here they amuse themselves zealously with talk of horse-races, runaway negroes, yesterday's play, politics, or it may be, with trafficking."[1] In the 1780s, horse-racing revived in South Carolina and to a lesser extent in Virginia, Maryland, and New York. By the 1790s it was thriving. Benjamin Latrobe in 1796 estimated that fifteen hundred people attended a horse race in Petersburg, Virginia. While Latrobe did not approve of the betting, the horse race pleased him. "Upon the whole, I think running matches a useful as well as a very amusing entertainment."[2] Theater companies gave plays in Baltimore, New York, and Richmond. In 1789, the Pennsylvania legislature repealed its act outlawing the theater. Ironically, theater curtains and proscenium arches were decorated with scenes glorifying the American Revolution.[3] The austerity of funerals dwindled after the Revolution. Disturbed by burgeoning extravagance, the Massachusetts General Court in 1797 urged the people to return to the regulations of 1774 in order to "perpetuate a national badge for mourning dress, suitable to the dignity of their independence."[4]

Cockfighting had an infusion of new blood in Philadelphia when

1. Johann David Schoepf, *Travels in the Confederation* (New York, 1788), translated from the German by Alfred J. Morrison (Philadelphia, 1911; reprinted New York, 1968), vol. 2:55.

2. Benjamin Henry Latrobe, *The Journal of Latrobe: Being the Notes and Sketches of an Architect, Naturalist and Traveler in the United States from 1796 to 1820* (New York, 1905), 23, 27.

3. Neil Harris, "The Making of an American Culture: 1750–1800," in Charles F. Montgomery and Patricia E. Kane, eds., *American Art: 1750–1800 Towards Independence* (Boston, 1976), 29.

4. Extracts from Massachusetts General Court Records in Joseph B. Felt, *The Customs of New England* (1853; reprinted New York, 1970), 203.

that city received a flood of immigrants from Santo Domingo in 1793. In 1809 a broadside publicly advertising a cock main and several matches was posted on the principal streetcorners of New York. The publicity elicited indignation. "The Mayor (De Witt Clinton) took measures to prevent this first instance, it is believed, of a publick Cock fight in the City of New York, where the inhuman practice has existed from time immemorial." In the South, cockfighting remained popular. Elkanah Watson attended a cockfight in Hampton County, Virginia, in 1787.

> We reached the ground, about ten o'clock the next morning. The roads, as we approached the scene, were alive with carriages, horses, and pedestrians, black and white, hastening to the point of attraction. Several houses formed a spacious square, in the centre of which was arranged a large cock-pit; surrounded by many genteel people promiscuously mingled with the vulgar and debased. Exceedingly beautiful cocks were produced, armed with long, steel-pointed gaffes, which were firmly attached to their natural spurs. The moment the birds were dropped, bets ran high. The little heroes appeared trained to the business; and were not the least disconcerted by the crowd or shouting. They stepped about with great apparent pride and dignity; advancing nearer and nearer, they flew upon each other at the same instant, with a rude shock, the cruel gaffes being driven into their bodies, and, at times, directly through their heads. Frequently one, or both, would be struck dead at the first blow; but they often fought after being repeatedly pierced, as long as they were able to crawl, and in the agonies of death would often make abortive efforts to raise their heads and strike their antagonists.

Watson was sickened at the sight and retired to the shade of a widespread willow where he was better entertained by a "voluntary" fight between a wasp and a spider. Years later, Mark Twain was also sickened at the sight. "When cocks had been fighting some little time, I was expecting them momently to drop dead, for both were blind, red with blood, and so exhausted that they frequently fell down. Yet they would not give up, neither would they die." Like Watson, Twain retired, unable to endure the gore; but he concluded that cockfighting was less cruel than fox-hunting because the cocks enjoyed themselves, while the fox did not. Whatever the value of Twain's animal psychology, cockfighting was still going strong in New Orleans in

1882. Men and boys of all ages, colors, and nationalities shouted "prodigiously" and "lost themselves in frenzies of delight."[5]

The moral movement of the American Revolution had a brief existence. On an oneiric level far removed from the political issues of taxation and representation, the funeral offers an appropriate symbol for a moral movement based on proscribed behavior. Such a specific and negative movement, which encapsulated values in plays, cock-fights, horse-races, and funeral gloves, produces a strangely terminal impression. A funeral procession, when it reaches the grave, has nowhere else to go. Negative moral movements also have no future. In a sense, the funeral, with its intimations both of finality and of doubt, is an appropriate symbol for a people hung between a rejected past and an unpredictable future. Colonists could come together as a people on the value of frugality, symbolized in the avoidance of useless expenditures; but in the long run they would need more than abstinence from horse-racing and the theater, more than the deco-rum of subdued funerals, to sustain them. The morality of negation is too insubstantial to build a lasting structure on. Americans soon devised psychological strategies for keeping in theory the ideology and values of the American Revolution, while relinquishing their inconvenient consequences. They became great consumers and, among other things, bought objects that glorified the American Revolution—a political movement that was launched on an ethic of nonconsumption.[6]

The moral movement helped bring the colonists together as a

5. Mrs. Ann Ridgely, Dover, Delaware, to George W. Ridgely, Carlisle, Pennsylvania, 15 January 1796, in *A Calendar of Ridgely Family Letters, 1742–1899, in the Delaware State Archives*, 3 vols., Leon deValinger, Jr., ed. (Dover, Dela., 1948) I:142; John H. Powell, *Bring Out Your Dead* (Philadelphia, 1949), 4–7; broadside in the New-York Historical Society with handwritten condemnation; *Men and Times of the Revolution; or Memoirs of Elkanah Watson, including his Journals of Travels in Europe and America, from the year 1777 to 1784, and his Correspondence with Public men, and Reminiscences and Incidents of the American Revolution*, Winslow C. Watson, ed. (New York, 1856), 261–62; Mark Twain, *Life on the Mississippi* (1883; New York, 1944), 264–65.

6. For psychological strategies for dealing with the tension between Revolutionary ideology and material prosperity, see my article "Republican Bees: The Political Economy of the Beehive in Eighteenth-Century America," *Studies in Eighteenth-Century Culture* 18 (1988): 39–77. For the development of trade in souvenirs of the American Revolution, see my article "Consumption and Republican Ideology in the Early Republic," in *Everyday Life in the Early Republic* (W. W. Norton, forthcoming).

people with a will and a character. On July 4, 1776, they declared themselves a people different from the British people. They were different from the British because they were virtuous and because they believed that all men were created equal. The character Americans established for themselves did have positive consequences, but they were limited. Equality did emerge from the Revolution in bits and pieces: reduction in property requirements for voting, some state laws against slavery and the slave trade, the disestablishment of the Anglican church, the abolition of primogeniture and entail. But slaves still worked the plantations of the South. Americans' belief in their own virtue and in equality did give them the confidence to establish thirteen republican governments and one confederated republic. But the national government under the Articles of Confederation had little power.

Eventually the Revolution did culminate in the formation of a national republic with power to operate effectively. But it was a republic founded on the sovereignty of a people, not on their character—on balanced interests, not on virtue. The concept of the sovereignty of the people bridged the gap between the states and the federal government. All power resided in the people, who could delegate some power to state governments, some to the federal government. But while a sovereign people succeeded in forming a union out of states of different sizes, sovereignty as a concept imposed no characterological constraints on the people, nor any ideology. A sovereign people could be slothful, extravagant, racist, and sexist. A sovereign people could believe in equality, but then again they could believe in inequality.

Was the political concept of sovereignty of the people enough to hold a people together, or did they, as George Washington felt, need a character and a defined moral commitment? The American Revolution was never taken over by radicals who pushed the ideals of the Revolution to new limits. Sovereignty as a concept offered an escape from the need to define values. James Madison, in urging Americans to ratify the Constitution, argued that, despite the accepted notion to the contrary, a republic *could* in fact operate successfully over an extensive area. The great variety of interests in an extensive area would prevent the formation of a majority that could persecute a minority. Madison envisioned a republic of balanced interests, not a republic of virtue, morality, or principle. On April 12, 1861, seventy-four years after the Constitutional Convention drew up the Constitution, General Beauregard fired his guns on Fort Sumter and shattered the tranquillity of balanced interests. In a sense, the Civil War was the reign of terror of the American Revolution—a time when people resurrected the values for which the Revolution had been fought and in four bloody years pushed them to new limits.

INDEX

Printed in the United States
52999LVS00002B/194